W9-BMY-717

Consulting Authors

Michael A. DiSpezio
Global Educator
North Falmouth, Massachusetts

Marjorie Frank
Science Writer and Content-Area Reading
Specialist
Brooklyn, New York

Michael Heithaus
Director, School of Environment and Society
Associate Professor, Department of Biological
Sciences
Florida International University
North Miami, Florida

Donna Ogle
Professor of Reading and Language
National-Louis University
Chicago, Illinois

Program Advisors

Paul D. Asimow
Professor of Geology and
Geochemistry
California Institute of Technology
Pasadena, California

Bobby Jeanpierre
Associate Professor of Science
Education
University of Central Florida
Orlando, Florida

Gerald H. Krockover
Professor of Earth and Atmospheric
Science Education
Purdue University
West Lafayette, Indiana

Rose Pringle
Associate Professor
School of Teaching and Learning
College of Education
University of Florida
Gainesville, Florida

Carolyn Staudt
Curriculum Designer for Technology
KidSolve, Inc.
The Concord Consortium
Concord, Massachusetts

Larry Stookey
Science Department
Antigo High School
Antigo, Wisconsin

Carol J. Valenta
Associate Director of the Museum and
Senior Vice President
Saint Louis Science Center
St. Louis, Missouri

Barry A. Van Deman
President and CEO
Museum of Life and Science
Durham, North Carolina

Power up with Science Fusion!

Your program fuses . . .

e-Learning & Virtual Labs

Labs & Explorations

Write-In Student Edition

. . . to generate new science energy for today's science learner— *you.*

SCIENCE
FUSiON

fusion [FYOO • zhuhn] a combination of two or more things that releases energy

This Write-In Student Edition belongs to

Poppy Kenner

Teacher/Room

Home

 HOUGHTON MIFFLIN HARCOURT

HOUGHTON MIFFLIN HARCOURT

Front Cover: *crab* ©Mark Webb/Alamy; *Great Basin National Park* ©Frans Lanting/Corbis; *tree frog* ©DLILLC/Corbis; *beaker* ©Gregor Schuster/Getty Images; *rowers* ©Stockbyte/Getty Images.

Back Cover: *Giant's Causeway* ©Rod McLean/Alamy; *digital screen* ©Michael Melford/Stone/Getty Images; *mountain biker* ©Jerome Prevost/TempSport/Corbis; *gecko* ©Pete Orelup/Getty Images.

Copyright © 2012 by Houghton Mifflin Harcourt Publishing Company

All rights reserved. No part of this work may be reproduced or transmitted in any form or by any means, electronic or mechanical, including photocopying or recording, or by any information storage and retrieval system, without the prior written permission of the copyright owner unless such copying is expressly permitted by federal copyright law. Requests for permission to make copies of any part of the work should be addressed to Houghton Mifflin Harcourt Publishing Company, Attn: Contracts, Copyrights, and Licensing, 9400 South Park Center Loop, Orlando, Florida 32819.

Printed in the U.S.A.

ISBN   978-0-547-71936-8

20 0877 22 21 20 19
4500785625   CDEFG

If you have received these materials as examination copies free of charge, Houghton Mifflin Harcourt Publishing Company retains title to the materials and they may not be resold. Resale of examination copies is strictly prohibited.

Possession of this publication in print format does not entitle users to convert this publication, or any portion of it, into electronic format.

Write-In
Student Edition

Be an active reader and make this book your own!

Write your ideas, answer questions, make notes, and record activity results right on these pages.

Learn science concepts and skills by interacting with every page.

Gravity
Gravity pu...
force that k...
on the road...

...ushes
...nd **PULL**...

...ses objects
object... stop moving

Active Re... ...As you read these t...ges, draw circles around
two words th... ...e types of forces.

...hat have you pus... ...r pulled
...ay? Maybe you p...ed open a
...d on your shoes... ...sh or a
...ce. Suppose you wa... ...change
...omething is moving. A...
...an object's speed or dire...

Many ...rces act on you. Gravity is a for...
that pulls o...ects down to Earth. Gr...
keeps you on the ground or...
Friction is a fo...
against the direc...
slow things down...

Labs & Activities

Science is all about doing.

Ask questions and test your ideas.

Draw conclusions and share what you learn.

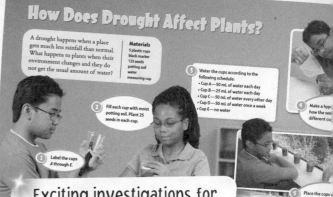

How Does Drought Affect Plants?

A drought happens when a place gets much less rainfall than normal. What happens to plants when their environment changes and they do not get the usual amount of water?

Materials
5 plastic cups
black marker
125 seeds
potting soil
water
measuring cup

1. Label the cups A through E.

2. Fill each cup with moist potting soil. Plant 25 seeds in each cup.

3. Water the cups according to the following schedule:
   • Cup A—50 mL of water each day
   • Cup B—25 mL of water each day
   • Cup C—50 mL of water every other day
   • Cup D—50 mL of water once a week
   • Cup E—no water

4. Make a hypo... how the see... different cup...

5. Place the cups ... windowsill. Obs... cups for two we...

Exciting investigations for every lesson.

e-Learning & Virtual Labs

Digital lessons and virtual labs provide e-learning options for every lesson of *ScienceFusion*.

What Are Organs and Body Systems?

The "Oddball Planets"

On your own or with a group, explore science concepts in a digital world.

360° of Inquiry

Contents

© Houghton Mifflin Harcourt Publishing Company

© Houghton Mifflin Harcourt Publishing Company (b) HMH

LIFE SCIENCE

© Houghton Mifflin Harcourt Publishing Company   (b) HMH

© Houghton Mifflin Harcourt Publishing Company (bl) ©Lee Beel/Alamy Images; (br) ©Juniors Bildarchiv/Alamy Images

© Houghton Mifflin Harcourt Publishing Company (b) ©David Noton/Alamy Images

Houghton Mifflin Harcourt Publishing Company (b) ©David Noton/Alamy Images

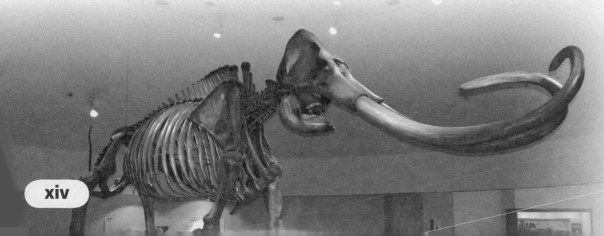

© Houghton Mifflin Harcourt Publishing Company (b) ©Martin Shields/Alamy Images

© Houghton Mifflin Harcourt Publishing Company

PHYSICAL SCIENCE

© Houghton Mifflin Harcourt Publishing Company (t) ©Getty Images/Digital Vision

© Houghton Mifflin Harcourt Publishing Company   (r) HMH; (l) HMH; (c) HMH

© Houghton Mifflin Harcourt Publishing Company (b) ©NASA

UNIT 1
How Scientists Work

© Houghton Mifflin Harcourt Publishing Company (inset) ©Mike Briner/Alamy; (bg) ©David Kennedy/Alamy; (border) ©NijsAge Fotostock

Big Idea

Scientists answer questions by careful observations and investigations.

I Wonder Why

Why do some scientists work outdoors and others work inside a laboratory? *Turn the page to find out.*

Here's why Scientists work to answer questions. Some questions can be answered with outdoor investigations. Other questions require tools in a lab.

In this unit, you will explore the Big Idea, the Essential Questions, and the Investigations on the Inquiry Flipchart.

Levels of Inquiry Key ■ DIRECTED ■ GUIDED ■ INDEPENDENT

Track Your Progress

Big Idea Scientists answer questions by careful observations and investigations.

Essential Questions

Now I Get the Big Idea!

Science Notebook

Before you begin each lesson, be sure to write your thoughts about the Essential Question.

© Houghton Mifflin Harcourt Publishing Company (Inset) ©Mike Briner/Alamy; (bg) ©David Kennedy/Alamy; (border) ©INDseAge Fotostock

What Is Science?

🧠 Engage Your Brain!

Find one answer to the following question in this lesson and write it here.

What are some science skills you could use when studying fish in an aquarium?

_____

_____

_____

Active Reading

Lesson Vocabulary

List the terms. As you learn about each one, make notes in the Interactive Glossary.

_____

_____

_____

_____

Use Headings

Active readers preview headings and use them to pose questions that set purposes for reading. Reading with a purpose helps active readers focus on understanding what they read in order to fulfill the purpose.

© Houghton Mifflin Harcourt Publishing Company (bkgd) ©Frans Lemmens/Getty Images

What All Scientists Do

Digging up fossils. Peering through telescopes. Mixing chemicals in a lab. Using computers to make weather predictions. These are only a few of the things scientists do.

Active Reading As you read these two pages, turn the heading into a question in your mind, and underline sentences that answer the question.

Does solving puzzles and searching for buried treasures sound like fun? If so, you might like being a paleontologist. Paleontologists are scientists who study the history of life on Earth. Like all scientists, they try to explain how and why things in the natural world happen. They answer questions by doing investigations. An **investigation** is a procedure carried out to carefully observe, study, or test something in order to learn more about it.

In addition to knowing a lot about living things of the past, paleontologists have to use many skills. In fact, all scientists use these skills. All scientists **observe**, or use their five senses to collect information. And all scientists **compare**, finding ways objects and events are similar and different.

Observe

Write one observation you could make about the fossil.

_____

_____

4

© Houghton Mifflin Harcourt Publishing Company (bkg) ©Tim Boyle/Getty Images

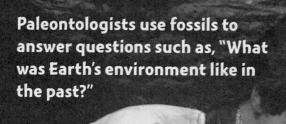

Paleontologists use fossils to answer questions such as, "What was Earth's environment like in the past?"

Paleontologists also work in labs, cleaning and studying fossils.

This paleontologist needs to observe the landscape to predict where fossils might be hidden. Once he finds the fossils, he compares them to fossils found in other parts of the world.

Paleontology is just one branch of science. **Science** is the study of the natural world and involves making observations and performing investigations. Scientists learn by thinking critically about the results of their investigations.

Compare

Observe these two skulls. List two ways they are similar and two ways they are different.

Similarities	Differences
_____	_____
_____	_____
_____	_____

© Houghton Mifflin Harcourt Publishing Company (bkgd) ©Tim Boyle/Getty Images; (t) ©MARIANA BAZO/Reuters/Corbis; (c) ©Robert Malone/Alamy; (b) ©Scott Camazine/Photo Researchers, Inc.

Prove It!

In the 1600s, there were not many ways to keep meat fresh. Rotting meat quickly filled with squirming, worm-like maggots. Yuck! Where did the maggots come from?

Active Reading On these two pages, circle the examples of evidence.

Rotten Meat turns into Maggots!

▶ Draw a large *X* through the explanation that was shown *not* to be true.

Travel back in time to the 1660s. Most people think flies, worms, and mice come from nonliving objects and rotting food. As *evidence*, or proof, they show how a dead animal's body soon becomes loaded with squirming maggots.

To a scientist, **evidence** is information collected during a scientific investigation. Some evidence, such as seeing a fossil dinosaur skull, is direct evidence that the dinosaur existed. Evidence can be indirect, such as finding a fossil footprint of a dinosaur.

Meet Dr. Francesco Redi, a scientist in Italy. A book Dr. Redi reads leads him to think maggots come from the eggs of flies. Redi **plans and conducts investigations** to gather evidence. He traps some maggots

© Houghton Mifflin Harcourt Publishing Company (all) ©PhotoDisc/Getty Images

The meat in the open jar soon became "wormy," while the meat in the sealed jar did not.

Redi placed fresh meat in two jars. He covered one jar and left the other jar uncovered.

▶ Fill in the blanks in this sequence graphic organizer.

Make observations and ask _____.

↓

Plan and conduct _____.

↓

Use _____ to explain observations.

inside jars with pieces of meat. He watches the maggots turn into adult flies. He observes adult flies laying eggs and more maggots come out of these eggs.

Redi then sets up an experiment. He places meat in several jars. Some jars are sealed and others are left open to the air. Redi observes that only the meat in jars he left open have maggots.

Redi experiments many times over. He tries dead fish, frogs, and snakes. All the evidence supports his idea: Living insects can only come from other living insects.

Maggots Hatch from eggs that flies lay.

© Houghton Mifflin Harcourt Publishing Company (all) ©PhotoDisc/Getty Images

A Sticky Trap

Humans are too big to get stuck in a spider's web. But there are some sticky traps you need to avoid when thinking like a scientist.

Active Reading As you read these two pages, turn the main heading into a question in your mind. Then underline sentences that answer the question.

▶ Look at the words in the spider web below. Star the things you *should* use to draw conclusions properly. Cross out the others.

Opinions

Favorites

Observations

Inferences

Evidence

Feelings

How to Draw Conclusions

Scientists **draw conclusions** from the results of their investigations. Any conclusion must be backed up with evidence. Other scientists judge the conclusion based on how much evidence is given. They also judge how well the evidence supports the conclusion.

Don't jump to conclusions too quickly. That's a sticky trap in science! As Dr. Redi did, repeat your investigations. Think about what you can **infer** from your observations. And then—only then—draw your conclusions.

Suppose you spend a week observing spiders. You might conclude that all spiders build webs to catch their food. This may be true of the spiders you observed, but it's not true of all spiders. Some spiders, such as wolf spiders, hunt for their prey instead.

© Houghton Mifflin Harcourt Publishing Company (bkg) ©Hu Zhao/Alamy

Observation Information collected by using the senses	The insect is stuck in the spider web.
Inference An idea or a conclusion based on an observation	A spider is going to use the bug for food later.
Opinion A personal belief that does not need proof	Spiders are really gross!

Opinion or Evidence?

An **opinion** is a belief or judgment. It doesn't have to be proved, or backed up with evidence. It might be your opinion that spiders are gross and disgusting. Others may disagree, but you are welcome to stick with your opinion!

Personal feelings and opinions should not affect how you do investigations. Nor should they affect your conclusions. It's hard to do, but science is about keeping an open mind. For example, don't ignore evidence just because you don't like what it means.

▶ Write one observation, one inference, and one opinion about what you see in the photo.

Observation	some spiders are hairy, colorful, scary.
Inference	spider can be big or small
Opinion	some spiders are cute!

© Houghton Mifflin Harcourt Publishing Company (bkg) ©Hu Zhao/Alamy; (t) ©Layne Kennedy/Corbis; (b) ©Jeffrey Coolidge/Getty Images

Knowledge Grows

How is a man investigating electricity and wires more than 350 years ago connected to the latest video game release?

Stephen Gray, a scientist born in 1666, was working at home when he discovered that electrical energy could move along a short metal wire. Gray carried his materials to friends' homes. He showed them how the materials worked and, together, they made the wire longer and longer.

Today there are so many ways for scientists to **communicate**, or share, the results of investigations. When scientists communicate clearly, others can repeat their investigations. They can compare their results with those of others. They can expand on one another's ideas. In these ways, scientific knowledge grows.

energy by living organisms

DATA

Communicate

List several ways you can communicate.

Sighn Langwidg,
wrighting
talking
emotions

© Houghton Mifflin Harcourt Publishing Company ©Nicole Hill/Getty Images

1729 Stephen Gray shows that electrical energy can be carried through a wire.

1882 Thomas Edison opens the first electricity generating station.

Knowledge grows when it is communicated. Each science discovery leads to new questions. More is learned and new things are invented.

The first video game was invented in 1958. The inventor was a scientist named William Higinbotham. The reason? To make Visitor's Day at his lab more interesting for the public! Hundreds of people lined up to play the game.

Take a look at the timeline. The science behind Higinbotham's game goes back hundreds of years or more.

1947 The transistor, needed to make radios and computers, is invented.

1953 The first computer is sold.

1958 William Higinbotham invents the first video game.

1967 First handheld calculator invented.

The first arcade games were not very complex.

1971 First coin-operated arcade video games in use.

1972 The first home video game systems are sold.

1977 The first handheld video games are sold.

2009 Scientists use super-fast video game cards inside computers to investigate the structure of molecules.

The video games of today are fast, complex, and interactive.

© Houghton Mifflin Harcourt Publishing Company   (t) ©North Wind Picture Archives/Alamy; (c) ©Bettmann/Corbis; (b) ©Andersen Foss/Getty Images

Meet Scientists

There are more people working as scientists today than ever before in history. Yet, there are plenty of unanswered questions left for you to answer!

Active Reading As you read these two pages, underline what each type of scientist studies.

Astronomer

Astronomers ask questions about how the universe works. Because novas, black holes, and galaxies are so far away, they use time/space relationships to investigate them. For example, astronomers measure space distances in units called light-years. That's how far light can travel in one Earth year.

Do the Math!
Use Fractions

Earth and Mars travel around the sun. Each time Earth makes one complete trip, Mars makes about $\frac{1}{2}$ of its trip.

1. How many trips does Earth make around the sun in the time it takes Mars to make one trip?

   ~~Art~~ two times.

2. In the drawing below, put an X where Mars will be after Earth completes five trips around the sun.

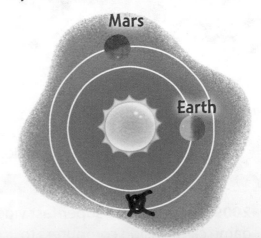

Mars

Earth

You don't have to be a pro to do astronomy. People have discovered many comets and exploding stars using telescopes in their back yards!

© Houghton Mifflin Harcourt Publishing Company ©Tetra Images/Alamy

Order

When you **order**, you place objects or events one after another in the correct sequence. Write the numbers *1, 2, 3,* and *4* to show the order of the images below.

Botanist

Botanists investigate questions about plants. For example, some botanists study how environmental conditions affect a plant's life cycle.

Taxonomist

Taxonomists are scientists who identify types of living things and classify them by how they are related. When you classify, you organize objects or events into categories based on specific characteristics.

Classify

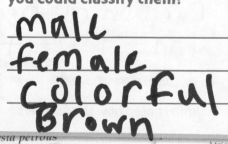

Look at the butterflies on this page. What are some ways you could classify them?

male
female
colorful
Brown

Lexias damalis
Asia

Yom...

...yrnia smolfildia
Africa

Agria...

...lena

Doxopoca agathina
America

Marpesia petrous
America

...us

...na emophon
America

Prepona dexamenes
America

...Africa

© Houghton Mifflin Harcourt Publishing Company (b) ©Mauro Fermariello/Photo Researchers, Inc.; (t) ©Noel Hendrickson/Getty Images; (inset) ©Roy McMahon/Corbis

Sum It Up!

When you're done, use the answer key to check and revise your work.

Read the summary, and fill in the missing words.

The goal of a scientist is to understand the natural world. To do this, a scientist plans and conducts 1. _____ .

Scientists use the 2. _____ they gather to draw 3. _____ .

A good scientist does not let his or her personal beliefs, or 4. _____, influence their study.

There are many important skills that scientists use. For example, when scientists 5. _____ , they use their observations and prior knowledge to determine what is happening.

Read each of the statements below. Write the science skill that each student used.

6. Angela made a list of how the two planets were alike.

_____

7. Krystal sorted the rocks into five groups based on their color.

_____

8. Robbie explained the results of his investigation to his classmates.

_____

9. Dmitri noted how the feathers looked and felt.

_____

10. Juan organized the steps of the process from first to last.

_____

© Houghton Mifflin Harcourt Publishing Company   ©Corbis

Answer Key: 1. investigations 2. evidence 3. conclusions 4. opinions 5. infer 6. compare 7. classify 8. communicate 9. observe 10. order

Name _____

Word Play

1 Complete the crossword puzzle. If you need help, use the terms in the yellow box.

Across

1. The study of the natural world through investigation
5. Collecting information by using the senses
6. An idea or a conclusion based on an observation
7. Facts and information collected over time
8. To put things into groups
9. A belief or a judgment

Down

2. The sharing of information
3. The observations and information that support a conclusion
4. The process of studying or testing something to learn more about it
5. To arrange things by when they happened or by their size

| classify | communication | evidence* | inference | investigation* |
| knowledge | observing | opinion* | order | science* |

* Key Lesson Vocabulary

© Houghton Mifflin Harcourt Publishing Company

Apply Concepts

2 Compare these two birds. List how they look similar and different.

All different

Similarities:
They are both Birds but don't have other similaraties

Differences:
color, Patern, Beaks, and shape.

3 Suppose someone tells you they saw a bird never before seen in your state. What kinds of evidence would you ask for?

Size, color, Beak, were did the find it, and if it was migrating.

4 What, in your opinion, is the scariest animal on Earth? How should this affect your investigations?

Spiders. Spiders can be poisinos, deadly and scare you!

5 One morning you see an outdoor garbage can tipped over. Plastic bags are torn open. What could you infer?

I infer that a racoon or bear got into the trash looking for food

Take It Home!

How can you communicate with people around the world, collect real data, and help answer a question? Research citizen science projects online. Choose an interesting project. Participate with your family.

© Houghton Mifflin Harcourt Publishing Company

1 A meteorologist is a person who studies weather.

2 Meteorologists use tools to measure temperature, wind speed, and air pressure.

6 THINGS
You Should Know About
Meteorologists

3 Meteorologists use data they collect to forecast the weather.

4 Computers help meteorologists share weather data from around the world.

5 Keeping good records helps meteorologists see weather patterns.

6 Meteorologists' forecasts help people stay safe during bad weather.

© Houghton Mifflin Harcourt Publishing Company

Be a Meteorologist

Answer the questions below using the Weather Forecast bar graph.

1 What was the temperature on Thursday? ~~73°~~ 90°F

2 Which day was cloudy and rainy? ~~Saterday~~ Wedn..

3 How much cooler was it on Tuesday than Thursday?
~~13°~~ 10°F

4 Which day was partly cloudy? Monday ~~Sunday~~

5 Compare the temperatures on Tuesday and
Friday. Which day had the higher temperature?
Friday

6 In the forecast below, which day has the highest
temperature Thursday ? The lowest?
Tuesday

WEATHER FORECAST

Temperature °F

90

85

80 — Partly cloudy (Monday) — Sunny (Tuesday) — Rainy (Wednesday) — Sunny (Thursday) — sunny (Friday)

75

70

| Monday | Tuesday | Wednesday | Thursday | Friday |

Day of week

© Houghton Mifflin Harcourt Publishing Company

Name _____

Essential Question

How Do Scientists Learn About the Natural World?

Set a Purpose
What will you learn from this investigation?

_____

_____

_____

_____

Think About the Procedure
How did you choose what predictions to write on your origami predictor?

_____

_____

_____

_____

Record Your Data
In the table below, record your results.

Date	Origami Prediction	Weather Service Prediction	Actual Weather

© Houghton Mifflin Harcourt Publishing Company

Draw Conclusions

Of the two kinds of weather predictions, which one was more likely to be correct? Explain.

_____

_____

_____

_____

Analyze and Extend

1. What results do you think you would get if you continued your investigation for a whole month?

_____

_____

_____

2. How do you think the weather service makes its predictions?

_____

_____

_____

3. Why is it important that scientists make good weather predictions?

_____

_____

_____

_____

4. The line graph shows average October air temperatures in Houston, TX. Can you predict the air temperature in Houston next October? If so, how?

_____

_____

_____

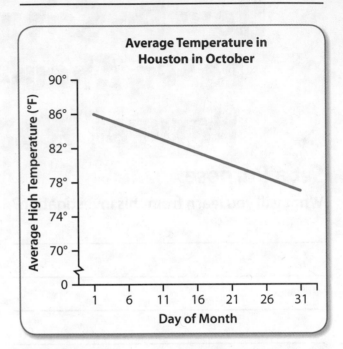

Average Temperature in Houston in October

5. What else would you like to find out about how scientists make predictions? Write each idea as a question.

_____

_____

_____

_____

_____

_____

© Houghton Mifflin Harcourt Publishing Company

Directions

1. Carefully tear this page out of your book.

2. Cut out the square below. You will use it to make your origami weather predictor.

3. On each set of lines, write a weather prediction.

4. Follow the instructions on the back of this page to fold and use your origami weather predictor.

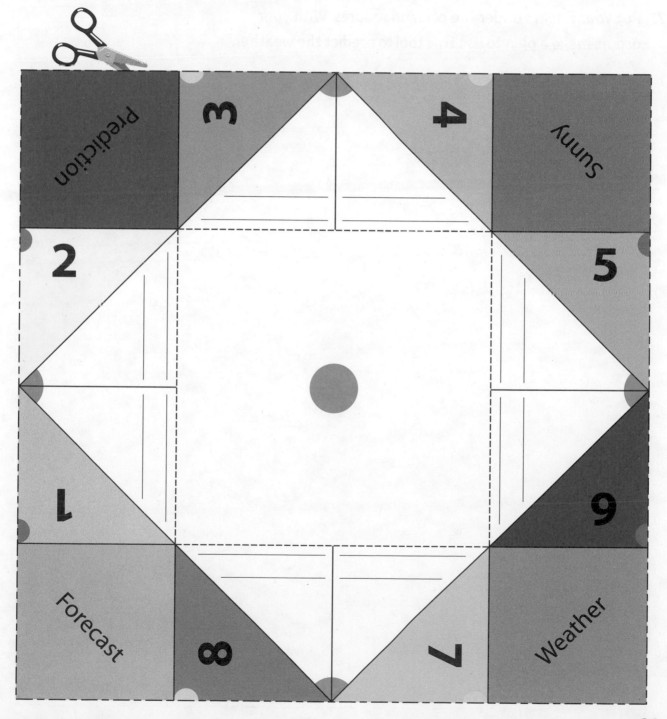

© Houghton Mifflin Harcourt Publishing Company

Directions (continued)

5. Fold the blue dots into the blue circle. Turn the paper over, and fold the green dots into the green circle.

6. Fold the paper in half so that the yellow dots touch each other. Make a crease, and unfold the paper. Fold it in half again so that the pink dots touch each other.

7. Put your fingers under the colorful squares. With your group, make a plan to use this tool to predict the weather.

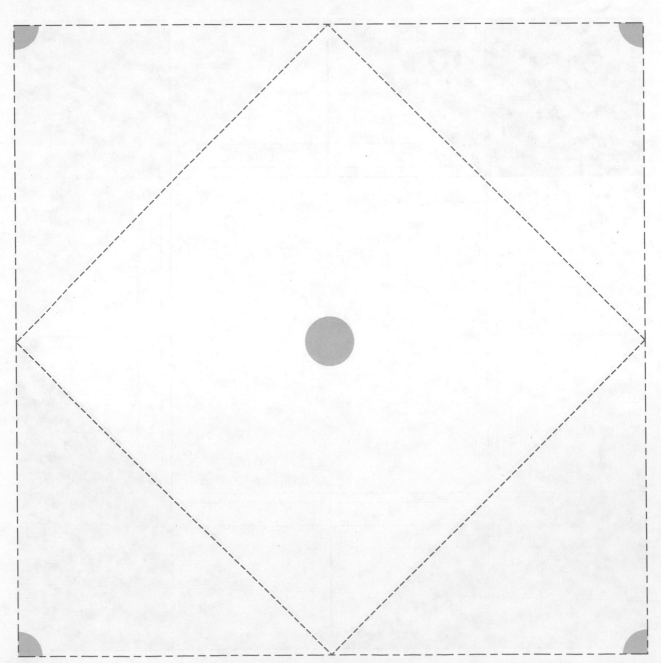

© Houghton Mifflin Harcourt Publishing Company

Essential Question

What Are Some Types of Investigations?

 **Engage Your Brain!**

Find one answer to the following question in this lesson and write it here.

What did this scientist do prior to starting her experiment with plants?

_____

_____

_____

_____

Active Reading

Lesson Vocabulary

List the terms. As you learn about each one, make notes in the Interactive Glossary.

_____

_____

_____

_____

Main Ideas

The main idea of a paragraph is the most important idea. The main idea may be stated in the first sentence, or it may be stated elsewhere. Active readers look for main ideas by asking themselves, What is this paragraph mostly about?

© Houghton Mifflin Harcourt Publishing Company ©Cultura/Alamy

A Process for Science

Testing bridge models, mapping a storm's path, searching the sky for distant planets—each of these investigations uses scientific methods.

Active Reading As you read these two pages, draw a line under each main idea.

How does the shape of the room affect the sound of a voice?

How does having a cold affect a person's singing?

Can a human voice shatter glass?

How high a note can a singer sing?

Start with a Question

Scientists observe the world and then ask questions that are based on their observations. But not all questions are the same. A good scientific question is one that can be answered by investigation. A scientific investigation always begins with a question.

Plan an Investigation

Once a scientist has a testable question, it is time to plan an investigation. **Scientific methods** are ways that scientists perform investigations. There are many ways that scientists investigate the world. But all scientific methods use logic and reasoning.

▶ Suppose you've just heard an opera singer warm up her voice. Write your own science question about the sounds a singer makes.

_____

_____

© Houghton Mifflin Harcourt Publishing Company   (br) ©GEORG HOCHMUTH/epa/Corbis

Experiments

In an experiment, scientists control all the conditions of the investigation. Scientists study what happens to a group of samples that are all the same except for one difference.

Repeated Observations

Scientists use repeated observation to study processes in nature that they can observe but can't control.

Using Models

Scientists use models when they cannot experiment on the real thing. Models help scientists investigate things that are large (like a planet), expensive (like a bridge), or uncontrollable (like the weather).

Investigations Differ

The method a scientist uses depends on the question he or she is investigating. An **experiment** is an investigation in which all of the conditions are controlled. Models are used to represent real objects or processes. Scientists make repeated observations to study processes in nature without disturbing them.

Drawing Conclusions

Whatever scientific methods are used, scientists will have results they can use to draw conclusions. The conclusions may answer the question they asked before they began. They may point to other questions and many more ideas for investigations.

▶ Write the type of investigation you should use to answer the following questions.

How do different bridge designs react to strong winds?

_____

How fast does the wind blow where a bridge will be built?

_____

Which type of paint works best to keep a bridge from rusting?

_____

© Houghton Mifflin Harcourt Publishing Company   (tr) ©Laura Ciapponi/Getty Images

Explosive Observations

How does a hurricane affect animals? Are coral reefs dying? How do whales raise their young? These are some science questions that can be answered with repeated observation.

Active Reading As you read these two pages, place a star next to three examples of repeated observation.

Old Faithful

Some science questions can only be answered by making observations. This is because some things are just too big, too far away, or too uncontrollable for experiments. However, much can be learned from repeated observation.

In Yellowstone National Park, heated water and steam shoots out of holes in the ground. This is called a geyser. Old Faithful is a famous geyser that erupts about every hour. Observations of the geyser collected over many years can be used to predict when the next eruption will occur. A prediction is a statement, based on information, about a future event.

The time until Old Faithful's next eruption is affected by how long the previous eruption lasted. Suppose the last eruption was at 3:05 p.m. and lasted 3 minutes 15 seconds. Predict when it will erupt next.

How long an eruption lasts	1 min 30 sec	2 min	2 min 30 sec	3 min	3 min 30 sec	4 min	4 min 30 sec	5 min
Time until next eruption	50 min	57 min	65 min	71 min	76 min	82 min	89 min	95 min

© Houghton Mifflin Harcourt Publishing Company • (bkgd) ©Laura Ciapponi/Getty Images

The first observation of a whale is often its spout.

Scientists have many questions about whales—the largest mammals on Earth. How long do whales live? How do they communicate? How do they care for their young? How far can they travel in a year? These questions can be answered with repeated observation.

For example, the tail flukes of whales are different from one whale to another. Scientists take photos of the flukes and use them to identify individual whales. Once they know which whale is which, they can recognize them each time they are seen in the ocean.

© Houghton Mifflin Harcourt Publishing Company (t) ©Wolfgang Kaehler/Corbis; (c) ©Game McGimsey/epa/Corbis

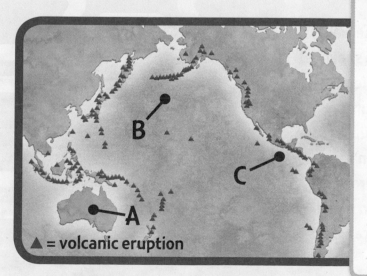

▲ = volcanic eruption

Predict

Scientists have observed and recorded volcanic eruptions for hundreds of years. The map to the left shows that data. Which location—A, B, or C— is most likely to have a volcanic eruption? _____
Why do you think scientists call this region the "Ring of Fire"?

_____

_____

Super Models

How does a bat fly? How might Saturn's rings look close up? How does a heart work? These are some science questions that can be answered with models.

Active Reading Circle different types of models that are described on these two pages.

Complex models can be made on a computer. This model shows where the most damage would occur if an earthquake were to strike.

When Modeling Is Needed

When scientists cannot experiment with the real thing, they can use models. Scientific models are needed to understand systems that have many hidden parts, such as an ant colony or the Internet. Scientists draw conclusions and make predictions by studying their models.

The closer the model represents the real thing, the more useful it is. So scientists change their models as they learn more.

Types of Models

Models are made in different ways. One way is to build a physical model. An earthquake shake table with model buildings on it is a physical model. Another way is to program computer simulation models. Scientists can speed up time in computer models so that they can see what might happen long in the future. Drawing diagrams and flow charts is a third way to make models. These two-dimensional models can be used to show how ideas are related.

Earthquakes are difficult to predict, and they can cause damage. New structures are designed to prevent damage.

© Houghton Mifflin Harcourt Publishing Company (t) ©Haruyoshi Yamaguchi/Sygma/Corbis (t) ©NASA/JPL/UCDavis

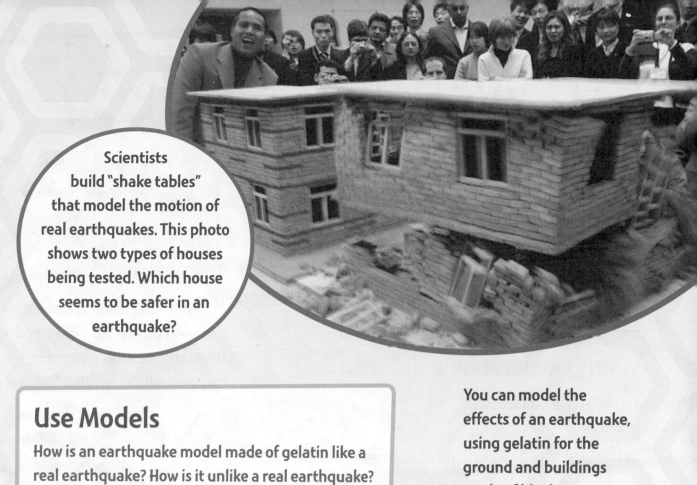

Scientists build "shake tables" that model the motion of real earthquakes. This photo shows two types of houses being tested. Which house seems to be safer in an earthquake?

Use Models

How is an earthquake model made of gelatin like a real earthquake? How is it unlike a real earthquake?

Alike: _____

_____

Different: _____

_____

You can model the effects of an earthquake, using gelatin for the ground and buildings made of blocks.

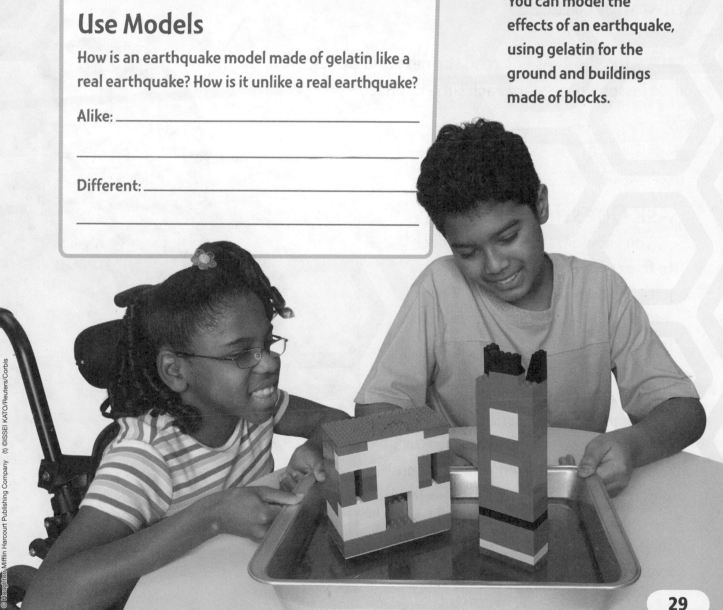

© Houghton Mifflin Harcourt Publishing Company (t) ©ISSEI KATO/Reuters/Corbis

How to Excel *in* Experimentation

You're enjoying a frozen juice pop. The heat of your tongue melts the pop. As you slurp the liquid, you think about how different substances freeze.

I know that water freezes at 0 degrees Celsius. How does adding other substances to water affect the temperature at which it freezes?

Active Reading As you read the next four pages, circle lesson vocabulary each time it is used.

Ask Questions

You know a freezer is cold enough to freeze water. You also know that juice is mostly water. You ask "Does adding substances to water affect its freezing point?"

Many science questions, including this one, can be answered by doing experiments. An **experiment** is a procedure used to test a *hypothesis*. It's a good idea to make some observations before stating a hypothesis. For example, you might put a small amount of orange juice in a freezer. Then you'd check it every few minutes to look for changes.

30

© Houghton Mifflin Harcourt Publishing Company

Hypothesize

A hypothesis is a statement that can be tested and will explain what can happen in an investigation. In the case of the freezing question, you think about what you already know. You can also talk to other people. And you can do research such as asking an expert.

You find out that the freezing point and melting point of a material should be the same temperature. An expert suggests that it is better to measure the melting point than the freezing point.

Design an Experiment

A well-designed experiment has two or more setups. This allows you to compare results among them. For the freezing/melting experiment, each setup will be a cup of liquid.

A **variable** is any condition in an experiment that can be changed. In most experiments, there are many, many variables to consider. The trick is to keep all variables the same in each setup, except one. That one variable is the one you will test.

Among the setups should be one called the control. The **control** is the setup to which you will compare all the others.

You've decided to dissolve different substances in water and freeze them. Then you plan to take them out of the freezer and use a thermometer to check their temperatures as they melt.

Hypothesize

Fill in the blank in the hypothesis. Any substance dissolved in water will _____ the temperature at which the mixture freezes and melts.

Identify and Control Variables

When you **identify and control variables**, you determine which conditions should stay the same and which one should be changed. Circle the variable that will be tested. Underline the variables that will remain the same.

- the kinds of cups
- the amount of water
- the material that is dissolved in the water
- the temperature of the freezer
- the types of thermometers
- the amount of time you leave the cups in the freezer

© Houghton Mifflin Harcourt Publishing Company

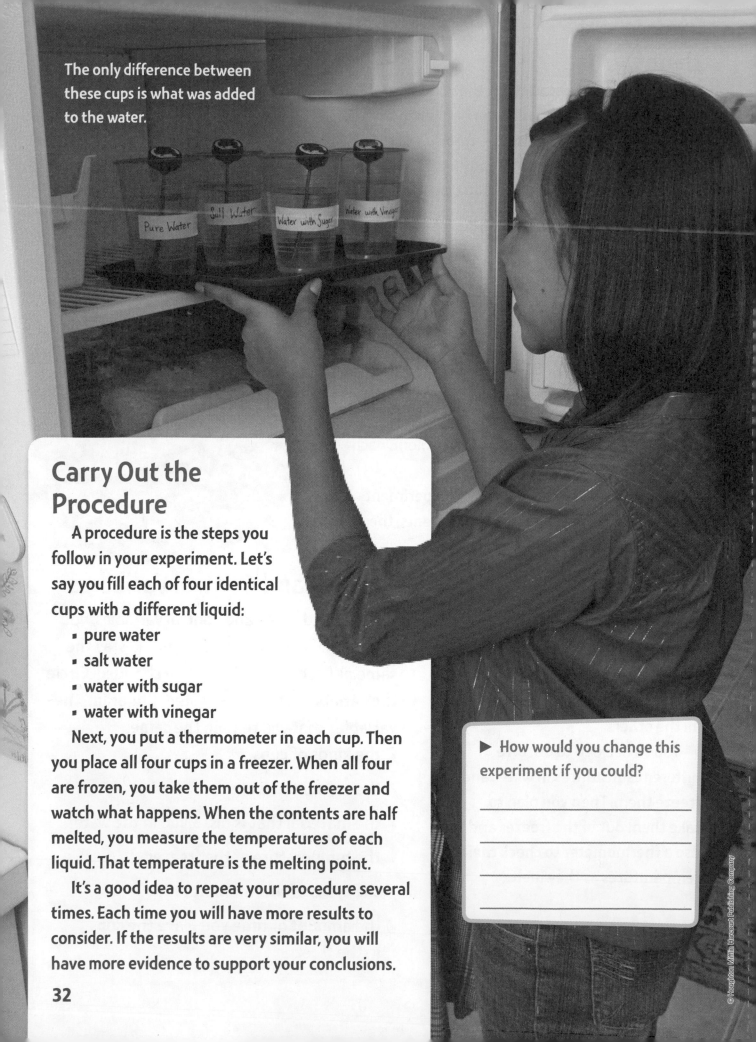

The only difference between these cups is what was added to the water.

Carry Out the Procedure

A procedure is the steps you follow in your experiment. Let's say you fill each of four identical cups with a different liquid:

- pure water
- salt water
- water with sugar
- water with vinegar

Next, you put a thermometer in each cup. Then you place all four cups in a freezer. When all four are frozen, you take them out of the freezer and watch what happens. When the contents are half melted, you measure the temperatures of each liquid. That temperature is the melting point.

It's a good idea to repeat your procedure several times. Each time you will have more results to consider. If the results are very similar, you will have more evidence to support your conclusions.

▶ How would you change this experiment if you could?

_____

_____

_____

_____

© Houghton Mifflin Harcourt Publishing Company

Record and Analyze Data

You could write down your observations as sentences. Or you could make a table to fill in. No matter how you do it, make sure you record correctly. Check twice or have a team member check.

Once the experiment is completed and the data recorded, you can analyze your results. If your data is in the form of numbers, math skills will come in handy. For example, in the data table below, you'll need to know how to write, read, and compare decimals.

Melting Point Experiment	
Substance	Melting Point (°C)
Pure water	0.0
Salt water	−3.7
Sugar water	−1.8
Vinegar water	−1.1

Draw Conclusions and Evaluate the Hypothesis

You draw conclusions based on your results. Remember that all conclusions must be supported with evidence. The more evidence you have, the stronger your conclusion.

Once you've reached a conclusion, look at your hypothesis. Decide if the hypothesis is supported or not. If not, try rethinking your hypothesis. Then design a new experiment to test it. That's what scientists do—build on what they learn.

Draw Conclusions

What conclusion can you draw based on this experiment?

_____

_____

_____

_____

_____

_____

© Houghton Mifflin Harcourt Publishing Company

Special Delivery: Data Displays

Once you've completed a science investigation, you'll want to share it. What's the best way to communicate the data you collected?

As part of their investigations, scientists collect, record, and interpret data. There is more than one way to display, or communicate, your data. Some kinds of displays are more suited to certain kinds of data than others.

Line graphs are suited to show change over time, especially small changes. If you want to show how much you grow each year, use a line graph.

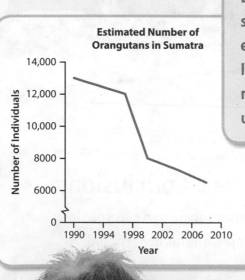

Estimated Number of Orangutans in Sumatra

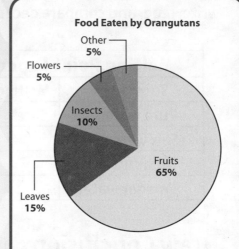

Food Eaten by Orangutans

- Other 5%
- Flowers 5%
- Insects 10%
- Fruits 65%
- Leaves 15%

Circle graphs are suited to comparing parts to the whole. If you want to show fractions or percents, use a circle graph.

Orangutan Using Tool to Feed

Diagrams are suited to show data that do not include numbers. This diagram shows how an orangutan uses a tool to eat seeds in fruit.

© Houghton Mifflin Harcourt Publishing Company   ©PhotoDisc/Getty Images

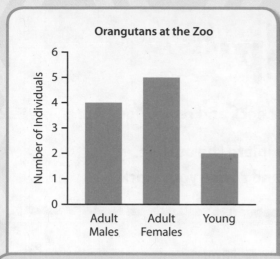

Orangutans at the Zoo

Number of Individuals

Adult Males | Adult Females | Young

Bar graphs are suited to compare things or groups of things. When your data are in categories, use a bar graph.

Do the Math!
Draw a Bar Graph

Draw a bar graph on this page. Use the data in the table below. Decide whether you want the bars to be vertical or horizontal. Carefully label the intervals on each axis. Draw the bars. Then title and label all the parts of your graph.

Number of Orangutans Counted	
Day	Number
Monday	7
Tuesday	13
Wednesday	10
Thursday	2
Friday	6

© Houghton Mifflin Harcourt Publishing Company ©PhotoDisc/Getty Images

Sum It Up!

When you're done, use the answer key to check and revise your work.

The outline below is a summary of the lesson. Complete the outline. When you are done, use the answer key to check and revise your work.

Summarize

I. Scientific Methods

  A. All start with a question

  B. Investigations differ

    1. experiments

    2. **1** _____

    3. **2** _____

  C. All have results from which to

    3 _____

II. Repeated Observations

  A. Some things are just too big, too far away, or too uncontrollable for experiments

  B. Examples

    1. volcanoes

    2. **4** _____

III. Using Models

  A. Needed to understand systems that have many hidden parts

  B. Types of models

    1. diagrams and flow charts

    2. **5** _____

    3. **6** _____

IV. Controlled Experiments

  A. Ask questions

  B. Hypothesize

  C. **7** _____

  D. Carry out the procedure

  E. **8** _____

  F. Draw conclusions

V. Organizing and Displaying Data

  A. Data displays help communicate

  B. Kinds of data displays

    1. circle graphs

    2. **9** _____

    3. **10** _____

    4. **11** _____

Answer Key: 1. models 2. repeated observations 3. draw conclusions 4. geysers or whales 5. computer simulation models 6. physical models 7. Design an experiment 8. Record and analyze data 9. line graphs 10. bar graphs 11. diagrams

© Houghton Mifflin Harcourt Publishing Company

Name _____

Word Play

1 Read each clue. Then find and circle the term in the word search puzzle.
Clues

1. All the ways scientists do investigations:
_ _ _ _ _ _ _ _ _ _ _ _ _ _
_ _ _ _ _ _ _ _ _

2. These should be as similar as possible to the real thing: _ _ _ _ _ _ _ _

3. The part of an experiment used to compare all the other groups:
_ _ _ _ _ _ _

4. What scientists do that is the basis for their investigations:
_ _ _ _ _ _ _ _ _ _ _ _ _ _ _

5. Any condition in an experiment that can be changed: _ _ _ _ _ _ _ _ _ _

6. A type of graph suited to show change over time: _ _ _ _ _ _ _ _ _ _ _ _ _

7. A statement that can be tested and that explains what you think will happen in an experiment:
_ _ _ _ _ _ _ _ _ _ _ _ _ _

8. The steps you follow in your experiment:
_ _ _ _ _ _ _ _ _ _ _ _

9. To use patterns in observations to say what may happen next:
_ _ _ _ _ _ _ _ _

10. An investigation that is controlled:
_ _ _ _ _ _ _ _ _ _ _ _

CHALLENGE: How many other important words from this lesson can you find in the word search? Write them below.

_____
_____
_____
_____
_____
_____

```
R T A S N O I T S E U Q K S A R S
C O L L E C T D A T A R S A T S I
S C I E N T I F I C M E T H O D S
B B N Z X E J E O E S T S A U Y E
A Z E Y N P I D D V U L O T Q S H
R F G L A C E A A U F Q E A T V T
G W R A M D N R E P L P T D V L O
R C A N C I I R I W N C I D O D P
A E P A C A D G R M I U N R A M Y
P I H A B G K N I D E P T O B Z H
H N K L Y R H L E A H N Y C C U A
R Y E W D A X R V M O A T E N R A
A N G L B M P R O C E D U R E Y D
```

© Houghton Mifflin Harcourt Publishing Company

Apply Concepts

2 For each question, state which kind of investigation works best: repeated observations, using models, or controlled experiments. Then explain how you would do the investigation.

What kinds of birds visit a feeder at different times of the year?

_____

_____

_____

Does hot water or cold water boil faster?

_____

_____

_____

What are the parts of an elevator and how does it work?

_____

_____

How does the length of a kite's tail affect the way it flies?

_____

_____

3 Ryan hypothesizes that darker colors heat up faster. He places a thermometer inside a red wool sock, a green cotton glove, and a black nylon hat. What's wrong with his procedure?

_____

_____

_____

_____

Take It Home!

Use scientific methods to help your family enjoy a healthy snack. Design an experiment to find out whether coating apple slices in lemon juice can stop them from turning brown. Perform your experiment.

© Houghton Mifflin Harcourt Publishing Company

Name _____

Essential Question

How Do You Perform a Controlled Experiment?

Set a Purpose
What will you learn from this experiment?

_____
_____
_____
_____
_____
_____

Think About the Procedure
What is the tested variable in this experiment?

_____

Each time you try the same test, it is called a trial. Why is it important to do repeated trials of this experiment?

_____
_____
_____
_____

Record Your Data
In the table below, record your results.

Surface Material	Height Ball Bounced					
	Trial 1	Trial 2	Trial 3	Trial 4	Trial 5	Average

© Houghton Mifflin Harcourt Publishing Company

Draw Conclusions

What can you conclude based on your experiment?

_____

_____

_____

_____

Analyze and Extend

1. **Think about the materials the ball bounced on. What was it about them that affected the height of the bounce?**

    _____

    _____

    _____

    _____

2. **What other floor materials could you test? Predict the results.**

    _____

    _____

    _____

    _____

3. **Tennis is played on three types of surfaces: grass, packed clay, and hard courts. Hard courts are often made from asphalt, the black road surface material, with paint on top. Predict how these surfaces would affect ball bounces. Then do some research. Find out the pros and cons of each type.**

    _____

    _____

    _____

    _____

    _____

    _____

4. **What else would you like to find out about how balls bounce?**

    _____

    _____

    _____

    _____

    _____

    _____

    _____

© Houghton Mifflin Harcourt Publishing Company

Essential Question

What Are Some Science Tools?

Engage Your Brain!

Find the answer to the following question in this lesson and write it here.

This scientific equipment is filled with liquids. What tools can scientists use to measure the volume of a liquid?

_____

_____

_____

Active Reading

Lesson Vocabulary

List the terms. As you learn about each one, make notes in the Interactive Glossary.

_____

_____

_____

_____

Compare and Contrast

Many ideas in this lesson are connected because they explain comparisons and contrasts—how things are alike and different. Active readers stay focused on comparisons and contrasts when they ask themselves, How are these things alike? How are they different?

© Houghton Mifflin Harcourt Publishing Company ©MOODBOARD/age fotostock

Field Trips

If you like school field trips, you might want to become a field scientist. Field scientists travel around the world studying science in the wild. They pack their tools and take them along.

Active Reading As you read these two pages, box the names of all the science tools.

Field scientists go "on location" to investigate the natural world. Their investigations are often in the form of repeated observations. They use tools to increase the power of their senses. Their choices of tools depend on the questions they ask.

Collecting Net

What kinds of animals swim near the shore of a pond? A scientist might use a collecting net and an observation pan to answer this question. By carefully pulling the net through the water, they can catch small animals without harming them.

© Houghton Mifflin Harcourt Publishing Company (bc) ©Steven May/Alamy; (t) ©Arville/Getty Images; (tc) ©Stockdisc/Getty Images; (r) ©Don Hammond/Design Pics/Corbis

Hand Lens

How does an ant move? How does it use its mouthparts? A hand lens might help answer these questions. Hold the hand lens near your eye. Then move your other hand to bring the object into view. Move the object back and forth until it is in sharp focus.

Cameras

What do lion fish eat? How do they catch their food? To investigate, a scientist might use an underwater video camera. Cameras help scientists record events.

Do the Math!
Estimate by Sampling

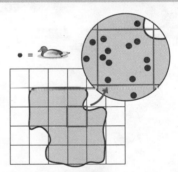

Scientists photograph ducks from a plane and then draw a grid over the photo. How many ducks do you estimate are on the whole lake?

_____

Why might your estimate differ from the actual number of ducks?

_____

_____

_____

© Houghton Mifflin Harcourt Publishing Company · (t) ©Pascal Goetgheluck/Photo Researchers, Inc.; (b) ©Imagebroker/Alamy

Into the Lab

What's living in a drop of pond water? Lots of tiny critters! Some behave like animals. Others are like plants. All are too small to be seen with only a hand lens.

Active Reading As you read these two pages, draw lines connecting the pairs of tools being compared to each other.

Science tools can be heavy and expensive. If you want to observe the tiniest pond life, you'll need science tools that are too big or too delicate to be carried into the field. For example, scientists use computers to record and analyze data, construct models, and communicate with other scientists.

Use Numbers

Some tools help scientists count things. Some scientists estimate, while others perform complex mathematical calculations. All scientists must be comfortable **using numbers**.

▶ To find the magnification of a light microscope, multiply the power of the eyepiece lens by the power of the objective lens. The letter X stands for how many times bigger objects appear.

Eyepiece Magnification	Objective Magnification	Total Magnification
10X	40X	
15X	60X	
8X	100X	

© Houghton Mifflin Harcourt Publishing Company   (t) ©Image Source/Corbis; (tc) ©Arville/Getty Images; (b) ©CDC/PHIL/Corbis

Light Microscope

The tiny living things in pond water are **microscopic**, or too small to see with just your eyes. A light microscope magnifies things, or makes them look bigger. The object to be viewed is placed on a clear slide. Light passes through the object and two lenses. You look through the eyepiece and turn knobs to focus an image.

Dropper

A dropper is a tube with a rubber bulb on one end. Squeeze the bulb and then dip the tip into a liquid. Release the bulb, and the liquid will be sucked up the tube. When you slowly squeeze the bulb, the liquid drops out.

Electron Microscope

Light microscopes have been around for 500 years. But technology, or people's use of tools, has improved. Today a scanning electron microscope (SEM) can magnify an object up to one million times. The SEM shoots a beam of electrons at the object. An image of the surface of the object appears on a computer screen.

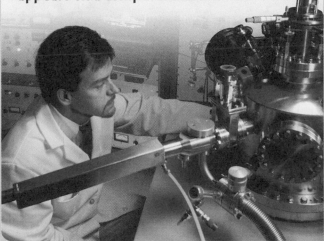

Pipette

A pipette is a tool like a dropper, but it's more exact. It is used to add or remove very small amounts of liquids. Pipettes often have marks on the side to measure volume. One kind of pipette makes drops so tiny that they can only be seen with a scanning electron microscope!

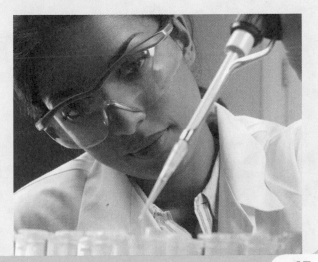

© Houghton Mifflin Harcourt Publishing Company   (tl) ©Laguna Design/Photo Researchers, Inc.; (tc) ©Hll Street Studios/Blend Images/Corbis; Inc.; (tr) ©Simon Jarratt/Corbis; (br) ©Tek Image/Photo Researchers, Inc.; (bl) ©Tom Tracy Photography/Alamy

Measuring Up

What do a digit, a palm, a hand, a dram, a peck, a rod, and a stone have in common? They all are, or were at one time, units of measurement!

Active Reading As you read the next four pages, circle all the units of measurement.

When you **measure**, you make observations involving numbers and units. Today most countries use the International System (SI) units in daily life. If you were to visit these countries, you'd purchase fruit or cheese by the *kilogram*. In the United States, most everyday measurements use units from the time when English colonists lived in America.

However, scientists around the world—including those in the United States—use the SI, or metric system.

The metric system is based on multiples of 10. In the metric system, base units are divided into smaller units using prefixes such as *milli-, centi-,* and *deci-*. Base units are changed to bigger units using prefixes such as *deca-* and *kilo-*.

Measuring Length

Length is the distance between two points. The base metric unit of length is the *meter*. Rulers, metersticks, and tape measures are tools used to measure length.

A caliper can be used to measure the distance between the two sides of an object.

© Houghton Mifflin Harcourt Publishing Company   (bl) ©Frans Lanting/Corbis; (br) ©Stuart O'Sullivan/Corbis

Measuring Time

Time describes how long events take. The base unit of time is the second. Larger units are the minute, the hour, and the day. Smaller units include the millisecond and microsecond. Clocks, stopwatches, timers, and calendars are some of the tools used to measure time.

Measure Your Science Book

Use a metric tool and units to measure the length, width, and thickness of your science book.

Length: _____

Width: _____

Thickness: _____

Measuring Temperature

Temperature describes how hot or cold something is. Thermometers are used to measure temperature. Scientists measure temperature in degrees Celsius. So do most other people around the world. In the United States, degrees Fahrenheit are used to report the weather, to measure body temperatures, and in cooking.

© Houghton Mifflin Harcourt Publishing Company   (tl) ©Stephen Dalton/Photo Researchers, Inc.; (bc) ©Artville/Getty Images; (br) ©WILscape/Alamy

With this balance, you can directly compare the masses of two objects. Put one object in each pan. The pan that sinks lower contains the greater mass.

Pan Balance

A **balance** is a tool used to measure mass. *Mass* is the amount of matter in an object. The base unit of mass is the kilogram. One kilogram equals 1,000 grams.

To measure in grams, place an object in one pan.

Always carry a balance by holding its base.

Add gram masses to the other pan until the two pans are balanced. Then add the values of the gram masses to find the total mass.

This pan balance has drawers where the masses are stored.

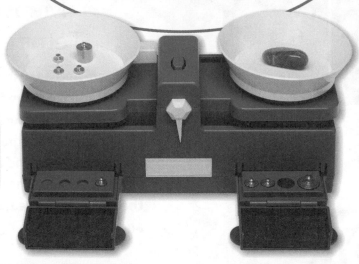

Three Beams

A triple-beam balance measures mass more exactly than the pan balance. It has one pan and three beams. To find the number of grams, move the sliders until the beam balances.

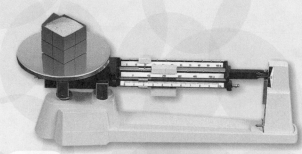

Digital Mass

An electronic balance calculates the mass of an object for you. It displays an object's mass on a screen.

© Houghton Mifflin Harcourt Publishing Company   (bl) ©Sam Dudgeon/HRW

How Strong?

A **spring scale** is a tool used to measure force. Force is a push or a pull. When an object hangs down from the scale, the force of gravity, or weight, is measured. When the spring scale is used to pull an object, it measures the force needed to move the object. Either way, the base unit is called a newton.

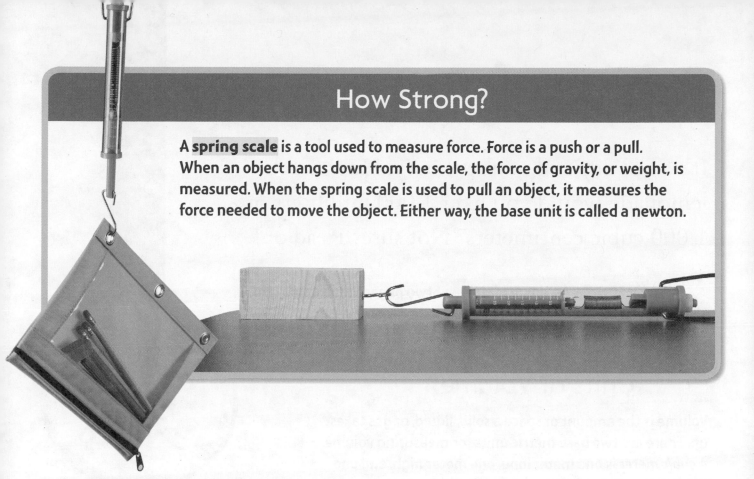

▶ Draw lines to match the tools to what they measure and the units.

Tool	What It Measures	Units
	▪ force ▪	▪ seconds, minutes, hours, days, years, etc.
	▪ temperature ▪	▪ grams, milligrams, kilograms, etc.
	▪ length ▪	▪ newtons
	▪ mass ▪	▪ degrees Celsius, degrees Fahrenheit
	▪ time ▪	▪ meters, kilometers, millimeters, etc.

© Houghton Mifflin Harcourt Publishing Company (thermometer) ©Eyewire/Getty Images

More Measuring

It's a hot day and you're thirsty. How much lemonade would you like? 1,000 milliliters or 1,000 cubic centimeters? Not sure? Read on!

Active Reading As you read the next two pages, circle important words that are defined, and underline their definitions.

Units of Volume

Volume is the amount of space a solid, liquid, or gas takes up. There are two base metric units for measuring volume. A *cubic meter* is one meter long, one meter high, and one meter wide. The *liter* is the base unit often used for measuring the volume of liquids. You're probably familiar with liters because many drinks are sold in 1-liter or 2-liter bottles. These two metric units of volume are closely related. There are 1,000 liters (L) in one cubic meter (m^3).

▶ One cubic centimeter (cm^3) is equal to 1 milliliter (mL). Both are equal to about 20 drops from a dropper.
Which is greater—1,000 mL or 1,000 cm^3?

_____

1 cm
1 cm
1 cm

© Houghton Mifflin Harcourt Publishing Company (b) ©Medioimages/Photodisc/Getty Images; (c) ©D. Hurst/Alamy

Finding Volume

You can find the volume of a rectangular prism by multiplying length times width times height. To find the volume of a liquid, use a measuring cup, beaker, or graduated cylinder. Use water to find the volume of an irregular solid. Put water in a graduated cylinder. Note the volume. Then drop the object in and note the new volume. Subtract the two numbers to find the volume of the object.

The surface of a liquid in a graduated cylinder is curved. This curve is called a *meniscus*. Always measure volume at the bottom of the meniscus.

Accurate Measurements

When a measurement is close to the true size, it is **accurate**. Try to measure as accurately as you can with the tools you have. Make sure a tool is not broken and that you know how to use it properly. Also pay attention to the units on the tools you use. Accurate measurements are important when doing science investigations, when baking, and when taking medicines.

Follow these tips to improve your accuracy:

☑ Handle each tool properly.

☑ Use each tool the same way every time. For example, read the measurement at eye level.

☑ Measure to the smallest place value the tool allows.

☑ Measure twice.

☑ Record your measurements carefully, including the units.

▶ Write the math sentence for finding the volume of the toy.

_____

© Houghton Mifflin Harcourt Publishing Company   (b) ©Ronnie Kaufman/Larry Hirshowitz/Getty Images

Sum It Up!

When you're done, use the answer key to check and revise your work.

There are many kinds of tools that scientists use. Tools help scientists observe, measure, and study things in the natural world. Fill in the blank boxes with examples of tools that scientists use.

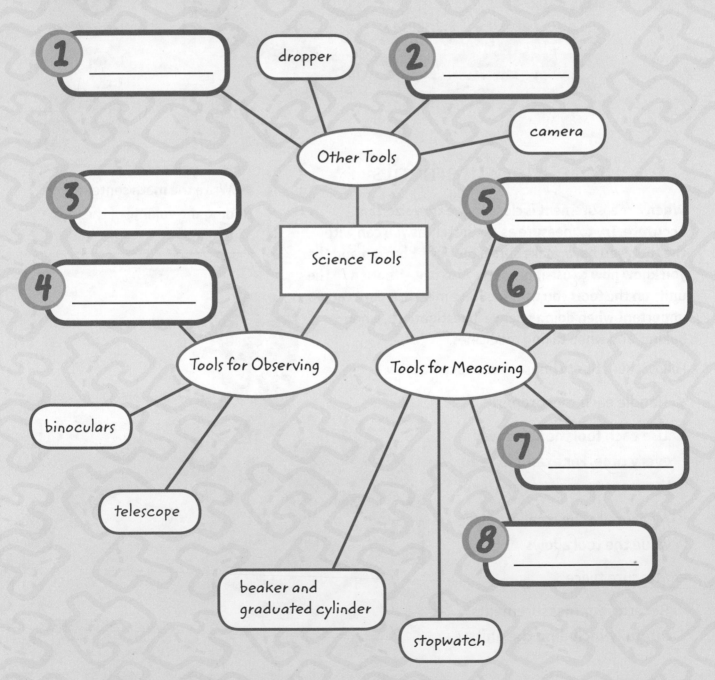

1 _____

dropper

2 _____

camera

Other Tools

3 _____

4 _____

5 _____

6 _____

Science Tools

Tools for Observing

Tools for Measuring

binoculars

telescope

beaker and graduated cylinder

7 _____

8 _____

stopwatch

© Houghton Mifflin Harcourt Publishing Company

Answer Key: 1 and 2—computer or collecting net; 3 and 4—microscope or hand lens; 5, 6, 7, and 8—thermometer, balance, spring scale, and ruler or meterstick.

Name _____

Word Play

1 Put the scrambled letters in order to spell a science term.

1. **treem** ⃝_ _⃝_ _ _ A metric unit of length

2. **amrg** _ _⃝_ _ A metric unit of mass

3. **rdsgeee seCisul** _ _ _ _ _ _⃝_
   _ _ _ _⃝_ _ _ A metric unit for temperature

4. **taceurca** _ _ _⃝_ _ _⃝_ _ A measurement close to the true size

5. **townne** _ _ _⃝_ _ _ _ A unit used to measure force

6. **trile** _ _ _ _⃝_ A metric unit of volume

7. **acnsrl spgei** _ _ _ _ _ _⃝_ A tool used to measure force

8. **nap cablane** ⃝_ _ _
   _ _ _ _ _ _ A tool used to measure mass

9. **dceson** ⃝_ _ _ _ _ A metric unit of time

10. **veumol** _ _ _⃝_ _ _ The amount of space a solid, liquid, or gas takes up

11. **tagurdade lycnidre** ⃝_ _ _ _ _ _ _ _
    _ _ _ _ _⃝_ _ A tool used to measure volume

Riddle: Place the circled letters in order to solve the riddle below.

Why did the captain ask for a balance?

He wanted to _ _ _ _ _ _ _ _ _

the mass of the _ _ _ _ _ _ _ _ _ _ _ _ _ .

© Houghton Mifflin Harcourt Publishing Company

2 Tell how you use one or more of these tools to investigate each question.

How are two fossil teeth similar and different?

_____

_____

_____

Which kinds of butterflies are found in a field?

_____

_____

_____

What do scientists already know about the bottom of the ocean?

_____

_____

_____

Does the mass of a ball affect how far it rolls?

_____

_____

_____

3 Identify what each tool measures and the metric units it uses.

_____   _____   _____

_____   _____   _____

Take It Home!

At your school or public library, find a book about how scientists work or the tools they use. Read and discuss the book with your family. Prepare a brief summary to present to your classmates.

54

© Houghton Mifflin Harcourt Publishing Company

Name _____

Essential Question

How Can Scientists Learn from Observations?

Set a Purpose
What will you learn from this investigation?

_____

_____

_____

_____

Think About the Procedure
What planning must I do before this investigation?

_____

_____

_____

_____

_____

What tools are used in this investigation. What measurements, if any, are taken with them?

_____

_____

_____

_____

_____

Record Your Data
In the space below, record your results.

Soil Sample: _____

My Observations:

Amount of water held by
100 mL of soil: _____

Mass Before Drying: _____

Mass After Drying: _____

© Houghton Mifflin Harcourt Publishing Company

Draw Conclusions

Compare your data with the data from other groups. What can you conclude?

_____

_____

_____

_____

Analyze and Extend

1. Why is it important that soils be able to hold some water?

_____

_____

_____

_____

2. Why would a farmer want to know about the soil on his or her farm?

_____

_____

_____

_____

3. How was this investigation different from a controlled experiment?

_____

_____

_____

_____

4. Why was it important to know the mass of the soil before it was dried for one week?

_____

_____

_____

_____

5. What else would you like to find out about different types of soils?

_____

_____

_____

_____

_____

© Houghton Mifflin Harcourt Publishing Company

Unit 1 Review

Vocabulary Review

Use the terms in the box to complete the sentences.

> balance
> control
> evidence
> experiment
> microscopic
> opinion
> spring scale
> variable

1. An investigation in which all conditions are controlled is

   a(n) _____.

2. Jane wants to measure the mass of a rock. The tool she should

   use is a(n) _____.

3. Any condition in an experiment that can be changed is

   a(n) _____.

4. The setup to which you compare all the others in an experiment

   is the _____.

5. The information that scientists collect as they investigate the

   natural world is _____.

6. Objects that are too small to see with your eyes alone are

   _____.

7. Jaime wants to find out how much force it takes to pull a toy car
   up a ramp. The tool he should use is

   a(n) _____.

8. A belief or judgment that is not supported by investigation is

   a(n) _____.

© Houghton Mifflin Harcourt Publishing Company   HMH Credits

Science Concepts

Fill in the letter of the choice that best answers the question.

9. Josh has been growing plants that received $\frac{1}{2}$ cup of water two times per week. Now he wants to see what happens when the amount of water is reduced, as shown in the chart.

Plant	Amount of Water
1	$\frac{1}{2}$ cup two times per week
2	$\frac{1}{2}$ cup once per week
3	$\frac{1}{2}$ cup once every two weeks
4	no water

Which plant is the control?

(A) Plant 1   (B) Plant 2

(C) Plant 3   (D) Plant 4

10. Observations are made using the five senses. We can use observations to draw conclusions. Which of the following is a conclusion?

(A) "The object is flat."

(B) "The flower smells like mint."

(C) "Crickets chirp to attract mates."

(D) "The food tastes salty."

11. Four students threw darts at the center of a dartboard. Which target shows the most accurate results?

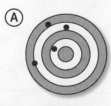
(A)

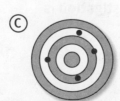
(C)

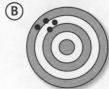
(B)

(D)

12. Samara observes and sketches the phases of the moon during a five-week period. Her drawings are shown here.

Which statement best describes Samara's investigation?

(A) It involves modeling.

(B) It involves experimentation.

(C) It involves repeated observations.

(D) It involves both experimentation and repeated observations.

13. Sometimes the results of an investigation are not what were expected. When this happens, what should a scientist do?

(A) change the results

(B) defend the results as correct

(C) plan another investigation to test the results of the first one

(D) ignore the first set of results and plan a different investigation

14. Why do scientists repeat their experiments?

(A) to avoid making observations

(B) to throw out the information they collected earlier

(C) to develop a new procedure that they can use later

(D) to make sure that the information they collect is reliable

© Houghton Mifflin Harcourt Publishing Company   HMH Credits

15. Maria counts the number of people who attend several basketball games. She displays her data using a bar graph.

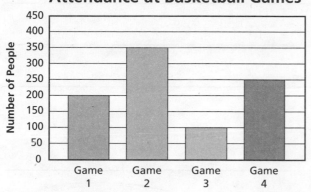

Attendance at Basketball Games

How many more people did Maria observe at Game 2 than at Game 1?

- (A) 100
- (B) 150
- (C) 200
- (D) 550

16. Jen wants to find out which of four surfaces produces the least friction when a ball rolls over it. She designs an experiment in which the same type of object rolls over each material under the same conditions. She repeats the experiment three times for each material, averaging how far the object travels before stopping during the three trials. Which would be the **best** way for Jen to record her observations and data?

- (A) in a table
- (B) as a line graph
- (C) as a circle graph
- (D) in a Venn diagram

17. Lia measured the volume of a liquid using a graduated cylinder. The following illustration shows three positions from which she could take a reading.

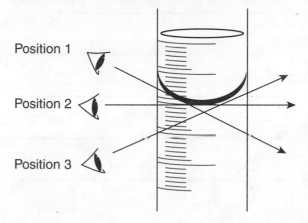

From which position will Lia get an accurate reading?

- (A) Position 1
- (B) Position 2
- (C) Position 3
- (D) All of the positions give accurate readings.

18. Asa watches his mom rub soap on her finger to help her get a ring unstuck. He thinks the soap must reduce friction. He designs an investigation to test his idea. He pulls a weight across a board and records the force with a spring scale. He then puts soap on the board and pulls the weight again at the same speed. Which of the following variables is Asa measuring?

- (A) the speed with which the weight is pulled
- (B) the amount of weight being pulled
- (C) the force needed to pull the weight
- (D) the type of surface the weight is being pulled across

© Houghton Mifflin Harcourt Publishing Company   HMH Credits

Apply Inquiry and Review the Big Idea

19. Aaliya knows that sliced apples turn brown when left out in the open air. She also knows that pouring certain liquids on them will keep this from happening. Aaliya thinks that water, ginger ale, or lemon juice may do the trick. How could Aaliya set up an experiment to find out which one will work? What are the variables? What will she use as a control?

_____

_____

_____

_____

20. Yamil is observing a fossil insect preserved in amber.

What can Yamil learn about the fossil through observation? What tools might she use to make her observations?

_____

_____

_____

_____

21. Identify which statement below is a hypothesis, and explain why. How could you determine whether the hypothesis is correct?

  a. Ocean water is too salty.

  b. Water heats faster if it contains salt.

  c. Space probes have discovered small amounts of water on the moon.

_____

_____

_____

© Houghton Mifflin Harcourt Publishing Company   HMH Credits

The Engineering Process

Big Idea

Technology is all around us. Engineers apply their knowledge of science to design solutions to practical problems.

I Wonder Why

Mixers, rollers, cutters, tumblers, and hoppers, all run by electricity! I wonder why it takes so many machines to make a gumball?

© Houghton Mifflin Harcourt Publishing Company (bg) ©Mark Joseph/PhotoDisc/Getty Images (border) ©Jayme Thornton/Getty Images (inset) ©NDisc/Age Fotostock

Here's why Food processing relies on technology. Machines produce treats that always have the same taste, color, smell, and size. When a gumball pops out of the dispenser, you know exactly what you're getting!

In this unit, you will explore the Big Idea, the Essential Questions, and the Investigations on the Inquiry Flipchart.

Levels of Inquiry Key ■ DIRECTED ■ GUIDED ■ INDEPENDENT

Big Idea Technology is all around us. Engineers apply their knowledge of science to design solutions to practical problems.

Essential Questions

Now I Get the Big Idea!

Science Notebook

Before you begin each lesson, be sure to write your thoughts about the Essential Question.

© Houghton Mifflin Harcourt Publishing Company · (b) ©Mark Joseph/PhotoDisc/Getty Images; (bkgd) ©Jayme Thornton/Getty Images; (border) ©IODIS/Age Fotostock

© Houghton Mifflin Harcourt Publishing Company • ©Leslie Garland Picture Library/Alamy

Essential Question

What Is the Design Process?

Engage Your Brain!

Find the answer to the following question in this lesson and record it here.

What are the steps for designing technology such as the robot arm you see here?

_____

_____

_____

_____

_____

_____

Active Reading

Lesson Vocabulary
List the terms. As you learn about each one, make notes in the Interactive Glossary.

_____   _____

_____   _____

Problem–Solution
Ideas in this lesson may be connected by a problem–solution relationship. Active readers mark a problem with a *P* to help them stay focused on the way information is organized. When multiple solutions are described, they mark each solution with an *S*.

Works of Ingenuity

Did you brush your teeth this morning? Did you run water from a faucet? Did you ride to school in a car or bus? If you did any of those things, you used a product of engineering.

Active Reading As you read these pages, underline the names of engineered devices.

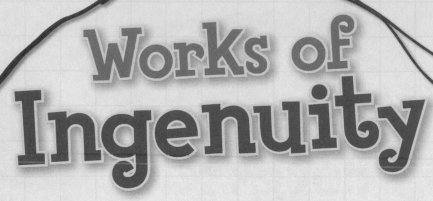
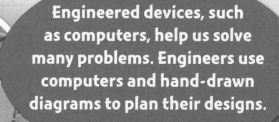

Engineered devices, such as computers, help us solve many problems. Engineers use computers and hand-drawn diagrams to plan their designs.

© Houghton Mifflin Harcourt Publishing Company (bl) ©Sami Sarkis/Getty Images; (tc) ©Tim Macpherson/Getty Images; (bc) ©George Steinmetz/Corbis

Engineers are problem solvers. They invent or improve products that help us meet our needs. Engineers use their knowledge of science and mathematics to find solutions to everyday problems. This process is called **engineering**.

From the start of each day, we use the products of engineering. Engineered devices are found all around us. They include simple tools and complex machines.

Engineers work in many fields. Some design and test new kinds of materials. Some work in factories or on farms. Others work in medical laboratories. Engineers also design the engines that may one day fly people to Mars!

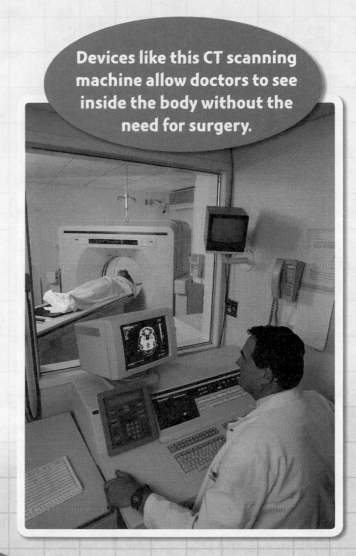

Devices like this CT scanning machine allow doctors to see inside the body without the need for surgery.

Sometimes engineers design devices with one purpose in mind—fun!

Engineering Diary

List some of the engineered devices you use every day. Explain the need that each device meets.

Device	Need

© Houghton Mifflin Harcourt Publishing Company   (tr) ©Corbis

The Right Tool for the Right Job

When you see or hear the word *technology*, you may think of things such as flat screen TVs, computers, and cell phones. But technology includes more than just modern inventions.

Active Reading As you read these two pages, underline sentences that describe how technology affects our lives.

Stone tools, the wheel, and candles were invented a long time ago. They are examples of technology. **Technology** is any device that people use to meet their needs and solve practical problems.

Technology plays an important role in improving our lives. Tools and machines make our work easier or faster. Medicines help us restore our health and live longer. Satellites help us predict weather and communicate.

Technology changes as people's knowledge increases and they find better ways to meet their needs. For example, as people's knowledge of materials increased, stone tools gave way to metal tools. As people learned more about electricity, washboards and hand-cranked washing machines gave way to electric washers.

Centuries ago, many people washed their clothes on rocks in a river. The invention of the washboard allowed people to wash their clothes at home.

© Houghton Mifflin Harcourt Publishing Company (bkgd) ©Max Mowbray/Alamy; (tcr) ©Photodisc/Getty Images; (r) ©Petrified Collection/Getty Images

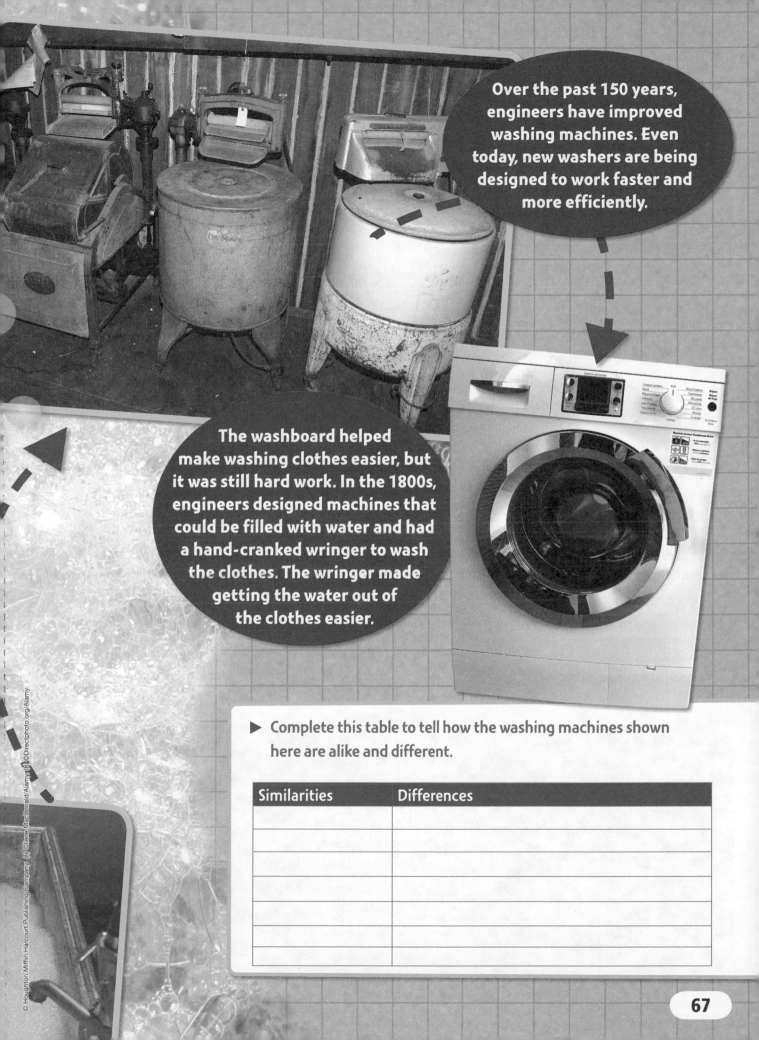

Over the past 150 years, engineers have improved washing machines. Even today, new washers are being designed to work faster and more efficiently.

The washboard helped make washing clothes easier, but it was still hard work. In the 1800s, engineers designed machines that could be filled with water and had a hand-cranked wringer to wash the clothes. The wringer made getting the water out of the clothes easier.

► Complete this table to tell how the washing machines shown here are alike and different.

Similarities	Differences

© Houghton Mifflin Harcourt Publishing Company (tl) ©Jane MacDonald/Alamy (b) ©Directphoto.org/Alamy

The Design Process (Part 1)

Technology is all over—video games, 3D TVs, microwaves. But technology doesn't just happen. It comes about through a step-by-step process.

Active Reading As you read these pages, bracket sentences that describe a problem. Write *P* in the margin. Underline sentences that describe a solution. Write *S* by them.

When engineers design new technologies, they follow a *design process*. The process includes several steps. Here's how the process starts.

1. Find a Problem Engineers must first identify a need, or a problem to be solved. They brainstorm possible solutions. There may be more than one good solution.

2. Plan and Build Engineers choose the solution they think is most practical. They build a working model, or **prototype**, to test.

Throughout the design process, engineers keep careful records. Good records include detailed notes and drawings. Records help them remember what they have done and provide information to others working on similar problems. If the prototype doesn't work, the records can provide clues to a solution that *might* work next time.

The design process begins with finding a problem to solve. Roller skates work great on smooth surfaces, like the skating rink floor. They don't work very well on rough surfaces such as grass.

© Houghton Mifflin Harcourt Publishing Company HMH Credits

Engineers make detailed drawings for their prototypes, as well as notes about the materials they plan to use. The notes and drawings are a record that they can study as they build and make changes to the prototype.

Engineers use their notes and drawings to build the first prototype. This prototype is a skate that is designed to work on rough surfaces.

Problem Solved!

The first step in the design process is identifying a problem and thinking up solutions.
Complete the table with a problem or a solution.

Problem	Solution
Cord for the computer mouse keeps getting tangled	
	Watch face that lights up
	Hand-held electronic reader
Injuries in car crashes	

© Houghton Mifflin Harcourt Publishing Company · HMH Credits

The Design Process (Part 2)

Do you get nervous when you hear the word *test*? A test is a useful way to decide both if you understand science and if a prototype works.

Active Reading As you read these two pages, draw boxes around clue words that signal a sequence or order.

The skate designers are steadily working through the steps of the design process. They have found a problem and built a prototype. What's next?

3. Test and Improve After engineers build a prototype, they test it. **Criteria** are standards that help engineers measure how well their design is doing its job. The tests gather data based on the criteria. The data often reveal areas that need improvement.

4. Redesign After testing, engineers may decide that they need to adjust the design. A new design will require a new prototype and more testing.

A prototype is usually tested and redesigned many times before a product is made on a large scale and sold to consumers.

5. Communicate Finally, engineers communicate their results orally and in written reports.

Engineers use criteria to test a prototype. They may gather data on how fast someone can skate on a rough surface or the number of times the person falls. Speed and safety are two criteria in the test you see here.

© Houghton Mifflin Harcourt Publishing Company HMH Credits

The design is modified if it doesn't meet all criteria. An unsafe design will be reworked even if the design meets all other criteria. The engineers focus on improvements. They revise their drawings and keep notes on design changes.

This is the redesigned skate. It has larger wheels that work better on rough surfaces. The skater can skate faster for longer distances without falling.

Do the Math!
Solve a Problem

Engineers tested a wheel that was 100 mm in diameter. Then they tested a wheel that was 15% larger.

Convert 15% to a decimal.

_____

What is the size of the larger wheel?

_____

© Houghton Mifflin Harcourt Publishing Company HMH Credits

71

If At First You Don't Succeed...

Suppose Thomas Edison asked himself, "How many times must I make a new prototype?" What do you think his answer was?

Many things affect how long it takes to reach the final product for new technology. The kinds of materials needed, the cost, the time it takes to produce each prototype, and safety are just some of the criteria engineers consider.

Thomas Edison tried 1,000 times to develop a light bulb that didn't burn out quickly. It took him nearly two years to develop a bulb that met the criterion of being long-lasting.

Some of Edison's early bulb prototypes

© Houghton Mifflin Harcourt Publishing Company (b) ©Daniel Dempster Photography/Alamy Images; (r) ©SuperStock/Getty Images

© Houghton Mifflin Harcourt Publishing Company (t) ©Tim Wright/Corbis; (c) ©Paolo Patrizi/Alamy Images; (r) ©Nicemonkey/Alamy Images; (b) ©Daniel Dempster Photography/Alamy Images

Cars must pass crash tests before they can be sold to the public.

Cars of the future may look different or run on fuels different from those of today. Years of testing and redesign occur before a new car is brought to market.

Finding materials that work well affects the design process. Edison found that the materials used to make light bulbs must stand up to heat.

Some technologies cost a lot of money to develop. For example, prototypes for many electronic devices are expensive to build. The cost of building the prototype, in turn, affects the cost of the final product.

It may take many years to develop new cars, because they must undergo safety and environmental testing. Environmental laws limit the pollutants that a car may release and determine the gas mileage it must get.

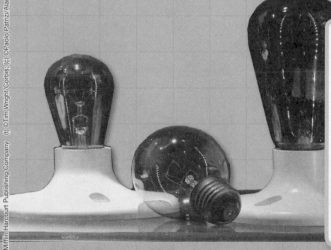

Criteria Match Up

Draw a line from the technology to criteria that must be considered during the design process.

Technology	Must Be Considered
Hydrogen car	Lightweight, sturdy
Laptop computer	Finding fuel
Bicycle	Portable, long battery life

Sum It Up!

When you're done, use the answer key to check and revise your work.

In the blanks, write the word that makes the sentence correct.

| engineering | technology |

1. The things that engineers design to meet human needs are _____

2. _____ is the process of designing and testing new technologies.

3. Toothbrushes, washing machines, and computers are examples of _____

4. _____ uses math and science to test devices and designs.

Summarize

Fill in the missing words to explain how engineers conduct the design process. Use the words in the box if you need help.

| communicating | engineering | keep good records |
| needs | problem | prototype |

5. _____ is the use of science and math to solve everyday problems. Engineers invent and improve things that meet human 6. _____ . The design process that engineers follow includes finding a 7. _____ , building and testing a 8. _____ , and 9. _____ results. During each step of the design process, engineers 10. _____ .

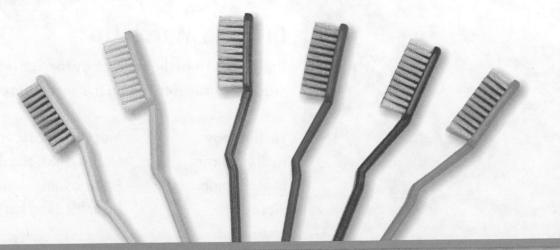

Answer Key: 1. technology 2. Engineering 3. technology 4. Engineering 5. Engineering 6. needs 7. problem 8. prototype 9. communicating 10. keep good records

© Houghton Mifflin Harcourt Publishing Company   (b) ©Getty Images Royalty Free/Stockbyte

Word Play

1 Beside each sentence, write *T* if the sentence is mostly about using technology. Write *E* if the sentence is mostly about the engineering design process.

_____ 1. Sarah sent a text message to Sam on her cell phone.

_____ 2. The nurse used a digital thermometer to measure the patient's temperature.

_____ 3. Henry tested three brands of blender. He wanted to see which one made the creamiest smoothies.

_____ 4. Workers at the factory use machines to bottle spring water.

_____ 5. Jessica invented a better mousetrap. She patented her invention.

_____ 6. Eli used math to figure out how much weight a bridge could hold.

_____ 7. The nurse is using a new x-ray machine.

_____ 8. Mayling is designing a refrigerator that uses less electricity.

_____ 9. Guillermo's new snowblower makes snow removal faster and easier.

_____10. Laptop computers are designed to be smaller, lighter, and easier to carry.

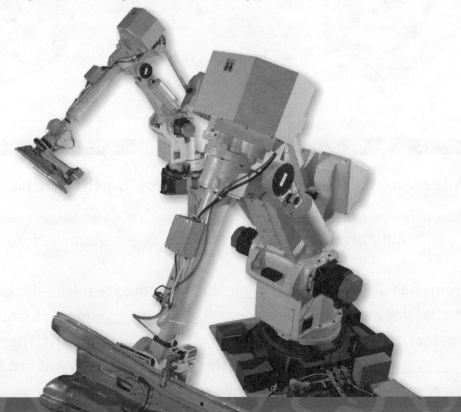

© Houghton Mifflin Harcourt Publishing Company ©Leslie Garland Picture Library/Alamy

Apply Concepts

2 Match the picture of the technology to the need it fulfills. Draw a line from the picture to the matching need.

go to school

get up on time

see clearly

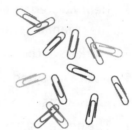

make a cake

fix a broken bone

keep papers together

3 Write the missing words in the sentences below. Use the word box if you need help.

| brainstormed | good records | problem | prototype |

Jeremy had a _____ that he wanted to solve—his go-cart was too slow. Jeremy and his friend Todd _____ ideas to make it faster. Together, they designed a _____ and tested it. They kept _____ that showed that the go-cart really was faster.

© Houghton Mifflin Harcourt Publishing Company   (tl) ©PhotoDisc/Getty Images;   (tr) ©Jupiterimages/Getty Images;   (bl) ©PhotoDisc/Getty Images

4 Circle the words or phrases that are criteria for designing skates that will be safe. Cross out those that are *not* criteria for safety.

roll smoothly   brake easily   come in different styles

fit snugly   come in different colors   sturdy

5 Look at the flow chart showing the steps of the design process. Then read the list of steps for designing a thermos. These steps are not in order. Write the letter of each step in the appropriate box of the flow chart.

The Design Process

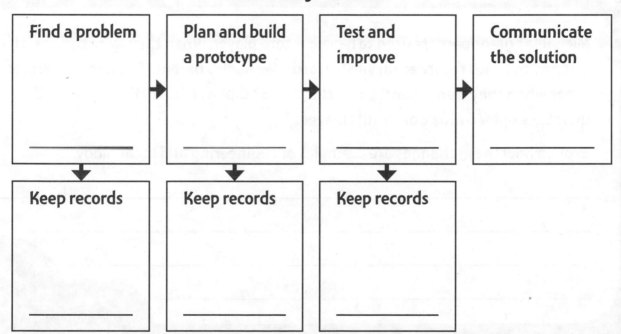

| Find a problem | Plan and build a prototype | Test and improve | Communicate the solution |
| _____ | _____ | _____ | _____ |

| Keep records | Keep records | Keep records |
| _____ | _____ | _____ |

Steps for Designing a Thermos

A Keep data tables.

B Write a report

C Write down ideas.

D Make drawings.

E Measure the temperature inside the container.

F Keep hot things hot and cold things cold.

G Use insulating materials to make a container.

© Houghton Mifflin Harcourt Publishing Company

6 Sylvia is an engineer. Her friend Martin is an artist who paints with oil paints. Martin tells Sylvia that cleaning oil paint out of brushes takes a lot of time. It's messy, too. Write three or more sentences explaining what Sylvia would do to engineer a solution to Martin's problem.

_____

_____

_____

_____

_____

7 Michaela's grandparents used to have a record player. When they were her age, they listened to songs recorded on vinyl records. Michaela's parents listened to cassette tapes when they were young. Later, they got a CD player. Now, Michaela's family members upload music onto MP3 players.

Explain how these changes are examples of engineering and technology.

_____

_____

_____

_____

Take It Home! Ask an older person about a technology that has changed since he or she was young. Discuss how engineering has changed that technology over the years.

© Houghton Mifflin Harcourt Publishing Company

Name _____

Essential Question

How Can You Design a Solution to a Problem?

Set a Purpose

What is the purpose of this investigation?

_____

_____

State Your Hypothesis

Sketch a raft with pennies on it to show what you think will be the best design. Write a brief description of your raft's key features.

_____

_____

Think About the Procedure

What variables can affect the results of this investigation?

_____

_____

_____

_____

Record Your Data

In the space below, make a table in which you record your results. Be sure to include information about each raft design and the number of pennies and their placement.

© Houghton Mifflin Harcourt Publishing Company

Draw Conclusions

Why did some of your model rafts work better than others?

_____

_____

_____

_____

Analyze and Extend

1. Sketch a raft design you think would NOT float. Explain why.

_____

_____

_____

_____

2. Mary and Sarah built identical raft models. Mary's raft sank after adding only 6 pennies. Sarah's raft held 12 pennies before it sank. Suggest a possible reason for the difference.

_____

_____

_____

_____

3. Scientists often build and test models to solve problems. What are the advantages of solving problems in that way?

_____

_____

_____

_____

_____

4. Think of other questions you would like to ask about designing solutions to a problem.

_____

_____

_____

_____

© Houghton Mifflin Harcourt Publishing Company

Essential Question

How Does Technology Improve Our Lives?

Engage Your Brain!

Find the answer to the following question in this lesson and record it here.

It looks like a map of a city with streets and buildings of all sizes. But all those bumps and lines are actually the "brain" of a computer! How has the invention of technology such as computers changed the way people communicate?

_____

_____

_____

_____

Active Reading

Lesson Vocabulary

List the terms. As you learn about each one, make notes in the Interactive Glossary.

_____

_____

Cause and Effect

Some ideas in this lesson are connected by a cause-and-effect relationship. Why something happens is a cause. What happens as a result of something is an effect. Active readers look for effects by asking themselves, What happened? They look for causes by asking, Why did it happen?

© Houghton Mifflin Harcourt Publishing Company (bg) ©Jim Corwin/Alamy

The Technology Zone

Pick up your pencil, and look at it carefully.
You are holding technology in your hand.

Active Reading As you read these two pages, draw boxes around the names of two things that are being compared.

Most of the things you use every day are *technology*. Pencils, bikes, light bulbs, even the clothes you wear are technology. Cooking food uses technology. What makes something technology is not how modern it is. Technology doesn't need to be complex or require electricity to operate.

What technology must do is meet a human need. A pencil lets you write your thoughts or work math problems. Think about what needs are being met as you read about the technologies on these two pages. How would you meet those needs without these items?

▶ Bike helmets and doorknobs are both technology. What need does each meet?

_____

_____

© Houghton Mifflin Harcourt Publishing Company (br) ©Comstock/Getty Images

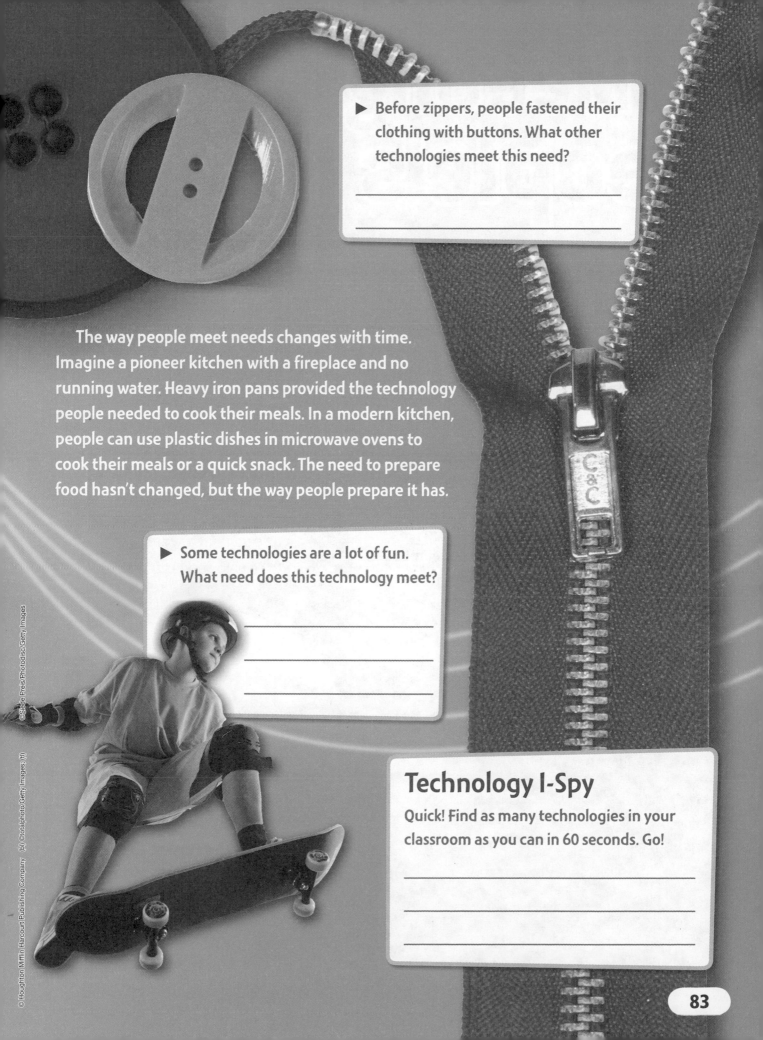

▶ Before zippers, people fastened their clothing with buttons. What other technologies meet this need?

_____

_____

The way people meet needs changes with time. Imagine a pioneer kitchen with a fireplace and no running water. Heavy iron pans provided the technology people needed to cook their meals. In a modern kitchen, people can use plastic dishes in microwave ovens to cook their meals or a quick snack. The need to prepare food hasn't changed, but the way people prepare it has.

▶ Some technologies are a lot of fun. What need does this technology meet?

_____

_____

_____

Technology I-Spy

Quick! Find as many technologies in your classroom as you can in 60 seconds. Go!

_____

_____

_____

© Houghton Mifflin Harcourt Publishing Company (b) ©totalphoto/Getty Images (t) ©Stade Preis/Photodisc/Getty Images

Meeting People's Needs

It's 1860. You want to contact a distant friend. Today, you might send a text message. What about then?

Active Reading As you read these two pages, draw one line under a cause. Draw two lines under its effect.

1869

When the transcontinental railroad opened, the time it took to move a letter across the country was cut down to a week or less.

1858

In the early 1800s, long-distance mail was carried by horseback riders, steamboats, and stagecoaches. A stage coach took 25 days to carry a letter 3,000 km (1,700 mi) from St. Louis to San Francisco.

1881

The time it took to send a message across the country was reduced to minutes with the invention of the telegraph.

© Houghton Mifflin Harcourt Publishing Company   (b) ©North Wind Picture Archives/Alamy Images   (bc) ©Ice/imagezoo/Getty Images   (c) ©Bank Fehmestock/Alamy Images   (t) ©North Wind Picture Archives/Alamy Images   (r) ©Ken Hackett/Alamy Images

In the early 1800s, communicating with someone far away might take weeks or months. Sometimes such communications were not possible at all. As people began to move westward across the growing United States, the need for reliable communication increased. The timeline on these pages shows ways technology changed in response to this need.

The time it took to communicate with someone across the country decreased as new technologies developed. What once took weeks, then days, then minutes now happens almost instantly! Today, people text back and forth almost as fast as they can talk in person. E-mails can be sent to many people at one time. New technologies for communicating seem to develop faster and faster. What could be next?

1915

Cross-country telephone service began in the United States.

1993

The first smart phone was developed.

Do the Math!
Solve a Problem

Suppose you can send 2 text messages per minute. How many text messages could you send in the time it took to deliver a letter by stagecoach from St. Louis to San Francisco in 1858?

_____

_____

_____

© Houghton Mifflin Harcourt Publishing Company   (c) ©Peter Carroll/Alamy Images; (b) ©Paul Fleet/Alamy Images (t) ©Ken Hackett/Alamy Images

Technology Risks and Benefits

A cell phone lets you communicate from almost anywhere. What happens when the phone dies or a newer, better model comes out?

Active Reading As you read these two pages, **underline** the things that are being contrasted .

Technology can have both positive and negative effects. Positive effects are called *benefits*. Benefits are the ways that a technology fills a need. For example, a cell phone lets friends and family communicate with you wherever you are. It might let you surf the Internet or download useful applications, too.

Negative effects are called *risks*. Cell phone technology changes fast, and some people switch to new models after just a few months. More resources are used up, and the old phones sometimes end up in a landfill. This risk is environmental.

No matter what the technology, there are both risks and benefits. Think about how each technology described here impacts your life. Are the benefits worth the risks?

Computers

BENEFITS	RISKS
Computers let you communicate with friends and family. They let you surf the Internet for information that can help with homework, and they let you play games.	Computer technology changes quickly, and many computers end up in landfills. Computers are expensive, and using the Internet can expose you to sites that are unsafe.

© Houghton Mifflin Harcourt Publishing Company (t) ©BrandX Pictures/Getty Images

Automobiles

BENEFITS	RISKS
Cars allow personal freedom by letting you go almost anywhere. They carry heavy items that you could not move on your own.	Cars use gasoline that is made from a limited resource—oil. They cause air pollution, and they can be dangerous if not driven properly.

MP3 Players

BENEFITS	RISKS
MP3 players let you download and listen to your favorite music without disturbing others.	Turning up the volume can damage your hearing. You may not be able to download some songs.

Risks Versus Benefits

Frozen foods and canned foods come prepackaged.
Write down some benefits and risks of using prepackaged foods.

BENEFITS	RISKS
_____	_____
_____	_____
_____	_____

© Houghton Mifflin Harcourt Publishing Company (l) ©Oleksiy Maksymenko/Alamy Images; (r) ©PhotoDisc/Getty Images

Living Technology

The many branches of science are often connected. Engineered devices are sometimes used on living things. This connects engineering and biology.

This plant cleans waste water to make it safe to return to the environment.

Engineers who work with living things are called bioengineers. When bioengineers apply the engineering design process to living things, they are practicing **bioengineering**.

A bioengineer may design a fish farm to raise large numbers of fish for food or other uses.

© Houghton Mifflin Harcourt Publishing Company (bg) ©Mark Burnett/Alamy; (t) ©Getty Images/PhotoDisc-Kent Knudson/PhotoLink; (br) ©Eitan Simanor/Alamy

An important part of bioengineering has to do with the environment. Bioengineers design tools to prevent or clean up pollution, for example. Any product used to benefit organisms or their environment is an example of **biotechnology**.

Bioengineering also deals with health and nutrition. For instance, plants can be engineered to grow faster or larger to feed more people. Food for livestock may be engineered to make the animals healthier.

Bioengineers also design biotechnology that helps detect or treat diseases. For example, scanners in hospitals can look inside the body. They let doctors see a diseased or damaged organ. Other devices help surgeons perform operations.

Some bioengineers design devices that replace human body parts. Artificial legs help people who have lost their own. Artificial skin helps people with burns. Bioengineers have even developed artificial hearts.

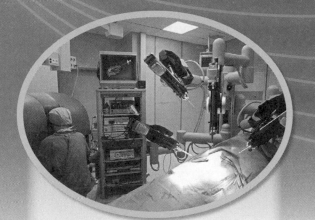
Surgeons today can use computer-assisted machines in delicate operations.

This artificial heart may not look like a real human heart, but it does the same job.

Bioengineering and Human Needs

Identify the human need met by each of these biotechnologies.

Biotechnology	Need
Water treatment plant	
Fish farm	
Robotic surgery	
Artificial heart	

© Houghton Mifflin Harcourt Publishing Company (bg) ©Mark Burnett/Alamy; (c) ©Patrick Landmann/Photo Researchers, Inc.; (cr) ©PHOTOTAKE Inc./Alamy

Sum It Up!

When you're done, use the answer key to check and revise your work.

Summarize

Fill in the missing words to explain how technology improves our lives. Use the words in the box if you need help.

benefits	bioengineering	risks
effect	need	technology

Technology may be simple or complex, but all technology meets a 1. _____ .

2. _____ changes as the needs of people change. Technology may have both a

positive and a negative 3. _____ on people. Positive effects are called

4. _____ . Negative effects are called 5. _____ . The application

of the engineering design process to living things is 6. _____ .

Draw a line from the picture to the statement that best summarizes what the picture shows.

7. Bioengineering may develop technologies that protect the environment, improve nutrition, or replace body parts.

8. A benefit of packaged food is convenience. A risk is an increase in the amount of trash.

9. Even a simple fastener is technology because it meets a human need.

10. Communication technology has changed greatly over time.

© Houghton Mifflin Harcourt Publishing Company   (b) ©PHOTOTAKE Inc./Alamy (r) ©Paul Fleet/Alamy Images

90

Answer Key: 1. need 2. Technology 3. effect 4. benefits 5. risks 6. bioengineering 7. line to artificial heart 8. line to canned food 9. line to zipper 10. line to smartphone

Name _____

Word Play

1 Use the words in the box below to help you unscramble the highlighted words in each statement. Then, write the unscrambled word on the line.

One **irsk** of using a computer is being exposed to unsafe Internet sites.

_____

A fish farm is an example of **hetooblyincgo**.

_____

otyleonchg is anything that meets a need or solves a problem.

_____

Engineers work with living organisms in the process of **nnneeeiiiggbor**.

_____

A **nefetib** of a car is that it allows personal freedom.

_____

benefit	bioengineering*	biotechnology*
risk	technology	

* Key Lesson Vocabulary

© Houghton Mifflin Harcourt Publishing Company (b) ©totalphoto/Getty Images;

Apply Concepts

2 Describe how changes in transportation have affected communication over long distances. Give an example.

_____

_____

3 Name two benefits and two risks for each of these technologies.

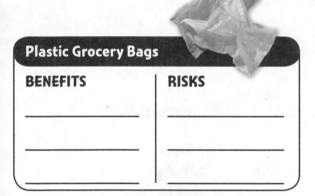

Plastic Grocery Bags

BENEFITS	RISKS
_____	_____
_____	_____
_____	_____

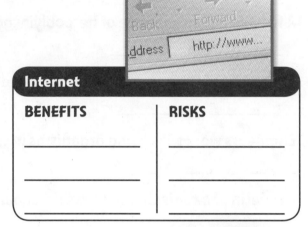

Internet

BENEFITS	RISKS
_____	_____
_____	_____
_____	_____

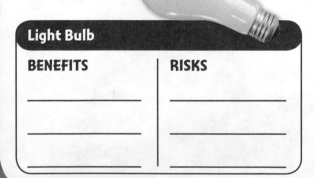

Light Bulb

BENEFITS	RISKS
_____	_____
_____	_____
_____	_____

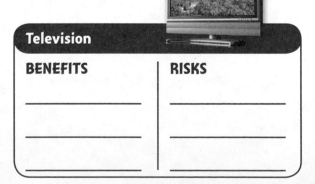

Television

BENEFITS	RISKS
_____	_____
_____	_____
_____	_____

Take It Home!

With a family member, identify five examples of technology in your home. Explain to the family member what needs are met by each of the technologies. Try to identify the risks and benefits of each one.

© Houghton Mifflin Harcourt Publishing Company (tl) ©Jonathan Kantor/Lifesize/Getty Images; (tr) ©Hemera Technologies/Photos.com/Jupiterimages/Getty Images; (bl) ©Cartville/Getty Images; (br) ©Yasuhide Fumoto/Digital Vision/Getty Images

1. Prosthetic designers help people who are missing a body part, such as a hand, arm, or leg.

2. The people they help may have lost a body part from an injury or a disease. Or it may have been missing from birth.

3. Prosthetic designers create the prosthesis that replaces the missing body part.

4. To design a prosthesis, prosthetic designers need to study how the human body moves.

5. A prosthetic designer looks for new ways to improve how a prosthesis is made.

6. They use both computers and traditional tools including drills.

7. A prosthesis is made to meet the needs of each user.

8. A person may need a special prosthesis to swim, run, bike, or golf.

9. A prosthesis is designed to move easily, naturally, and under the wearer's control.

10. Prosthetic designers can change people's lives!

10 THINGS
YOU SHOULD KNOW ABOUT
Prosthetic Designers

© Houghton Mifflin Harcourt Publishing Company (bkg) ©Jim White/Getty Images/PhotoDisc (inset) ©Richard T. Nowitz/Corbis

Designing
Sports Prostheses

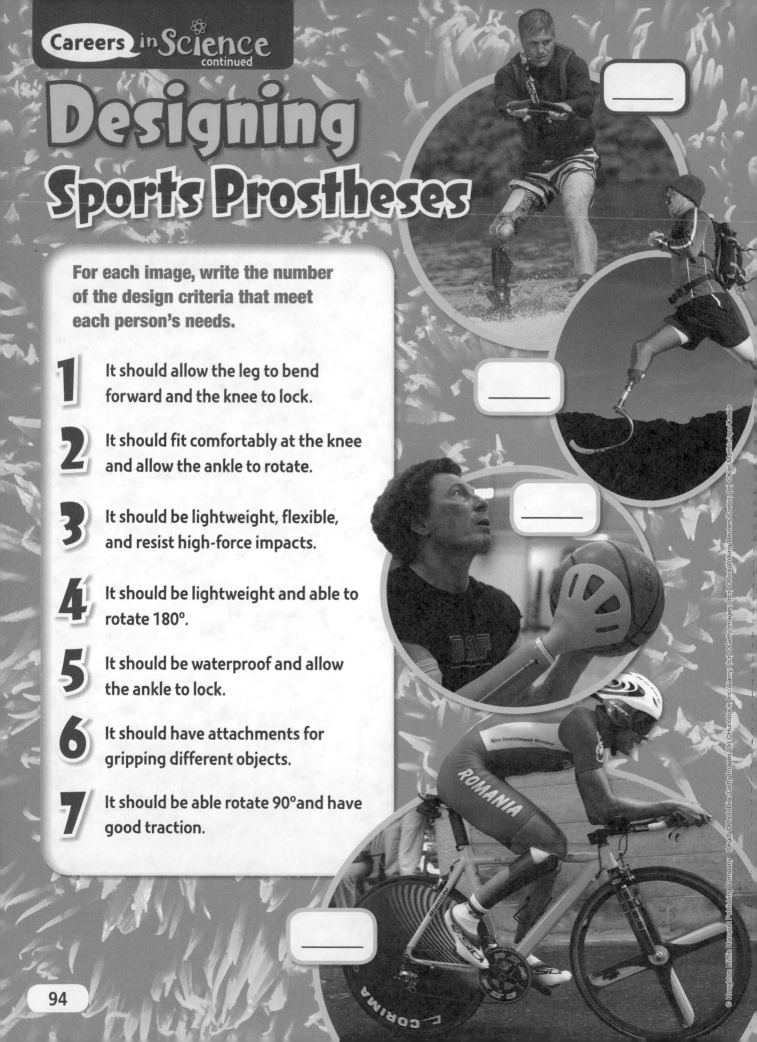

For each image, write the number of the design criteria that meet each person's needs.

1 It should allow the leg to bend forward and the knee to lock.

2 It should fit comfortably at the knee and allow the ankle to rotate.

3 It should be lightweight, flexible, and resist high-force impacts.

4 It should be lightweight and able to rotate 180°.

5 It should be waterproof and allow the ankle to lock.

6 It should have attachments for gripping different objects.

7 It should be able rotate 90°and have good traction.

© Houghton Mifflin Harcourt Publishing Company (bkgd) ©PhotoDisc/Getty Images; (tr) ©Rick Wilking/Reuters/Corbis; (bcr) ©Hurtstock, Inc./Alamy; (tr) ©Getty Images; (br) ©Karl Mathis/epa/Corbis

Name _____

Essential Question

How Can You Use Engineering to Solve a Problem?

Set a Purpose

What problem are you trying to solve?

_____

_____

How would a jar opener be useful?

_____

_____

_____

Think About the Procedure

What is a prototype?

_____

Describe two ideas for your prototype.

_____

_____

_____

_____

Record Your Data

Draw a detailed plan for your jar opener. Label the materials. Describe how it will work. Then build and test your prototype.

_____

_____

_____

© Houghton Mifflin Harcourt Publishing Company

95

Draw Conclusions

What criteria did you use to test your prototype?

_____

_____

_____

_____

Describe how you tested your prototype. Record any data you collected.

_____

_____

_____

Analyze and Extend

1. Did your prototype need improvements? Describe them.

_____

_____

_____

_____

_____

2. Summarize how you designed and tested your jar opener.

_____

_____

_____

_____

_____

_____

3. Describe another jar opener design that is possible using the materials provided.

_____

_____

_____

_____

_____

_____

4. Think of other designs you might make if you had different materials. How would that design work?

_____

_____

_____

_____

_____

© Houghton Mifflin Harcourt Publishing Company

Name _____

Vocabulary Review

Use the terms in the box to complete the sentences.

bioengineering
biotechnology
criteria
engineering
prototype
technology

1. The use of scientific knowledge to solve practical problems

   is _____.

2. Using science and math for practical purposes such as designing

   structures, machines, and systems is _____.

3. The standards for measuring a design's success

   are _____.

4. The process of applying the engineering design process to living

   things is _____.

5. The original or test model on which a product is based is

   a(n) _____.

6. Artificial legs are an example of _____.

7. Computer models, along with mathematical data, can help to provide which information to bioengineers?

   Ⓐ which prosthesis is more appealing

   Ⓑ which prosthesis would be less necessary

   Ⓒ what kinds of changes need to be made to a prosthetic device

   Ⓓ what kinds of adjustments need to be made to the marketing plan

8. This foot x ray is an example of which kind of science or engineering?

   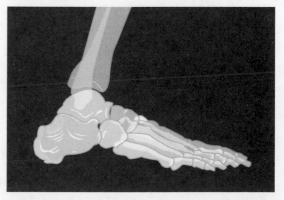

   Ⓐ biotechnology Ⓒ prototype design

   Ⓑ microbiology   Ⓓ prosthetic devices

© Houghton Mifflin Harcourt Publishing Company   HMH Credits

Science Concepts

Fill in the letter of the choice that best answers the question.

9. Suppose you are a bioengineer who is designing a prosthetic shoulder joint. You are building a prototype. Which is an **important** design criterion for a shoulder joint that you should include?

   (A) It should be realistic in color and appearance.

   (B) It should be capable of full movement within a shoulder socket.

   (C) It should keep the person for whom it is designed from injuring himself or herself again.

   (D) It should be stronger than a typical shoulder joint and support more weight.

10. A sports designer wants to produce a profitable product that will benefit the wearer. The data below show the result of a survey about students' favorite sport activities.

Sports Participation in High School	
Sport	Percentage of students
basketball	80
bicycling	60
soccer	50
swimming	30

    Which can you infer would be the **most** needed product among the students surveyed?

    (A) a helmet to protect from accidental head injuries

    (B) high-impact, ankle-supporting shoes

    (C) water-repelling racing swim trunks

    (D) shorts with padded backs

11. You and your design team have designed a new waterproof wristwatch made of a soft, flexible, clothlike material. Which of the following prototypes could be used to predict how well the watch would work in real life?

    (A) a graphic drawing of the watch

    (B) a computer model of the watch that actually moves

    (C) a wearable model of the watch made of plastic or cloth

    (D) a wearable version of the watch made of the new material

12. A company has developed a new skateboard that can more easily roll over gravel or grass. Some users of these new boards are wearing paths through the local park. What aspect of technology does this situation represent?

    (A) benefits and risks

    (B) design and redesign

    (C) computer models and prototypes

    (D) brainstorming and communication

© Houghton Mifflin Harcourt Publishing Company   HMH Credits

13. Bioengineers designed a prosthetic hand that is capable of grasping small objects between the thumb and index finger. The thumb was not one of the prosthetic hand's original design criteria. Which process was most responsible for including this feature in the final design?

(A) troubleshooting after manufacture

(B) safety concerns among doctors

(C) brainstorming sessions within the design team

(D) prototype testing and redesigning

14. You are determining the criteria you will use to decide how well your prototype racecar works. Which units would you use to determine the distance your car traveled?

(A) grams   (C) meters

(B) degrees   (D) liters

15. Engineers are investigating several materials that they think might be suitable for use in an artificial knee joint. They need to select a strong material that has a density (mass ÷ volume) in the range of 2.3–2.6.

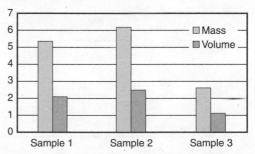

What can the engineers conclude using the data from the graph?

(A) All of the samples meet the density criteria that the engineers identified.

(B) Sample 3 has the least volume and should not be considered for the knee.

(C) Sample 2 has the greatest mass per volume and is the densest material.

(D) All samples are outside the acceptable range and show a mass of 5–6.

16. An engineering team is developing a device that will help individual farm families clean drinking water. The device must be inexpensive enough that families can afford to buy one. At what stage in the engineering process should the team take into account the need for the device to be affordable?

(A) before they build a prototype

(B) after the device is on the market

(C) before they identify the problem

(D) after the testing has been completed

© Houghton Mifflin Harcourt Publishing Company   HMH Credits

Apply Inquiry and Review the Big Idea

Write the answer to these questions.

17. Building a prototype of a prosthetic human body part means that you must use materials in ways that will resemble the actions of the real body parts. For example, you can use rubber bands to simulate the action of muscles on bones in order to move them. Describe **two** ways that rubber bands can imitate muscles in a model of a human arm.

(1) _____

_____

(2) _____

_____

18. A fully loaded backpack should not exceed 20 percent of a student's weight. However, most doctors recommend a 15-percent weight limit. These data are shown in the table below.

Body weight (lb)	Recommended limit of 15% (lb)	Maximum weight of 20% (lb)
70	$10\frac{1}{2}$	14
80	12	16
90	$13\frac{1}{2}$	18
100	15	20
110	$16\frac{1}{2}$	22
120	18	24

Materials that are often used to make backpacks have the following properties:

Material	Cost	Durability	Weight
plastic	low	low	low
canvas	moderate	average	medium
leather	high	high	high

a. What is the maximum weight a student who weighs 70 lb should carry?

_____

b. What is the range of weights for a student who weighs 80 lb?

_____

_____

c. Suggest a material for a backpack that will be used by a 70 lb student to carry 9 lb of books and materials. Support your answer.

_____

_____

© Houghton Mifflin Harcourt Publishing Company HMH Credits

Cells to Body Systems

© Houghton Mifflin Harcourt Publishing Company (c) ©Juniors Bildarchiv/Alamy; (inset) ©Peter Dear/Argipicture Images/Alamy; (bkgd) ©NDisc/Age Fotostock

Big Idea

All living things are made up of cells. Cells work together to make up tissues, organs, and organ systems.

I Wonder Why

Why do horses galloping across the frozen landscape make a sound like thunder? *Turn the page to find out.*

Here's why At the end of a horse's leg is a strong, hard structure called a hoof. When horses run, their hooves beat against the frozen ground making a sound like thunder.

In this unit, you will explore the Big Idea, Essential Questions, and Investigations on the Inquiry Flipchart.

Levels of Inquiry Key ■ DIRECTED ■ GUIDED ■ INDEPENDENT

Track Your Progress

Big Idea All living things are made up of cells. Cells work together to make up tissues, organs, and organ systems.

Essential Questions

Now I Get the Big Idea!

Science Notebook

Before you begin each lesson, be sure to write your thoughts about the Essential Question.

© Houghton Mifflin Harcourt Publishing Company (c) ©Juniors Bildarchiv/Alamy; (inset) ©Peter Dean/Agripicture Images/Alamy; (border) ©NDisc/Age Fotostock

What Are Cells?

🧠 Engage Your Brain!

Find the answers to the following questions in this lesson, and record them here.

What does a whale have in common with an amoeba? What makes them different?

_____

_____

_____

Active Reading

Lesson Vocabulary

List the terms. As you learn about each one, make notes in the Interactive Glossary.

_____ _____

_____ _____

_____ _____

_____ _____

Main Ideas and Details

Detail sentences give information about a topic. The information may include examples, features, characteristics, or facts. Active readers stay focused on the topic when they ask, What fact or information does this sentence add to the topic?

© Houghton Mifflin Harcourt Publishing Company   (c) ©Duncan Murrell/Steve Bloom Images/Alamy

Nerve cells

Skin cells

All Made of Cells

Do you know that the cells shown in these pictures are found in your body? Your body is made of nerve cells, skin cells, and many other kinds of cells. Together, the cells allow you to do everything you do!

Active Reading As you read the next page, underline the parts of the *cell theory*.

The bodies of all living things are made of cells. A **cell** is the basic unit of structure and function in a living thing. This means a cell is the smallest unit of life. Living things are also called **organisms**. Organisms may be made of one cell or trillions of cells. In animals with multiple cells, the different kinds of cells may have different functions.

▶ The shape of a cell can tell you what it does. Which of the cells is flat and protects you? Which cell is threadlike and sends messages?

_____

_____

_____

© Houghton Mifflin Harcourt Publishing Company   (t) ©Steve Gschmeissner/Photo Researchers, Inc.; (b) ©Biophoto Associates/Photo Researchers, Inc.; (tr) ©Kevin Peterson/PhotoDisc/Getty Images

Most cells are too small to be seen with the unaided eye—they are *microscopic.* In fact, before the 1600s, people didn't know cells existed because there were no microscopes. Today, we can see even the tiniest parts of cells using powerful microscopes.

In the 1800s, scientists put together their ideas about cells and developed the *cell theory.* The cell theory has three parts. (1) All living things are made of cells. From the largest organisms in the world to tiny one-celled amoebas, all organisms are made of cells. (2) All the processes of life take place in cells. Your cells take in oxygen, give off carbon dioxide, and make the energy you need. (3) New cells come from existing cells. Organisms need new cells for repair and growth.

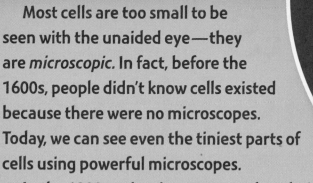

The amoeba's one cell carries out all the processes needed for life.

Robert Hooke observed dead cells from tree bark, like these cork cells. He named the structures *cells* because they looked like "tiny rooms."

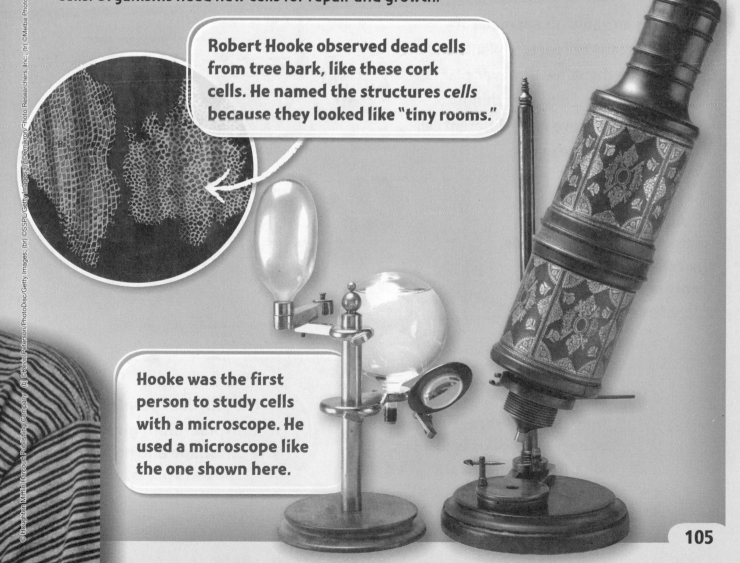

Hooke was the first person to study cells with a microscope. He used a microscope like the one shown here.

© Houghton Mifflin Harcourt Publishing Company (b) ©Kevin Peterson/PhotoDisc/Getty Images; (bl) ©SSPL/Getty Images; (l) ©Omikron/Photo Researchers, Inc; (tr) ©Melba Photo Agency/Alamy

What Parts Do Cells Have?

It's a lot of work to keep a body alive! Cells have parts that do certain jobs. Read about the jobs of cell parts on these two pages.

Active Reading As you read these two pages, circle the cell parts that plants and animals have in common. Underline the cell parts that are different.

Plants and animals are made of cells. Many cell parts of plants and animals are the same. However, plants and animals need different things to stay alive. They have some different cell parts to meet these needs.

The nucleus is enclosed in a membrane and directs all the cell's activities. Making more cells, producing energy, taking in materials, and getting rid of wastes are all functions the nucleus controls.

Animal Cell

All cells have a cell membrane that surrounds the cell and controls what enters and leaves the cell.

Cell parts called *mitochondria* [my•tuh•KAHN•dree•uh] release energy the cell uses to do its jobs. Mitochondria are called the "powerhouses" of the cell.

The jellylike *cytoplasm* [SY•tuh•plaz•uhm] gives the cell shape and holds the cell's parts.

© Houghton Mifflin Harcourt Publishing Company

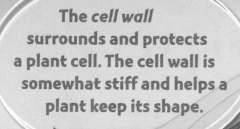

The *cell wall* surrounds and protects a plant cell. The cell wall is somewhat stiff and helps a plant keep its shape.

Plant Cell

The large *vacuole* [VAK•u•ol] in a plant cell stores water, nutrients, and wastes. Many animal cells have vacuoles, but they are much smaller than those in plants.

Each *chloroplast* [KLOHR•uh•plast] uses the energy from sunlight to make sugar. This sugar is food for the plant. Animals must take in food from their surroundings.

▶ Fill in the table to describe the parts found in cells.

Nucleus

Comparing Plant and Animal Cells

Cell Part	Plants, Animals, or Both	Function
Cell membrane	Both	
Nucleus		
Mitochondria		Release energy
Chloroplast	Plants	
Cell wall		Surrounds, protects cell

Mitochondria

Chloroplast

© Houghton Mifflin Harcourt Publishing Company

Cells Divide and Multiply

Have you ever wondered why cells divide? You might say that cells divide so they can multiply!

Active Reading As you read these two pages, underline the two reasons that cells divide.

Suppose you are with some friends, and you want to get a soccer game started. What is the first thing you do? You divide your group into two teams! To keep their activities going, cells must divide, too. The process of cell division allows single cells to multiply. Cells divide for two main reasons.

Growth A cell can't be very large. If a cell is too big, it won't be able to get enough of the materials it needs or get rid of wastes. So to become larger, or grow, an organism makes more cells.

Reproduction Organisms must reproduce. Most organisms reproduce sexually. They make egg and sperm cells through cell division. Parent egg and sperm cells then unite to produce new young organisms.

Growth begins when one cell divides and becomes two cells. The two cells then divide to produce four cells. Each of the four cells divides to make eight cells. At the eight-cell stage, the organism looks like a ball. Cell division continues as the organism grows.

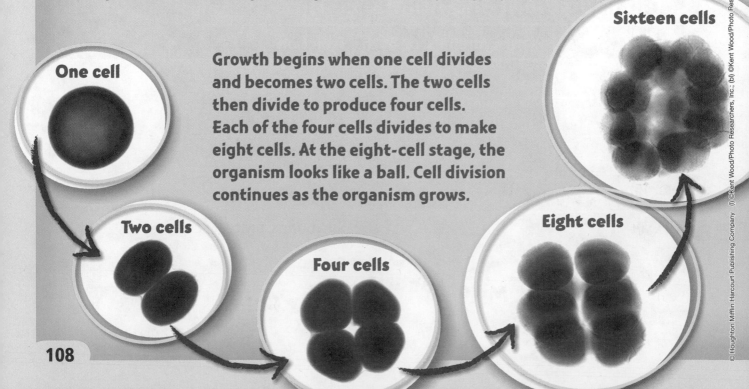

One cell

Two cells

Four cells

Eight cells

Sixteen cells

© Houghton Mifflin Harcourt Publishing Company   (l) ©Kent Wood/Photo Researchers, Inc.; (bl) ©Kent Wood/Photo Researchers, Inc.; (bc) ©Kent Wood/Photo Researchers, Inc.; (br) ©Kent Wood/Photo Researchers, Inc.; (r) ©Kent Wood/Photo Researchers, Inc.

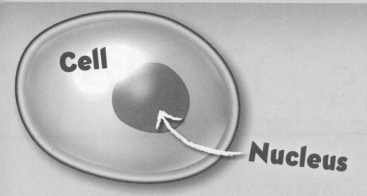

Cell

Nucleus

Chromosome

DNA

An organism has specific features. For example, your eyes are a certain color. Information that controls an organism's characteristics, such as eye color or height, comes from the parents' cells when they reproduce.

Within the nucleus of each of an organism's cells are structures called *chromosomes.* Chromosomes are made of DNA, the basic building block of life. DNA has sections called *genes.* Genes control an organism's characteristics.

Gene

Do the Math!
Cell Division

How long will it take a single cell to make new cells by cell division?

Suppose that a cell divides once every 5 minutes.

At 5 minutes: 1 cell × 2 = 2 cells

At 10 minutes: 2 cells × 2 = 4 cells

How long will it be before there are 16 cells?

_____

You can also calculate the number of cells there will be after a certain length of time. If the cells continue to divide every 5 minutes, how many cells will there be after one hour?

_____

© Houghton Mifflin Harcourt Publishing Company

How Cells Divide

If you cut a sandwich in half, do you get two whole sandwiches? No, you get two halves. Cells, however, divide in a process that makes complete new cells. It works one of two ways—through mitosis or meiosis.

Active Reading As you read these two pages, write numbers next to the steps of cell division to show their correct order.

Mitosis [my•TOH•suhs] occurs within body cells and allows for growth. Mitosis has five steps that occur inside the nucleus. A sixth step that is not part of mitosis takes place outside the nucleus. During that sixth step, the cytoplasm divides and two new cells are formed. These new cells will grow to the same size as the original cell. They will also have the same number of chromosomes as the starting cell.

Mitosis

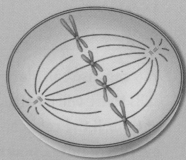

Before the cell divides, its DNA is copied. The DNA is contained in the nucleus in loose strands of chromosomes.

Next, the chromosomes condense into rodlike structures. The duplicated chromosomes are joined near their centers. The membrane of the nucleus disappears.

The duplicated chromosomes line up near the middle of the cell.

© Houghton Mifflin Harcourt Publishing Company

Meiosis [my•OH•suhs] forms sex cells—eggs and sperm. Egg and sperm cells each have only half as many chromosomes as a body cell. Egg and sperm cells join during *sexual reproduction* to form a new single cell. When the sex cells join, the new cell has a full set of chromosomes.

For example, humans have 46 chromosomes. Their sex cells have 23 chromosomes. When the sex cells joined, they formed a single cell with 46 chromosomes. The single cell divided by mitosis. It grew into a new individual.

▶ Knowing that human sex cells have half as many chromosomes as human body cells, take a look at the images to the right. Give a possible reason to explain why human sex cells have fewer chromosomes.

_____

_____

_____

_____

_____

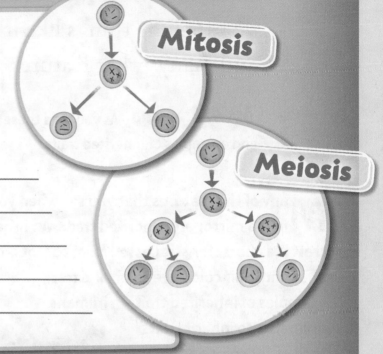

Mitosis

Meiosis

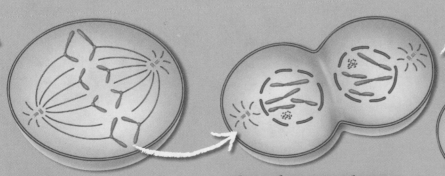

The duplicated chromosomes split and each half moves to opposite ends of the cell.

A nuclear membrane forms around the newly separated chromosomes. The cytoplasm pinches inward.

Finally, the cytoplasm divides. Cell division is complete. There are two new cells.

© Houghton Mifflin Harcourt Publishing Company

Where Do Traits Come From?

Look in a mirror, and describe what you see. Did you include things like hair and eye color? These, and many other features, came from your parents.

Active Reading As you read these two pages, underline the definition and examples of inherited traits.

Many of the features that you see when you look into a mirror are inherited traits. An **inherited trait** is a characteristic passed from parents to their offspring. Hair color, eye color, and freckles are a few examples of inherited traits in humans. Animals also inherit traits, such as fur color and texture. The kittens on this page inherited their fur color from their parents.

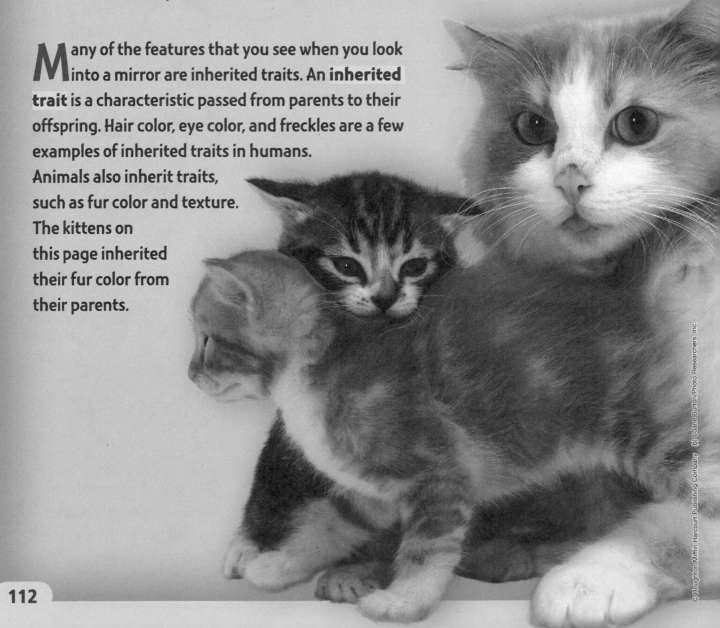

©Houghton Mifflin Harcourt Publishing Company   (b) ©Jane Burton/Photo Researchers, Inc.

Did you notice that one of the kittens on the left page has a fur color different from the mother's? That's because parents and their offspring have genetic differences. You can observe a similar thing in human families, like the one on this page. Family members have genetic differences that cause differences in traits.

Genetic differences are a result of meiosis. An organism receives only half its genes from each parent. So, the organism is not identical to either parent. Each offspring from a set of parents receives a different set of genes, too. That means offspring are not identical to each other, unless they are identical twins.

Inherited traits include skin color, hair color, the shapes of facial features, earlobe shape, and even your tone of voice!

My Inherited Traits

After reading the text and looking at the pictures, list your traits below.

_____

_____

_____

_____

The ability to roll your tongue is an inherited trait.

© Houghton Mifflin Harcourt Publishing Company   (b) ©Jane Burton/Photo Researchers, Inc.   (t) ©moodboard/Corbis

Dominant and Recessive Traits

Are your eyes a different color from your mom's? How can that happen?

Active Reading As you read these two pages, underline what causes a dominant trait to appear.

The boy and girl in the picture show a number of inherited traits. One has curly hair, and one has straight hair. One has dimples, and one doesn't. What determines whether a person displays these traits? In the 1800s, Gregor Mendel came up with an explanation. He noticed that pea plants were either short or tall. He investigated how the trait of height was passed on from parent plants.

Brown eyes, dark hair, curly hair, dimples, and freckles are dominant traits in humans.

114

Mendel hypothesized that a trait, such as plant height, is controlled by a pair of *factors*, one for tall and one for short. Each parent passes on one of its factors. In pea plants, tallness is a strong trait, or **dominant trait**. Shortness is a weak trait, or **recessive trait**. If an organism has one factor for a dominant trait, that trait appears. A recessive trait appears only if an organism has two recessive factors for the trait.

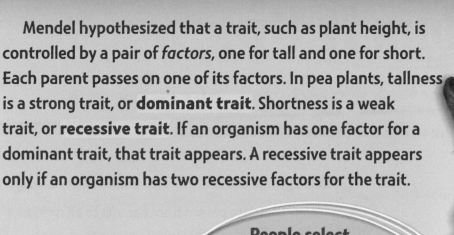

People select plants and animals to breed for certain traits. Selective breeding produced this angora rabbit. How different is it from these wild rabbits?

▶ Mendel bred tall and short pea plants together. The offspring were all tall. The picture shows what happened when Mendel then bred those tall offspring together. Some of their offspring were short. Which plants display dominant factors? Which plants display *only* recessive factors?

_____

_____

_____

_____

_____

© Houghton Mifflin Harcourt Publishing Company (bl) ©Science Source/Photo Researchers, Inc.; (r) ©Tierbild Okapia/Photo Researchers, Inc.; (cl) ©John Daniels/Ardea London Ltd.

Sum It Up!

When you're done, use the answer key to check and revise your work.

Draw a line from each statement to the picture that matches it.

1 Many traits are passed from parents to offspring. These traits are inherited.

2 Mitosis is the process by which body cells make more cells. It allows an organism to grow.

3 All cells have a cell membrane, nucleus, mitochondria, and cytoplasm.

4 The nucleus directs all the activities of the cell, including growth, producing energy, taking in materials, and getting rid of wastes.

5 Dominant traits appear if an organism has one factor for a trait. Two factors must be present for recessive traits to appear.

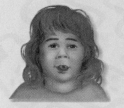

6 Plant cells have chloroplasts and cell walls, which animal cells lack. Plants also have a large vacuole.

© Houghton Mifflin Harcourt Publishing Company   HMH Credits

Answer Key: 1. fifth image: puppies 2. fourth image: mitosis 3. second image: animal cell 4. third image: nucleus 5. last image: tongue rolling 6. first image: plant cell

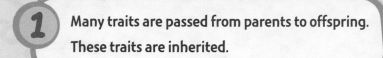
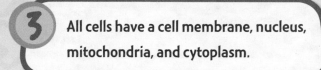

Word Play

Name

1 Unscramble the words on the right to fill in the blanks in each sentence.

A. An _____ is a living thing.

eisomsi

B. All cells are surrounded by a _____ that controls what enters and leaves a cell.

heetinrid aritt

C. The _____ of a cell is jellylike and holds the cell parts.

oysctlpma

D. The process of _____ produces cells with the same number of chromosomes as the original.

lecl nbemmera

E. The process of _____ produces sex cells.

ssiitom

F. The _____ protects a plant and helps it keep its shape.

csesiever rtait

G. An _____ is passed from parents to offspring.

gimsaron

H. A _____ is expressed only if both factors are present in an organism.

ellc lwal

Bonus: How many different parts of a cell can you name?

_____   _____

_____   _____

_____   _____

_____   _____

© Houghton Mifflin Harcourt Publishing Company   HMH Credits

Apply Concepts

2 Read each statement about the cell theory. Draw a line from the statement to the correct picture.

Cell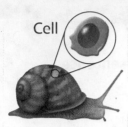

Oxygen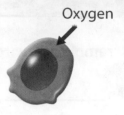

A. New cells come from existing cells.

B. Life processes take place inside cells.

C. All living things are made of cells.

3 Write the cell part that matches each living thing. Your answer may be *chloroplast*, *cell membrane*, or *both*.

A. Tree

_____

C. Insect

_____

B. Bird

_____

D. Sunflower

_____

4 Write *1, 2, 3, 4,* or *5* below each picture to show the correct sequence of cell divisions.

_____   _____   _____   _____   _____

© Houghton Mifflin Harcourt Publishing Company   HMH Credits

5 For each characteristic, write *inherited* or *not inherited* on the line.

A. Eye color

_____

B. Riding a bike

_____

C. Hair color

_____

D. Reading

_____

E. Hair texture

_____

6 For each trait listed, write *dominant* or *recessive* on the line.

A. Dimples

_____

B. Short pea plants

_____

C. Blue eyes

_____

D. Curly hair

_____

E. No freckles

_____

7 Select the kind of cell that matches each living thing. Write *A* or *B* below the picture.

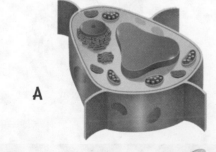

A

B

© Houghton Mifflin Harcourt Publishing Company HMH Credits

Read each statement. Decide if it describes *mitosis* or *meiosis*.

A. It produces sex cells. _____

B. New cells have the same number of
chromosomes as the original cell. _____

C. It allows for growth. _____

D. It produces two cells from one cell. _____

E. New cells have half the number of
chromosomes as the original cell. _____

F. It makes sexual reproduction possible. _____

9 The circles below show a cell undergoing mitosis. Assume that the original cell has two chromosomes. Draw the correct number of chromosomes in each of the circles.

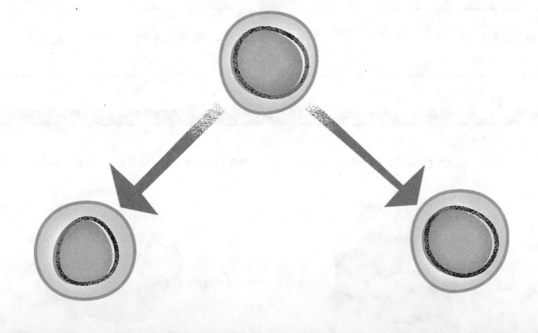

Take It Home! Use construction paper and string to make a model of a cell undergoing mitosis. Explain to a family member what happens to the chromosomes during mitosis.

© Houghton Mifflin Harcourt Publishing Company HMH Credits

Pumping Blood

1950s Early Machines
The first device to artificially keep blood flowing through the body was the heart-lung machine. It was used to keep a patient alive when the patient's heart was being operated on. These machines are still used in surgeries today. They remove blood from the body, transfer gases, and put the blood back in.

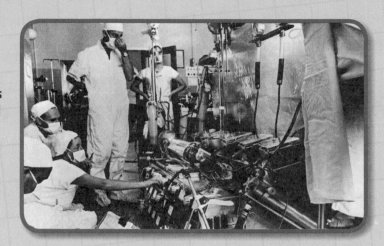

1964 Artificial Heart Program
The National Institutes of Health began a program to develop an artificial heart that could replace a defective human heart.

1982 First Artificial Heart
The first artificial heart was implanted into a person. This heart was designed to be temporary until the patient could receive a donor heart for a transplant.

1990s Heart Assist Devices
An LVAD (left ventricular assist device) is an implanted device that keeps a patient alive while waiting for a donor heart. A natural heart transplant is still the longest-term solution for patients.

2010s Artificial Hearts Today
This is the first self-contained artificial heart. It is designed as an alternative to a heart transplant.

Troubleshooting

How have mechanical devices that circulate blood improved over time?

_____

_____

_____

© Houghton Mifflin Harcourt Publishing Company (t) ©Hulton-Deutsch Collection/Corbis; (l) ©Smithsonian Institution/Corbis; (br) ©Ira Wyman/Sygma/Corbis

Artificial hearts are the last resort for patients who cannot survive without them, even just to wait long enough for a transplant of a donor heart.

Do research about how real human hearts work and the most modern artificial heart. Draw and label a diagram of the human heart and a replacement heart. Describe how each heart pumps blood.

You Decide

What are the advantages and disadvantages of artificial hearts? What improvements would reduce the disadvantages?

Build On It!

Rise to the engineering design challenge — complete **Owner's Manual: Using a Microscope** in the Inquiry Flipchart.

© Houghton Mifflin Harcourt Publishing Company

Name _____

Essential Question

How Can We Observe Cells?

Set a Purpose

What will you be looking for in this activity?

_____

_____

_____

What is the purpose of using food coloring to look at the plant cell?

_____

_____

_____

Think About the Procedure

When scientists observe, they use their senses to learn about objects and events. In the center of most cells are structures that direct how the cells function. Look for these structures. Based on what you observe, how many directing structures does each cell have?

_____

_____

What is this directing structure called?

_____

_____

Record Your Observations

Drawing of Plant Cell

[ ]

Drawing of Animal Cell

[ ]

© Houghton Mifflin Harcourt Publishing Company   HMH Credits

Draw Conclusions

What similarities do you observe between the two cells?

_____

_____

_____

What differences do you observe between the two cells?

_____

_____

_____

Why do you think a plant cell has a thicker outer covering than an animal cell?

_____

_____

_____

Analyze and Extend

1. Suppose that you found a mystery organism. How could you tell if it was a plant or an animal?

_____

_____

_____

2. Do you think other parts of the onion would look the same as the skin?

_____

_____

_____

3. You observe a piece of tissue under the microscope. Each cell of the tissue has a cell wall, a cell membrane, a nucleus, and organelles including chloroplasts and vacuoles. What type of organism did this tissue come from? How do you know?

_____

_____

4. What other questions would you like to ask about cells?

_____

_____

_____

5. Name two ways you could find the answer to your questions.

_____

_____

_____

124

© Houghton Mifflin Harcourt Publishing Company   HMH Credits

Essential Question

How Do Cells Work Together?

Engage Your Brain!

Find the answer to the following question in this lesson and record it here.

What senses can the girl use to experience the flower?

_____

_____

_____

_____

Active Reading

Lesson Vocabulary
List the terms. As you learn about each one, make notes in the Interactive Glossary.

_____ _____

_____ _____

_____

Sequence
Main ideas in this lesson are connected by a sequence, or order, that describes the steps in a process. Active readers stay focused on sequence when they mark the transition from one step in a process to another.

© Houghton Mifflin Harcourt Publishing Company   (c) ©Noam Armonn/Alamy

How Cells Are ORGANIZED

Your body has trillions of cells! Yet, they all work together so that you can eat, play, go to school, and read this page.

Active Reading As you read this page, number four parts of the body from simplest, 1, to most complex, 4.

You've read that each cell in your body has parts that allow it to do its jobs. Your cells must work with each other, too. Cells are organized to work together so your body functions smoothly.

Tissue Cells of the same type that work together to do a certain job make up a **tissue**. Your body has different kinds of tissues. These include *muscle tissue, connective tissue, nerve tissue,* and *epithelial* [ep•uh•THEE•lee•uhl) *tissue.*

Organ Several tissues that work together to do a certain job make up an **organ**. Your skin is an organ made of all four kinds of tissues. Your heart is an organ made mostly of muscle tissue.

Organ System Organs that work together to do a job for the body make up an **organ system**. Your heart is part of the circulatory system. The circulatory system sends blood that contains oxygen to all your body parts.

▶ Number the pictures in order from simplest, 1, to most complex, 4.

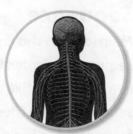

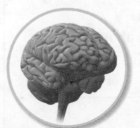

_____ _____ _____ _____

© Houghton Mifflin Harcourt Publishing Company

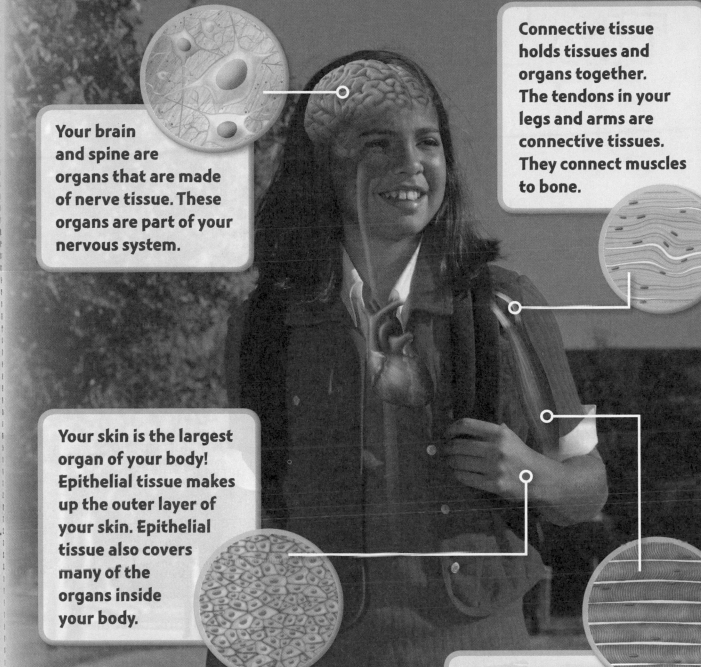

Your brain and spine are organs that are made of nerve tissue. These organs are part of your nervous system.

Connective tissue holds tissues and organs together. The tendons in your legs and arms are connective tissues. They connect muscles to bone.

Your skin is the largest organ of your body! Epithelial tissue makes up the outer layer of your skin. Epithelial tissue also covers many of the organs inside your body.

Muscle tissue makes up a large part of your body. Your arms and legs could not move and your heart could not beat without muscle tissue.

© Houghton Mifflin Harcourt Publishing Company

The Information HIGHWAY

Keep your eye on the ball! In just seconds you can see a ball, run toward it, and swing a racket! How does the body relay all of the information needed to do this? Read on to find out.

Active Reading As you read this page, underline the names of parts of the nervous system.

Sensing your surroundings and communicating information within the body are the main jobs of your *nervous system*. Your nervous system is made of tiny structures called *nerve cells*. Chains of long nerve cells make up nerves. Nerves carry information to and from the **brain**. The brain is the organ that processes information. It's like a computer made of millions of nerve cells working together.

A rope-like bundle of nerve tissue, called the *spinal cord,* runs along your backbone. Your spinal cord is the main pathway for information traveling to and from the brain. Nerves connect to your spinal cord from all over your body.

Some of these nerves send information to the brain. Other nerves receive signals from the brain.

Imagine that you're playing tennis. Nerves in your eyes sense light. These nerves, like other nerves in your head, send information directly to your brain without routing the signal through your spinal cord. You see the ball coming toward you. Your brain decides on an action. It sends instructions through your spinal cord to nerves in your body. The messages from your brain "tell" your legs to run across the court and your arms to swing the racket and hit the ball. All of this communication takes place in seconds!

© Houghton Mifflin Harcourt Publishing Company

Information Relay

Fill in the blanks to describe the path that a nerve signal might take in this tennis player.

1. The boy's _____ sense the ball coming toward him.

2. His _____ processes this information.

3. Messages from the _____ travel down the _____ _____.

4. _____ in his arms deliver the message from his brain to swing the racket.

© Houghton Mifflin Harcourt Publishing Company

SIGHT and SMELL

How do you see the whirl of color and smell the yummy aromas at a carnival?

Active Reading As you read this page, write numbers next to the appropriate sentences to show the order of events for the sense of sight.

Senses are your body's way of gathering information. Two of your senses are sight and smell.

Sight Your eye is the sense organ that lets you see the world. The part of the eye that gives your eye color is the *iris*. Light enters the eye through an opening in the iris called the *pupil*. Light then strikes the back of the eye, called the *retina*. Inside the retina are nerve cells that detect light. These nerve cells send signals along nerve pathways to the brain. The brain interprets this information, and you see.

Smell When you breathe air into your nose, structures inside your nose sense chemicals in the air. The structures are attached to nerve cells in the olfactory bulb that send messages to your brain about the chemicals. This makes up your sense of smell.

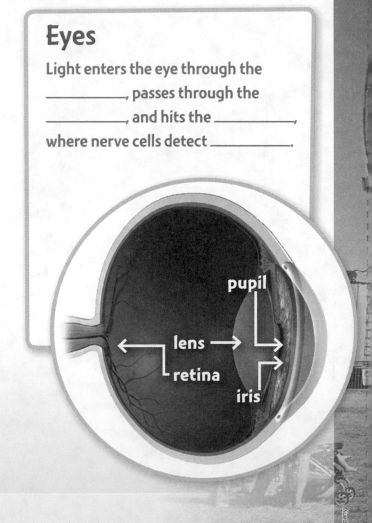

Eyes
Light enters the eye through the
_____, passes through the
_____, and hits the _____,
where nerve cells detect _____.

pupil

lens →

retina

iris

© Houghton Mifflin Harcourt Publishing Company

130

Nose

When you breathe, air travels through your organ of smell—your nose. Inside your nose, structures detect _____ in the air. These structures send messages to the _____ and then to the _____, where the message is interpreted.

olfactory bulb

nasal passages

© Houghton Mifflin Harcourt Publishing Company   (bg) ©Buddy Mays-Alamy; (inset) ©Jose Luis Pelaez/Getty Images

HEARING and TASTE

How do you hear the crunch and taste the juicy sweetness of an apple?

Active Reading As you read this page, write numbers next to the appropriate sentences to show the order of events in hearing.

Hearing The part of your ear that you see is your outer ear. The outer ear funnels sound into the middle ear. Inside the middle ear, sound causes the eardrum to vibrate. The vibrations are passed to tiny bones. These bones pass vibrations to the inner ear. There, a fluid-filled structure called the cochlea passes vibrations to tiny hairs attached to nerves. The nerves send messages about the vibrations to the brain, and you hear.

Taste Have you ever noticed small bumps all over your tongue? Inside these bumps are *taste buds*. Taste buds sense the chemicals in food. They are attached to nerves that send messages to the brain. The brain interprets this information as taste.

© Houghton Mifflin Harcourt Publishing Company

Do the Math!
Interpret Data in a Table

Taste buds on the tongue detect sweet, sour, salty, bitter, and meaty tastes. The table shows how sensitive the tongue is to each of these tastes. The smaller the number in the right column, the fewer the molecules that need to be present for you to detect the taste.

Tasting Ability	
Taste	Number of molecules per liter of solution
Salty	0.010
Sour	0.0009
Sweet	0.01
Bitter	0.000008
Meaty	0.0007

Place the tastes in order from the one to which the tongue is most sensitive to least sensitive.

_____

_____

_____

_____

_____

Ears

The organ of hearing is your ear. Sound enters the ear. Vibrations pass from the _____ to tiny bones called the hammer, anvil, and stirrup. Vibrations then pass through the _____ and to tiny hairs attached to nerves.

eardrum

hammer

anvil

outer ear

stirrup

cochlea

Tongue

The organ of taste is your tongue. When food enters the mouth, structures on the tongue sense _____ in the food. These structures are called _____.

taste buds

© Houghton Mifflin Harcourt Publishing Company (b) ©George Munday/Design Pics Inc./Alamy

The SKIN You're In

Some people don't think of skin as an organ, but it is. Our bodies couldn't survive without it.

Active Reading As you read, circle the different parts of the integumentary system described below.

Covering your body is a protective layer called **skin**. Skin is part of the *integumentary* [in•teg•yoo•MEN•ter•ee] *system.* Fingernails, toenails, and hair are, too. This system helps to protect the inside of your body.

Skin keeps germs out. If you've ever had a cut that got infected, you know how important it is to keep germs from entering your body. At the same time, skin keeps water inside your body. Your waterproof skin keeps you from becoming dehydrated.

What happens when you get too hot? Sweat helps cool your body. Also, tiny blood vessels near the surface of the skin help to cool your blood.

But what if you get cold? Hair helps to keep your head warm in cold weather. Hair also helps to protect your scalp from injury and shades your scalp from the sun's harmful rays.

Fingerprinting

Draw your own friction ridges in the circles at the tips of these fingers.

© Houghton Mifflin Harcourt Publishing Company   (bg) ©Arthur Selbach/Getty Images

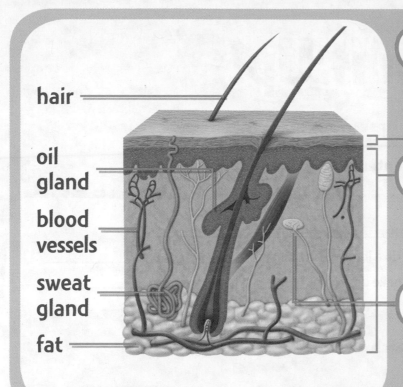

Epidermis

This is the outer layer of the skin. It is thin in some places, like your eyelids, and thick in others.

Dermis

This is the inner layer of the skin. It contains hair follicles, sweat glands, blood vessels, and nerve endings.

Nerve endings

These are special structures that sense touch, heat, cold, pain, pressure, and vibration.

hair

oil gland

blood vessels

sweat gland

fat

Look at your fingers. Do you see swirls, loops, and waves? These are friction ridges, which form your fingerprints. They allow your fingers to be more sensitive to touch.

© Houghton Mifflin Harcourt Publishing Company (bg) ©Arthur Seabach/Getty Images

Sum It Up!

When you're done, use the answer key to check and revise your work.

Fill in the blanks in the following sentences.

1

Cells that work together are called (a) _____ .

Several tissues working together to do a job are called an (b) _____ .

Several organs that work together make up an (c) _____ .

Read the summary statements. Match each statement with the correct image.

2 The brain, spinal cord, and nerves form the nervous system. The nervous system senses the environment, sends information to the brain, processes information, and sends instructions to the body.

_____

3 Light enters the eye through a hole in the iris called the pupil.

_____

4 Skin, hair, and nails are part of the human integumentary system. It protects internal organs, helps maintain body temperature, and provides waterproofing.

_____

5 The eyes, ears, nose, and tongue are sense organs. They have special parts that sense the environment.

_____

6 Four kinds of tissues are muscle, connective, nervous, and epithelial.

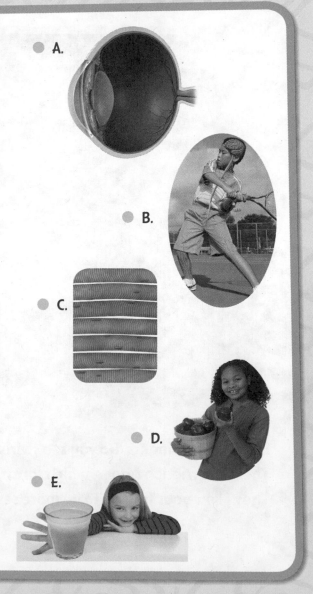

A.

B.

C.

D.

E.

© Houghton Mifflin Harcourt Publishing Company (green snake scales) ©Martin Harvey/Corbis; (bc) ©Arthur Selbach/Getty Images

Answer Key: 1a. tissues 1b. organ 1c. organ system 2.B 3.A 4.E 5.D 6.C

Name _____

Word Play

1 Unscramble the words on the right to fill in the blanks in each sentence.

1. The _ _ _ _ _ _ _ system sends messages throughout your body.

   s r n u o e v

2. The _ _ _ _ _ _ _ _ _ _ _ _ _ system protects the body's organs.

   n e n i g e m t t a y r u

3. The _ _ _ _ is the largest organ in the body. It covers and protects the other organs.

   i n k s

4. The _ _ _ _ _ receives messages from the body, processes the information, and sends instructions to the body.

   r b i n a

5. An _ _ _ _ _ system is a group of organs that work together to do a job.

   o g n r a

6. The _ _ _ _ _ _ include sight, taste, smell, hearing, and touch.

   s s s e e n

7. The fluid-filled _ _ _ _ _ _ _ passes sound vibrations to tiny hairs attached to nerves.

   l a c h e o c

8. Skin is made of _ _ _ _ _ _ _ _ _ _ _ tissue.

   h l e e a p i t l i

Bonus: How many body parts can you think of that have only three letters?

_____   _____

_____   _____

_____   _____

_____   _____

© Houghton Mifflin Harcourt Publishing Company

Apply Concepts

2 Some areas of the body have more sensory structures than others. Which do you think would have more? For each pair of body parts, circle the one you think would have more sensory structures. Then state your reason.

  Why? _____

_____

  Why? _____

_____

 _____

_____

 _____

_____

3 Draw a line to connect the tissue type to the correct body part.

Covers your body and many organs

Contracts to move blood

Sends messages about smells and sounds to the brain

4 How are the senses of taste and smell alike?

_____

_____

_____

_____

5 Which of the following structures have sweat glands?

a. olfactory bulb

b. retina

c. dermis

d. cochlea

Take It Home!

Make a model of the nervous system using items around the house, such as string and cardboard tubes. Explain to your family members what each part represents and how messages travel.

© Houghton Mifflin Harcourt Publishing Company

© Houghton Mifflin Harcourt Publishing Company (bkg) ©Martin Strmiska/Alamy

Essential Question

How Do Our Bodies Move, Breathe, and Circulate Blood?

Engage Your Brain!

Find the answer to the following question in the lesson, and record it here.

What organs make it possible for you to swing your arms and kick your legs as you swim freestyle?

_____

_____

Active Reading

Lesson Vocabulary
List the terms. As you learn about each one, make notes in the Interactive Glossary.

_____   _____

_____   _____

_____   _____

Main Ideas
The main idea of a paragraph is the most important idea. The main idea may be stated in the first sentence, or it may be stated elsewhere. Active readers look for main ideas by asking themselves, What is this section mostly about?

Strong Bones

Try picking up a pencil without bending your fingers. How different would life be without bones and joints?

Active Reading As you read this page, underline the main idea of each paragraph and put brackets [ ] around one detail sentence.

Bones, ligaments, and cartilage form the *skeletal system*. **Bones** are organs that support and protect the body, store minerals, and allow movement. For example, the ribs and skull protect internal organs while bones attached to muscles move arms and legs.

Bones have a hard outer layer that contains calcium. Inside bones is a spongy layer called marrow where blood cells are made. You may have seen marrow in the middle of a beef bone.

What Do Bones Do?

List five jobs of bones.

_____

_____

_____

_____

© Houghton Mifflin Harcourt Publishing Company (l) ©Photodisc

Use your fingers to wiggle the tip of your nose. What you feel beneath the skin is cartilage. Cartilage cushions the ends of bones and forms flexible parts like your ears and nose.

The place where two or more bones meet is a joint. *Ligaments* [LIG•uh•muhnts] connect bones together at joints. Some joints, like those in your skull, don't move. Other joints allow different kinds of movement.

Ball-and-Socket Joints Swing your arm in a complete circle. The ball-and-socket joint in your shoulder allows circular movement.

Hinge Joint Bend and straighten your lower leg. The hinge joint in your knee allows back-and-forth movement.

Pivot Joint Shake your head "No." The joint in your neck that allows you to rotate your head from side to side is a pivot joint.

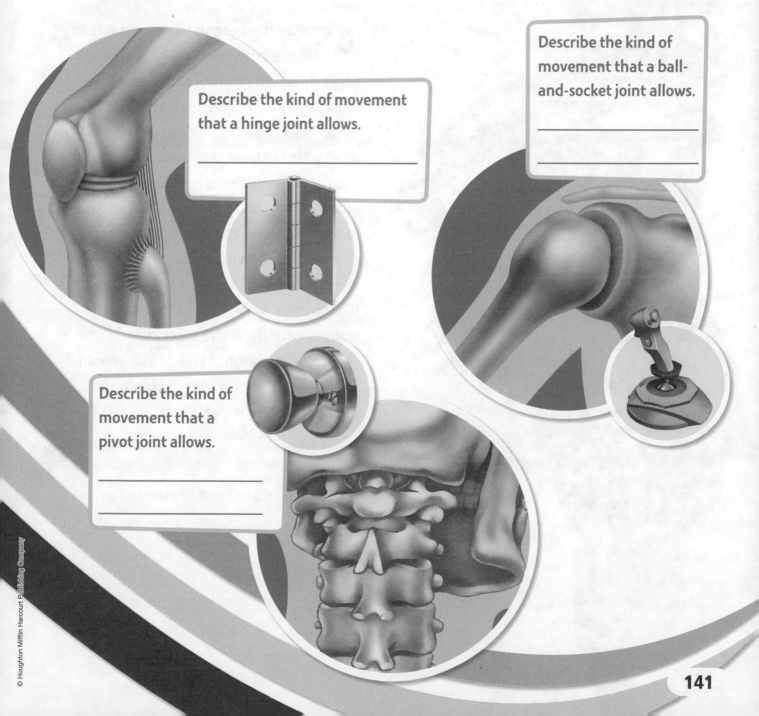

Describe the kind of movement that a hinge joint allows.

_____

Describe the kind of movement that a ball-and-socket joint allows.

_____

_____

Describe the kind of movement that a pivot joint allows.

_____

_____

© Houghton Mifflin Harcourt Publishing Company

Mighty Muscles

Smile! You just used at least ten muscles to form that grin on your face.

Active Reading As you read these two pages, draw one line under a cause. Draw two lines under the effect.

A **muscle** is an organ that contracts to produce body movement. There are three different kinds of muscles in the *muscular system*. The heart is made of one kind. Heart muscle is strong—it works all of your life pumping blood. Another kind of muscle makes up the walls of blood vessels and organs. As the muscle in a blood vessel contracts or relaxes, the diameter of the vessel changes, causing the amount of blood that moves through it to change. Muscles that make up the walls of your digestive tract contract to push food through. A third kind, known as skeletal muscle, pulls on your bones, enabling you to move.

Tell what the three kinds of muscle do.

_____

_____

_____

_____

© Houghton Mifflin Harcourt Publishing Company

What if you had to think about making your heart beat? Luckily, you don't! The beating of your heart and contracting and relaxing of blood vessels are *involuntary* movements, which means they happen without your thinking about them. Movements that you control are *voluntary*. Running and playing computer games are examples of voluntary movements.

Tendons are strong bands of tissue that connect skeletal muscles to bones. During voluntary movement, the contracting muscle pulls on the tendon, which then moves the bone. This happens when your legs pump as you run, or your fingers click on the keys of your computer.

Skeletal muscles connect the upper leg to the lower leg across the knee joint. What happens to the lower leg when the muscle above the knee contracts?

_____

Muscles can only contract to cause movement, which is why skeletal muscles work in pairs. When one muscle contracts, the other muscle in the pair relaxes. The contracting muscle moves the bone that it's attached to. When the opposite muscle contracts, the first muscle relaxes. What happens if both muscles contract at the same time?

Let's Get Moving

Circle the muscle that bends your arm.

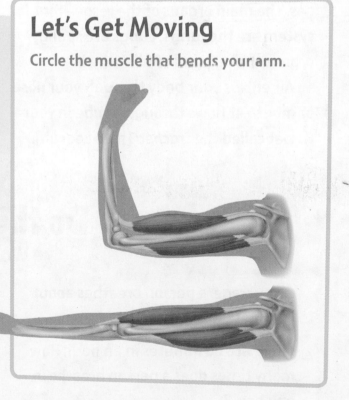

© Houghton Mifflin Harcourt Publishing Company

143

Breathe In, Breathe Out

Take a deep breath. Do you feel "inspired"? You should. *Inspire* is another word for breathing in. Breathing out is called *expiring*.

Active Reading As you read the text below, draw boxes around the five parts of the respiratory system that are described.

Organs in the *respiratory system* bring in oxygen that the body needs and release carbon dioxide, the body's waste gas. The main organs of the respiratory system are the **lungs**. Lungs are spongy organs that expand to fill with air.

Air enters your body through your nose or mouth. It flows through a tube in your throat called the *trachea* [TRAY•kee•uh].

The trachea branches into two smaller tubes called bronchi [BRAHNG•ky]. Where the bronchi enter the lungs, they branch into many bronchioles [BRAHNG•kee•ohlz]. At the end of each bronchiole are tiny sacs called alveoli [al•VEE•uh•ly]. Alveoli make up most of the lungs. When you inhale, air flows into the lungs and the alveoli inflate like tiny balloons. When you exhale, air flows back out of the alveoli and out of the lungs.

Do the Math!
Solve Word Problems

On average, a person breathes about 20 times per minute.

There are 60 minutes in an hour. How many times does a person breathe in one hour? _____

_____

There are 24 hours in a day. How many times does a person breathe every day?

_____

If you take in about 1 liter of air with each breath, how much air passes through your lungs every day?

_____

© Houghton Mifflin Harcourt Publishing Company

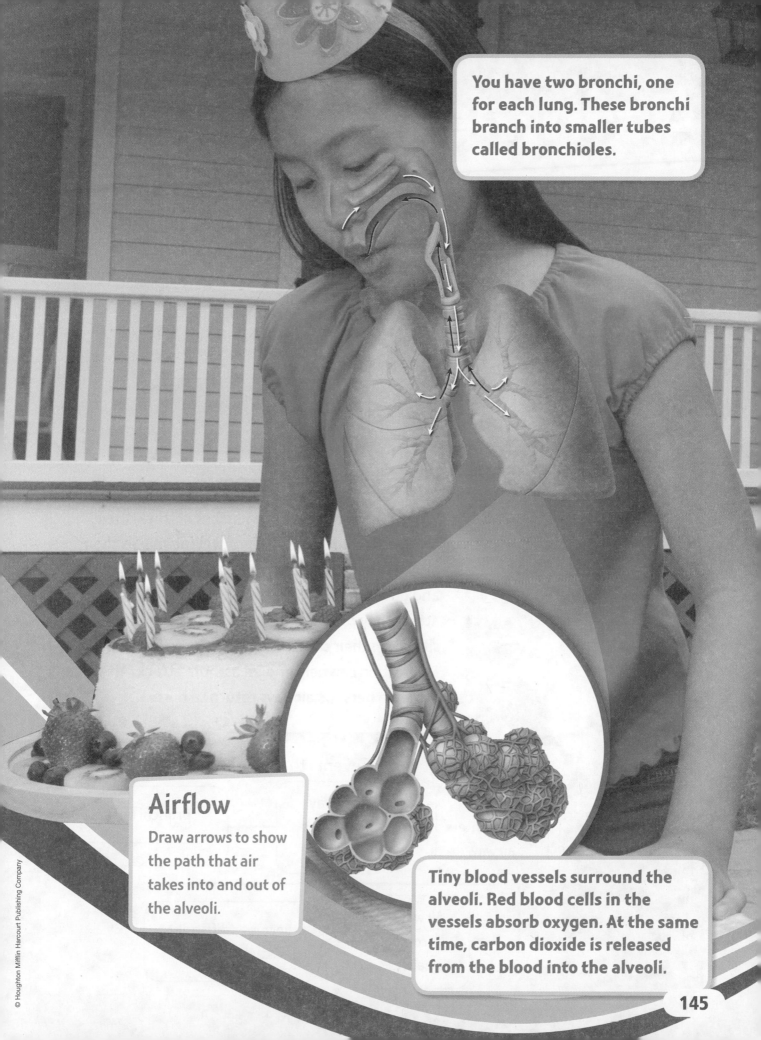

You have two bronchi, one for each lung. These bronchi branch into smaller tubes called bronchioles.

Airflow

Draw arrows to show the path that air takes into and out of the alveoli.

Tiny blood vessels surround the alveoli. Red blood cells in the vessels absorb oxygen. At the same time, carbon dioxide is released from the blood into the alveoli.

© Houghton Mifflin Harcourt Publishing Company

Asthma Attack

Asthma is an illness that makes it hard for a person to breathe. During an attack, some kids say it feels like breathing through a straw.

Active Reading As you read these two pages, draw a star next to what you consider to be the most important sentence, and be ready to explain why.

Constricted Airways

When people are having an asthma attack, their bronchi become swollen. The swelling makes their airways smaller. Air becomes much harder to get in and out of the lungs. People having an asthma attack may cough, wheeze, or feel like a weight is sitting on their chest. They struggle to breathe. Medication can help end an asthma attack. After the attack, a person's airways return to normal.

▶ Fill in the sequence of events that leads to an asthma attack.

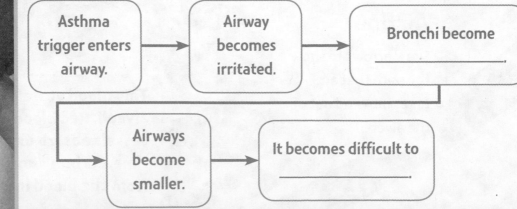

| Asthma trigger enters airway. | → | Airway becomes irritated. | → | Bronchi become _____. |

| Airways become smaller. | → | It becomes difficult to _____. |

© Houghton Mifflin Harcourt Publishing Company. (bg) ©Living Art Enterprises, LLC/Photo Researchers, Inc.; (l) ©Adam Gault/Science Photo Library/Corbis

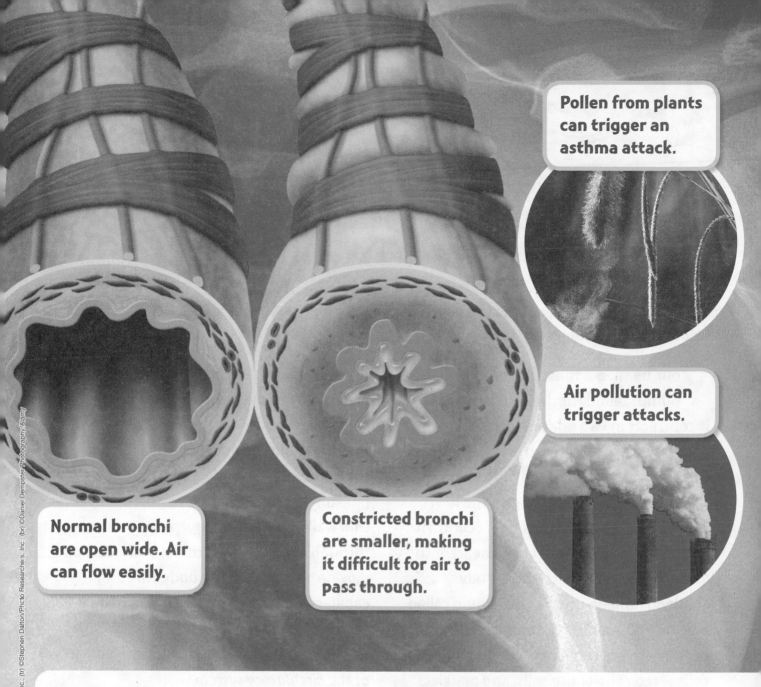

Pollen from plants can trigger an asthma attack.

Air pollution can trigger attacks.

Normal bronchi are open wide. Air can flow easily.

Constricted bronchi are smaller, making it difficult for air to pass through.

Triggers

The exact causes of asthma aren't known. Many people are born with it, but people sometimes develop asthma as they get older. Doctors do know that there are certain things that can cause an asthma attack. These things are called asthma triggers. Smoke, air pollution, and allergies are all possible triggers that start the process of an asthma attack.

Management

People who have asthma try to avoid things in the air that trigger attacks. However, a person can't always avoid triggers such as pollen or air pollution. A doctor can give people who suffer from asthma a device called an inhaler. An inhaler releases a mist of medicine that a person breathes in. This medicine can help open up airways during an attack. Other types of medicine help to prevent asthma attacks.

© Houghton Mifflin Harcourt Publishing Company (bg) ©Living Art Enterprises, LLC/Photo Researchers, Inc.; (tr) ©Stephen Dalton/Photo Researchers, Inc.; (br) ©Daniel Dempster Photography/Alamy

Beat It

Your heart is a powerful muscle. It never rests! The drumlike sound of your heart's contractions is called your heartbeat.

Active Reading As you read this page, underline the four parts of blood and their jobs.

Your **heart** is a muscular organ that pumps blood throughout your body. It contracts in two phases. When the top part is relaxed, it fills with blood. Then the top part contracts and the bottom part relaxes. Blood is squeezed into the lower part of the heart. The lower part contracts and squeezes blood out of the heart, into vessels, and to all parts of the body.

Blood is made up of a clear liquid called plasma and small structures called blood cells. There are three main types of blood cells—red cells, white cells, and platelets.

Arteries are blood vessels that carry blood away from the heart to different parts of the body. Veins are blood vessels that bring blood back to the heart from the lungs and the body. Capillaries [KAP•uh•lair•eez] are tiny vessels with very thin walls. Oxygen and nutrients can pass through capillary walls to the body. Carbon dioxide passes from the body, through capillary walls, and into the blood to be carried back to the lungs.

The heart, vessels, and blood are all part of the *circulatory system.*

Red blood cells carry oxygen throughout your body.

White blood cells help fight disease.

Platelets stop bleeding by sticking together and forming clots.

Plasma carries nutrients and blood cells throughout the body.

© Houghton Mifflin Harcourt Publishing Company (bg) ©Pauline St. Denis/Corbis

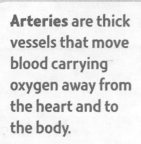

Arteries are thick vessels that move blood carrying oxygen away from the heart and to the body.

Veins move blood carrying waste material back to the heart and lungs so the process can begin again.

Capillaries connect arteries and veins. Capillaries have extremely thin walls that allow gases and nutrients to pass through.

Heartbeat Rate

How many times does your heart beat in a minute while you are sitting?

_____

Now, do 25 jumping jacks. How many times does your heart beat in a minute?

_____

© Houghton Mifflin Harcourt Publishing Company (bg) ©Pauline St. Denis/Corbis

Sum It Up!

When you're done, use the answer key to check and revise your work.

1 Read the summary statements below. Each one is incorrect. Change the part of the summary in blue to make it correct.

1. The circulatory system consists of bone, cartilage, and ligaments. Your lungs work in pairs to move your body.

   _____
   _____

2. The respiratory system brings in carbon dioxide for the body to use and releases oxygen as a waste product.

   _____
   _____

3. The muscular system carries blood through your body. It consists of the heart, blood vessels, and blood.

   _____

4. The respiratory system enables movement of materials inside the body and of the body itself.

   _____
   _____

5. Ball-and-socket joints allow for back-and-forth movement, hinge joints allow for side-to-side movement, and pivot joints allow for circular movement.

   _____
   _____
   _____

Answer Key: 1. skeletal, skeletal muscles 2. oxygen, carbon dioxide 3. circulatory 4. muscular 5. circular, back-and-forth, side-to-side or rotational

© Houghton Mifflin Harcourt Publishing Company

Brain Check

Word Play

Name _____

1 Use the clues to fill in the crossword puzzle.

Across

4. Organs that expand to fill with air
6. Body parts that work in pairs to help your body move
8. Organ that pumps blood through your body
9. The organ system that moves blood around your body
10. Place where two bones meet

Down

1. Tissue that connects bone to bone
2. Two tubes that connect to the trachea and to bronchioles
3. The organ system composed of tissue that can contract and relax
5. The organ system that moves air into and out of your body
7. The organ system that supports your body

© Houghton Mifflin Harcourt Publishing Company

Apply Concepts

2 Fill in the process chart below to describe the path that air takes through the respiratory system.

Air enters through the mouth or nose and travels through the

_____ .

Then it flows through the large tubes called _____

and the smaller tubes called

_____

until it reaches the

_____ .

There, oxygen enters the blood and

_____ _____

leaves the blood and enters the

_____ .

Then it passes through the

_____

and finally leaves the body through the mouth or nose.

The air flows back out through the

_____

and then through the larger

_____ .

3 How is the function of muscles and bones related?

_____

_____

Take It Home!

Make a model of a human skeleton using different types of pasta. Talk with your family about the different bones and what purpose they serve.

© Houghton Mifflin Harcourt Publishing Company

Essential Question

How Do Our Bodies Digest Food, Remove Wastes, and Send Messages?

Engage Your Brain!

Find the answer to the following question in this lesson and record it here.

If you could see through your body, this might be what you'd see when you look in the mirror. What is the coiled tube inside your belly, and what does it do?

_____

_____

_____

Active Reading

Lesson Vocabulary

List the terms. As you learn about each one, make notes in the Interactive Glossary.

_____   _____

_____   _____

_____

Using Charts

A chart adds information to the text that appears on the same page. Active readers pause their reading to review the chart and decide how the information in it adds to what they are reading.

© Houghton Mifflin Harcourt Publishing Company (bg) ©Custoimages/Photo Researchers, Inc.

What Goes In...

When you swallow food, it passes through a long tube in your body. As it travels, the food is broken down into smaller pieces, and all of the useful parts are absorbed by the body. All that is left over is waste.

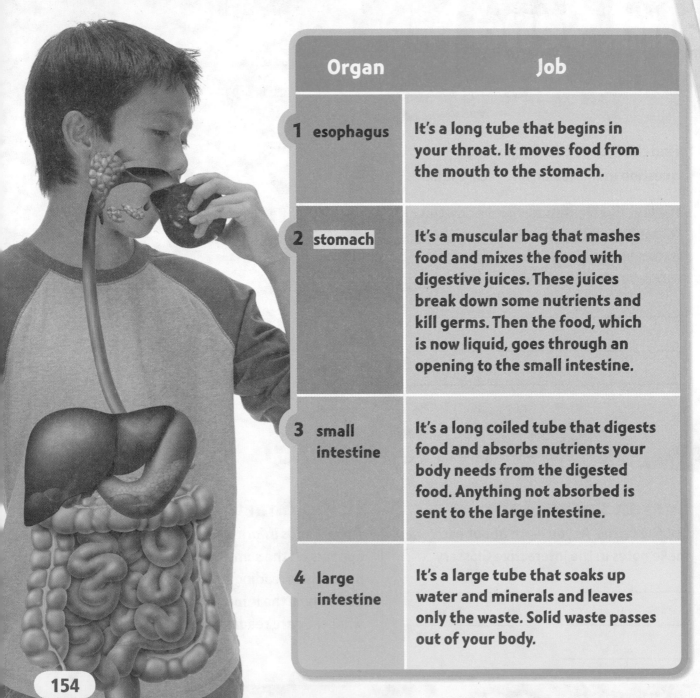

Organ	Job
1 esophagus	It's a long tube that begins in your throat. It moves food from the mouth to the stomach.
2 stomach	It's a muscular bag that mashes food and mixes the food with digestive juices. These juices break down some nutrients and kill germs. Then the food, which is now liquid, goes through an opening to the small intestine.
3 small intestine	It's a long coiled tube that digests food and absorbs nutrients your body needs from the digested food. Anything not absorbed is sent to the large intestine.
4 large intestine	It's a large tube that soaks up water and minerals and leaves only the waste. Solid waste passes out of your body.

© Houghton Mifflin Harcourt Publishing Company

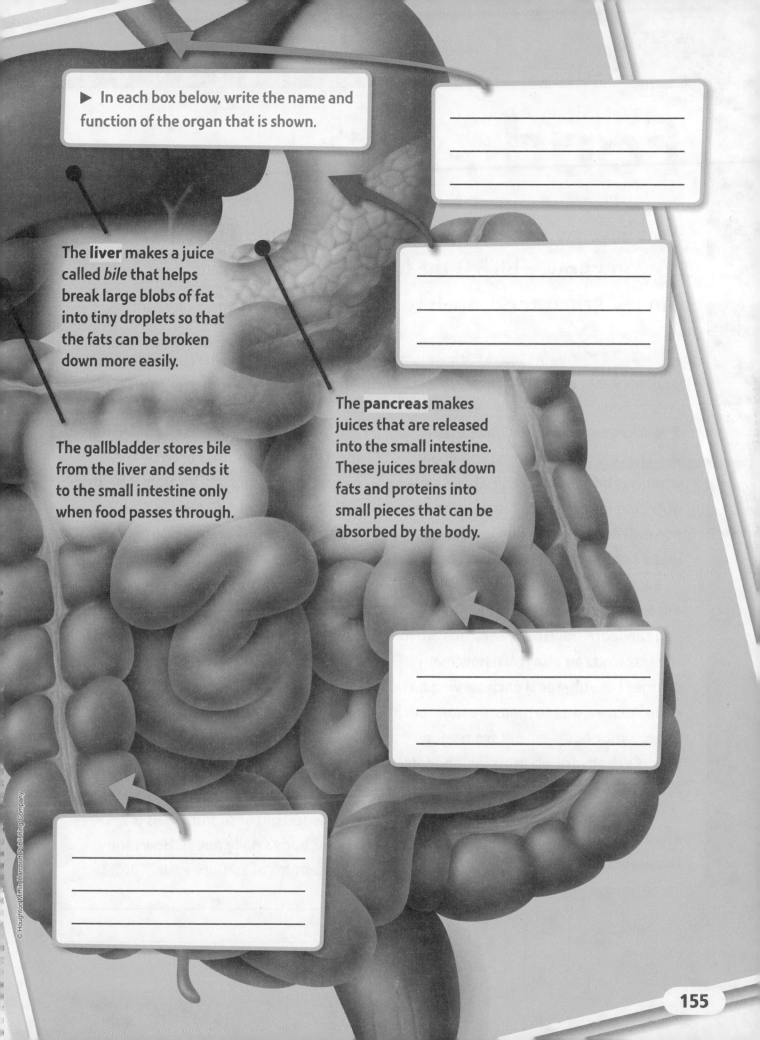

▶ In each box below, write the name and function of the organ that is shown.

The **liver** makes a juice called *bile* that helps break large blobs of fat into tiny droplets so that the fats can be broken down more easily.

The gallbladder stores bile from the liver and sends it to the small intestine only when food passes through.

The **pancreas** makes juices that are released into the small intestine. These juices break down fats and proteins into small pieces that can be absorbed by the body.

© Houghton Mifflin Harcourt Publishing Company

Food for Thought

You have two boxes of cereal in your hand. How do you know which is the healthier choice? You can read their food labels to help you decide.

Active Reading As you read these two pages, draw a star next to what you consider to be the most important sentence, and be ready to explain why.

Packaged foods must have a label that gives you information about what is inside the package. This is called nutrition information. Learning how to use nutrition information can help you make healthy food choices.

Each part of a nutrition label has different information. For example, you can learn how many servings are in the box. You can also learn how many calories [KAL•uh•reez] each serving has. Calories are a way to measure how much energy your body will get from your food. Carbohydrates, proteins, and fats are used by the body for energy.

The nutrition label has information about more than just energy. It also lists the amounts of important nutrients the food contains. Bones need calcium for strength. Sodium is used by the nerves to send signals. Vitamin A helps with your eyesight. Protein is used to build muscle. Fats are used to make important chemical signals and to store energy. As you can see, reading food labels can help you make choices that fulfill all of your body's nutrition needs.

Do the Math!
Solve Word Problems

One serving of this cereal provides you with 160 mg of sodium. This is 7% of your body's daily needs. How many milligrams of sodium equal 100%?

_____

_____

© Houghton Mifflin Harcourt Publishing Company (bg) ©imagebroker/Alamy

Nutrition Facts

Serving Size ¾ cup (30g)
Servings Per Container About 14

Amount Per Serving	Corn Crunch	with ½ cup skim milk
Calories	120	160
Calories from Fat	15	20

	% Daily Value**	
Total Fat 2g*	**3**%	**3**%
Saturated Fat 0g	**0**%	**0**%
Cholesterol 0mg	**0**%	**1**%
Sodium 160mg	**7**%	**9**%
Potassium 65mg	**2**%	**8**%
Total Carbohydrate 25g	**8**%	**10**%
Dietary Fiber 3g		
Sugars 3g		
Other Carbohydrate 11g		
Protein 2g		

*Amount in Cereal. A serving of cereal plus skim milk provides 2g fat, less 5mg cholesterol, 220mg sodium, 270mg potassium, 31g carbohydrate (19g sugars) and 6g protein.

**Percent Daily Values are based on a 2,000 calorie diet. Your daily values may be higher or lower depending on your calorie needs:

	Calories	2,000	2,500
al Fat	Less than	65g	80g
at fat	Less than	20g	25g
esterol	Less than	300mg	300mg
m	Less than	2,400mg	2,400mg
ium		3,500mg	3,500mg
rbohydrate		300g	375g
y Fiber		25g	30g

The serving size will help you make smart decisions about how much of a food you should eat to get the right amount of nutrients in your diet.

The "% Daily Value" tells you what percent of this nutrient a serving of this food will provide compared to how much you should get in a full day.

This section shows how many grams (g) or milligrams (mg) of each type of nutrient you should get each day, depending on how many calories you need.

▶ How many calories are in 1 serving, with 1/2 cup skim milk?

_____

©Houghton Mifflin Harcourt Publishing Company ©imagebroker/Alamy

...Must come Out

Digesting food produces one kind of waste. Using the nutrients produces another kind of waste. The *excretory system* rids the body of this waste and keeps your body's water and salt levels in balance.

Active Reading As you read this page, underline the different types of waste that are described.

Your body "burns" nutrients much like a fire burns wood. Your body doesn't produce ash, but the "burned" nutrients do make waste products. For example, as protein is broken down, ammonia is made. Ammonia is very toxic! The liver converts ammonia to urea [yoo•REE•uh], which is less toxic. But if urea builds up it makes you sick, so your body gets rid of it as urine. A small amount of urea is also released in sweat.

Like a fire, your body uses oxygen and produces a waste gas called carbon dioxide. Carbon dioxide is released by your lungs when you breathe out.

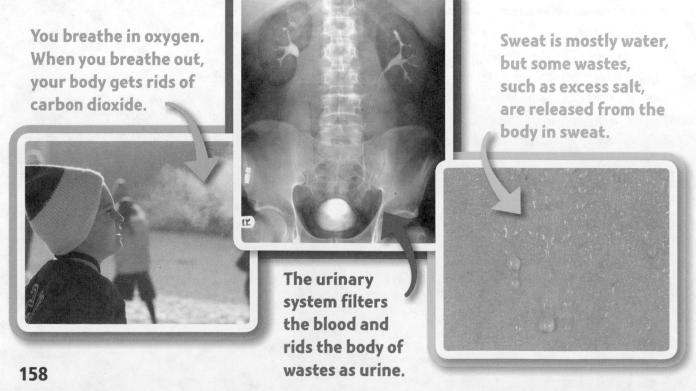

You breathe in oxygen. When you breathe out, your body gets rids of carbon dioxide.

The urinary system filters the blood and rids the body of wastes as urine.

Sweat is mostly water, but some wastes, such as excess salt, are released from the body in sweat.

© Houghton Mifflin Harcourt Publishing Company (bl) ©David R. Frazier Photolibrary, Inc./Alamy; (c) ©Medical Body Scans/Photo Researchers, Inc.; (br) ©Jason Hetherington

The Urinary System

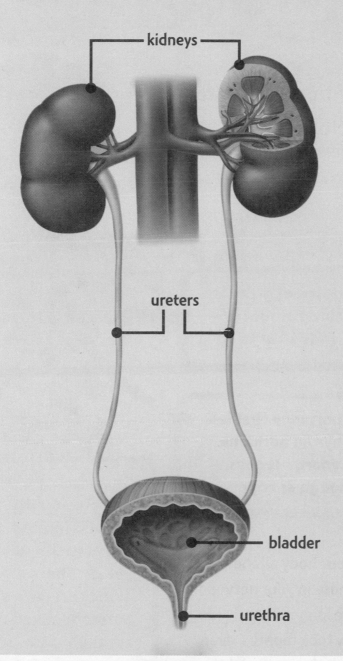

kidneys

ureters

bladder

urethra

1 The **kidneys** are organs that remove waste from the blood. They also help to conserve water and to make sure the blood does not have too much or too little salt.

2 After the kidneys filter the blood, the waste, *urine*, collects in tubes called *ureters* [YUR•ih•tuhrz]. These take the urine to the bladder.

3 The **bladder** stores urine and then releases it from the body. The bladder can stretch like a balloon. It can hold up to a pint of urine at a time!

4 The urethra [yu•REE•thruh] is a small tube that takes urine from the bladder to outside of the body.

Organize It—Sequence

Write the organs in order to show the path of urine through the urinary system.

© Houghton Mifflin Harcourt Publishing Company   HMH Credits

Chemical Messages

What happened to the boy in the picture?
Did he put on the wrong clothes?

Active Reading As you read these
two pages, draw one line under a cause.
Draw two lines under the effect.

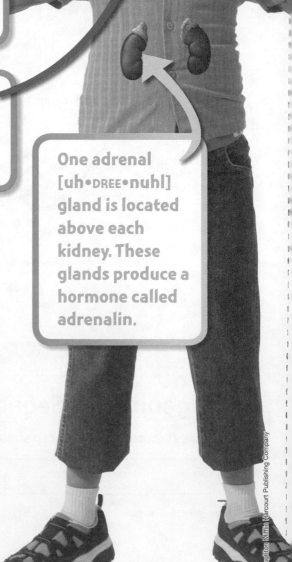

The pituitary [puh•TOO•uh•tair•ee] gland is
located underneath the brain. It produces
hormones that tell other glands what to do.

The thyroid produces a hormone that lets
your body use energy. Thyroid hormone
goes up when you need energy. It goes
down when you have enough energy.

One adrenal
[uh•DREE•nuhl]
gland is located
above each
kidney. These
glands produce a
hormone called
adrenalin.

Messages are traveling through your body all the
time. Some messages, such as those in your nervous
system, are lightning-fast. Others take longer. The
messages that caused the boy to grow took months, even
though he seemed to grow out of his clothes overnight!

Chemicals called *hormones* carry messages that cause
growth and other slow changes in the body. Hormones
travel from one part of the body to another and pass along
messages that result in different changes. Groups of cells
called *glands* produce hormones. Glands and hormones
make up the *endocrine system*.

© Houghton Mifflin Harcourt Publishing Company

The response you have when you are afraid happens fast. It is caused by adrenalin. Your heart beats faster, and you break into a sweat. This response prepares you to defend yourself or run away!

Your pancreas produces a hormone that controls the sugar in your blood. When the amount of sugar is high, the pancreas releases the hormone insulin. As blood sugar goes down, the pancreas stops releasing insulin.

The pituitary is called the master gland because it tells the other glands what to do. For example, it tells the thyroid and adrenal glands when to release hormones. The pituitary also releases growth hormone. Growth hormone causes changes in the body that lead to maturity. Growth hormone may cause rapid growth spurts that lead to "growing pains."

What Happens Next?

Fill in an effect that matches each cause.

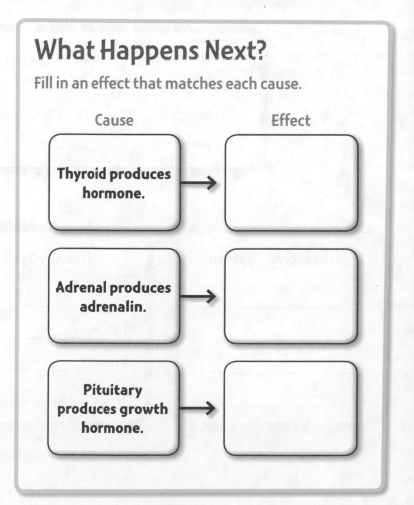

Cause	Effect
Thyroid produces hormone. →	
Adrenal produces adrenalin. →	
Pituitary produces growth hormone. →	

© Houghton Mifflin Harcourt Publishing Company

Sum It Up!

When you're done, use the answer key to check and revise your work.

Complete the summary paragraph by filling in the blanks. Then write each word listed below the paragraph in the appropriate system box at the bottom of the page.

Summarize

Your body is made up of many 1._____ that work together in systems. The 2._____ system is a long tube inside your body. It takes the nutrients out of food for your body to use. The 3._____ system is responsible for removing waste from your body. The 4._____ system produces hormones that cause changes such as growth.

pituitary	small intestine	thyroid
kidneys	adrenal	esophagus
stomach	large intestine	ureters
urethra	bladder	pancreas

Digestive System

5. _____

6. _____

7. _____

8. _____

Urinary System

9. _____

10. _____

11. _____

12. _____

Endocrine System

13. _____

14. _____

15. _____

16. _____

Answer Key: 1. organs 2. digestive 3. excretory 4. endocrine 5.–8. (in any order) esophagus, stomach, small intestine, large intestine 9.–12. (in any order) kidneys, ureters, bladder, urethra 13.–16. (in any order) pituitary, adrenal, thyroid, pancreas

© Houghton Mifflin Harcourt Publishing Company

Name _____

Word Play

1 Read the clues. Write the answers on the lines. Then find these words in the puzzle.

1. These bean-shaped organs filter the blood and remove wastes.
   _____

2. This long tube connects the mouth to the stomach.
   _____

3. This gland lets your body use energy.
   _____

4. This organ expands and fills up with urine until it is ready to be released.
   _____

5. In this organ, water is removed until the waste is solid.
   _____

6. This organ makes juices that break down protein in the small intestine.
   _____

```
d  u  r  i  n  a  r  y  l  a  t  o  d  i
n  o  p  t  n  a  o  i  i  e  s  r  p  a
t  v  e  t  e  l  o  s  v  v  s  k  a  t
l  a  r  g  e  i  n  t  e  s  t  i  n  e
t  e  o  u  u  g  r  d  r  c  t  d  c  s
i  n  d  i  g  e  s  t  i  v  e  n  r  t
i  d  c  e  d  y  t  b  i  e  p  e  e  h
t  o  c  e  f  l  o  v  h  r  d  y  a  y
i  c  t  d  r  c  m  y  e  o  e  s  s  r
n  r  u  i  b  l  a  d  d  e  r  r  e  o
t  i  v  i  t  k  c  p  n  d  o  n  t  i
a  n  e  s  o  p  h  a  g  u  s  e  e  d
e  e  a  d  v  s  s  r  g  l  a  n  d  e
i  r  u  e  c  c  v  r  m  r  p  r  y  k
```

7. This system moves food through your body and absorbs the nutrients.
   _____

8. This organ makes a juice that breaks large blobs of fat into smaller blobs.
   _____

9. This system sends chemical messengers through the body.
   _____

10. This structure is a group of cells that make hormones.
    _____

11. This organ mashes food and mixes food with digestive juices.
    _____

12. This system filters wastes from the blood.
    _____

© Houghton Mifflin Harcourt Publishing Company

Apply Concepts

2 Think about how organs depend on other organs to do their work. Complete each sentence.

1. Food couldn't reach the stomach without the _____ and the _____ .

2. Kidneys couldn't work without the _____ because _____ couldn't leave the body.

3. The small intestine couldn't work without the _____ because fats couldn't be broken down.

3 Explain why the structure shown here is called a master gland.

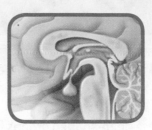

_____

_____

_____

4 Explain how each of the items shown below are alike.

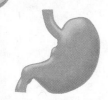   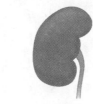

stomach and blender   **kidney and coffee filter**   **bladder and water balloon**

_____   _____   _____

_____   _____   _____

5 The pancreas is part of two different body systems. Name the two systems. Describe the job of the pancreas in each system. _____

_____.

_____.

Take It Home!

Write the words *small intestine, pancreas, esophagus, liver, large intestine, gall bladder,* and *stomach* on index cards. Eat a snack. Ask your family to explain how each organ helps to digest your food.

© Houghton Mifflin Harcourt Publishing Company

Meet the Grays of Biology

Henry Gray

Henry Gray was a surgeon in London. He was fascinated by the science of anatomy. Anatomy is the study of the parts of the body. In 1858, when he was only 31 years old, Henry Gray published a book on anatomy. It became one of the most famous scientific books of all time: *Gray's Anatomy*. The book included drawings of all of the organs and systems of the human body. Henry Gray died three years later from smallpox, but his work lives on. In 2009, the 40th edition of *Gray's Anatomy* was published. It is still used today by doctors, students, and other scientists.

Asa Gray

Asa Gray was an American botanist. He studied plants. He lived around the same time as Henry Gray, but the two men were not related. They never even met. Still, their work had some things in common. Asa Gray wrote a book known as *Gray's Manual*. Working with a scientific illustrator named Isaac Sprague, Asa Gray published a book that had information about almost every plant in the Northern United States. It was written more than a century ago. But *Gray's Manual* is still used by botanists today. Asa Gray is considered to be one of history's most important botanists.

© Houghton Mifflin Harcourt Publishing Company   (bkgd) ©Javarman/Alamy; (tl) ©Bettmann/Corbis;

Be a Scientific Illustrator

Try your hand at scientific illustrations! See how well you can produce an anatomical drawing of the bones of the human hand. Then try making a botanical illustration of the raspberry branch.

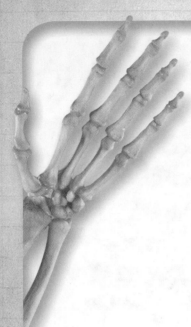

Bones of the Human Hand

Raspberry Branch

© Houghton Mifflin Harcourt Publishing Company (bkgd) ©Javarman/Alamy; (cl) ©Lester V. Bergman/Corbis; (tr) ©Getty Images Royalty Free; (br) ©Jeffrey Lepore/Photo Researchers, Inc.

Name _____

Essential Question

How Does the Body Stay Cool?

Set a Purpose
What will you learn from this experiment?

_____

_____

_____

State Your Hypothesis
Write your hypothesis, or testable statement.

_____

_____

_____

Think About the Procedure
Which sample is the control? What is its purpose?

_____

_____

_____

Record Your Data
Record your observations in a data table.

Draw Conclusions
How did your results compare with your hypothesis?

_____

_____

_____

_____

© Houghton Mifflin Harcourt Publishing Company

Analyze and Extend

1. What was the difference between the starting temperature and the ending temperature for each of your experimental groups? Show your work in the space below.

_____

_____

_____

_____

2. Make a bar graph in the space below to display your data.

3. How does this activity relate to the role of sweating?

_____

_____

_____

4. A swamp cooler is a type of air conditioner that blows air over a wet surface. Use your data to explain whether you think this would be an effective way to cool a building.

_____

_____

_____

_____

5. Why is it important that your body be able to cool itself?

_____

_____

_____

_____

_____

6. Think of other questions you would like to ask about evaporation and cooling.

_____

_____

_____

_____

© Houghton Mifflin Harcourt Publishing Company

Unit 3 Review

Vocabulary Review

Use the terms in the box to complete the sentences.

cell theory
heart
inherited trait
liver
nucleus
organ
stomach
tissue

1. The idea that all living things are made of cells, that all life processes take place in cells, and that new cells come from existing cells is known as _____.

2. The muscular organ that pumps blood through the rest of the circulatory system is the _____.

3. A body part made of smaller parts that work together to do a job is a(n) _____.

4. The part of a cell that controls taking in materials, producing energy, and getting rid of wastes is the _____.

5. The large organ that makes a digestive juice called bile is the _____.

6. A group of similar cells that work together make up _____.

7. A baglike organ in which food is mixed with digestive juices and squeezed by muscles is the _____.

8. A characteristic that is passed from parents to their offspring is a(n) _____.

Science Concepts

Fill in the letter of the choice that best answers the question.

9. David wraps five thermometers in strips of cloth. He dips four into different liquids. He leaves the fifth dry. He sets them in the shade for five minutes. The table below shows the temperature that he records for each thermometer.

Alcohol	Mineral oil	Salt water	Water	Dry
72 °F	82 °F	78 °F	78 °F	83 °F

Which liquid evaporates fastest?

(A) water

(B) alcohol

(C) salt water

(D) mineral oil

10. In David's experiment, why did he leave one thermometer dry?

(A) David had five thermometers but only four liquids, so he left one thermometer dry.

(B) David wanted to know what the temperature was in the room where he prepared his experiment.

(C) The dry thermometer is the variable to which he could compare the others.

(D) The dry thermometer is the control to which he could compare the others.

11. Which process is the function of the skeletal system?

(A) gas exchange

(B) structural support

(C) removal of waste

(D) temperature control

12. In the early days of telephone use, a person had to call an operator. The operator would connect two callers. The operator performed a function that is most similar to which human body part?

(A) brain

(B) nose

(C) eyes

(D) skin

13. During recess, Renée scraped her knee, so the nurse put a bandage on it. Which of the functions normally provided by skin is now being provided by the bandage?

(A) preventing dehydration

(B) regulating body temperature

(C) keeping bacteria out of the body

(D) sensing when it is being touched

14. You accidentally touch a hot stove and immediately pull your hand back. Which statement best describes the organ systems involved in this response?

(A) Only the nervous system is involved.

(B) Only the integumentary system is involved.

(C) Neither the integumentary system nor the nervous system is involved.

(D) Both the integumentary system and the nervous system are involved.

© Houghton Mifflin Harcourt Publishing Company   HMH Credits

15. The following picture shows some muscles and bones of the arm.

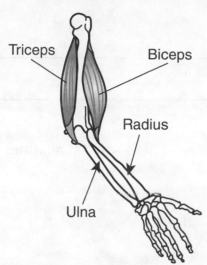

As this arm bends, which word describes what the biceps muscle is doing?

Ⓐ relaxing   Ⓒ contracting

Ⓑ retracting   Ⓓ constricting

16. An important body function is the taking in of oxygen from air and releasing carbon dioxide back to the atmosphere. Which organ performs this function?

Ⓐ heart

Ⓑ lungs

Ⓒ mouth

Ⓓ intestine

17. Urine is a product of the urinary system. What makes up normal human urine?

Ⓐ oxygen

Ⓑ nutrients

Ⓒ water and waste products

Ⓓ all the fluids a person drinks

18. Cells in the body use nutrients and oxygen for energy. Which body system transports oxygen and nutrients throughout the body?

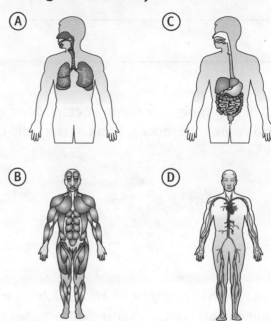

19. Digestion takes place in the digestive tract, shown here.

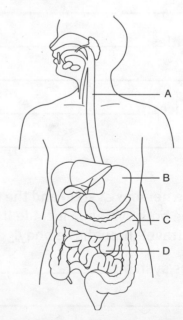

In what order does food move through the organs of the digestive tract?

Ⓐ A, B, C, D   Ⓒ A, B, D, C

Ⓑ A, C, B, D   Ⓓ A, D, B, C

© Houghton Mifflin Harcourt Publishing Company HMH Credits

Apply Inquiry and Review the Big Idea

Write the answer to these questions.

20. It is a warm summer day. Juan has been running fast while playing soccer with his friends. Using what you have learned about the human body, explain why he is breathing hard, his heart is pounding, and he is sweating.

_____

_____

21. All living things are made of cells. The cells of plants and animals have some similarities and some differences. Look at the cells below.

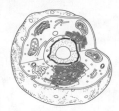

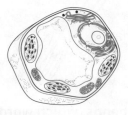

Cell A   Cell B

Tell which is a plant cell and which is an animal cell. Then describe three things these cells have in common, and three differences between the two types of cells.

a. Identify the cells. _____

_____

b. Similarities: _____

_____

c. Differences: _____

_____

22. Both the nervous system and the endocrine system send messages throughout your body. Describe both systems. Include how messages are sent and the length of time messages take to travel through the body.

a. Nervous system: _____

_____

b. Endocrine system: _____

_____

© Houghton Mifflin Harcourt Publishing Company   HMH Credits

How Living Things Grow and Reproduce

Big Idea

All living things have observable characteristics that allow them to be classified. Plants and animals pass these characteristics on to their offspring.

I Wonder Why

It's got spines like a porcupine. It has a long, sticky tongue like an anteater. And it lays eggs! What is this strange looking animal? I wonder why scientists would classify it as a mammal? *Turn the page to find out.*

© Houghton Mifflin Harcourt Publishing Company (bg) ©Dave Watts/Alamy; (inset) ©WILDLIFE GmbH/Alamy; (border) ©NIDst-Age Fotostock

Here's why Scientists classify the echidna as a mammal, even though it lays eggs. Most mammals give birth to live young. When the echidna's eggs hatch, the young are tiny. They are no bigger than a lima bean!

In this unit, you will explore the Big Idea, Essential Questions, and Investigations on the Inquiry Flipchart.

Levels of Inquiry Key ■ DIRECTED ■ GUIDED ■ INDEPENDENT

Track Your Progress

Big Idea All living things have observable characteristics and pass them to their offspring.

Essential Questions

Now I Get the Big Idea!

Science Notebook
Before you begin each lesson, be sure to write your thoughts about the Essential Question.

© Houghton Mifflin Harcourt Publishing Company · (tg) ©WILDLIFE GmbH/Alamy; (bordar) ©NDisc/Age Fotostock · (b) ©Dave Watts/Alamy; (inset) ©WILDLIFE GmbH/Alamy

Essential Question

How Are Living Things Grouped?

Engage Your Brain!

Find the answer to the following questions in this lesson and record them here.

Why is the grass classified as a plant? Why is the mushroom not classified as a plant?

_____

_____

_____

_____

Active Reading

Lesson Vocabulary

List the terms. As you learn about each one, make notes in the Interactive Glossary.

_____   _____

_____   _____

_____   _____

Main Ideas and Details

Detail sentences give information about a topic. The information may include examples, features, characteristics, or facts. Active readers stay focused on the topic when they ask, What fact or information does this sentence add to the topic?

© Houghton Mifflin Harcourt Publishing Company (bg) © John Devries/Photo Researchers, Inc.

Why Classify?

Would you classify, or group, insects and birds together just because they have wings? Of course not! So how do scientists classify organisms?

Active Reading As you read these two pages, put brackets around the main idea.

When you visit the grocery store to buy peanut butter, how do you find it? The store classifies, or groups, similar items so that you can find them easily. Scientists use **classification** to organize living things into similar groups.

Domains and kingdoms are the broadest levels of classification.

DOMAIN   KINGDOM

Bacteria → Bacteria

Archaea → Archaea

Eukarya → Animalia
Eukarya → Plantae
Eukarya → Fungi
Eukarya → Protista

This bird and this plant are both commonly called Birds of Paradise. Although they share this common name and are both colorful, they are very different. Clearly they should not be grouped together. But how can you classify them if the common name doesn't help?

© Houghton Mifflin Harcourt Publishing Company (bg) ©PictureNet/Corbis; (r) ©blickwinkel/Alamy; (bc) ©Douglas Peebles Photography/Alamy

What about this worm and this snake? They have similar forms, so why do we give them different names? In what ways are the snake and worm similar? In what ways are they different?

Scientists classify organisms so that they can understand how the organisms are related. Cell type, cell structure, and genetic information are three types of information used to classify organisms. Other features used to classify organisms include shape, size, and symmetry.

Scientists use different tools to identify and record data about differences in organisms. These differences can be used to identify an organism. A **dichotomous key** [di•KOT•uh•muhs KEE] is a chart with many choices that guide you to the name of the thing you want to identify. You can make a dichotomous key to identify all kinds of things.

Using a Dichotomous Key

Fill in the dichotomous key below to help someone determine which type of shoe he or she is observing.

Is the shoe red?

yes → Does the shoe have laces?
    yes →
    no →

no → Does the shoe have straps?
    yes →
    no →

sandal

sneaker

boot

pump

© Houghton Mifflin Harcourt Publishing Company (bg) ©PictureNet/Corbis; (l) ©blickwinkel/Alamy; (t) ©Polka Dot Images/Jupiterimages/Getty Images; (tl) ©Artville/Getty Images

Domain
Eukarya

Kingdom
Animalia

Classifying Living Things

Thc system scientists use to classify living things begins with groups that include many organisms. But it doesn't stop there!

Active Reading Underline the classification levels of a camel.

Organisms are classified into one of three domains. A **domain** is the broadest level of classification. Organisms are separated into domains by their cell structures. As you continue down each level of classification, the organisms are more closely related to each other.

KINGDOM

The camel is in Kingdom Animalia.

PHYLUM

Next, the organisms in kingdoms are grouped into phyla. The camel is in the phylum Chordata.

CLASS

A phylum can be broken into classes. The camel is in the class Mammalia.

ORDER

The next level of division is order. Camels are part of the order Artiodactyla.

178

© Houghton Mifflin Harcourt Publishing Company   (bg) ©PictureNet/Corbis

The organisms to the right are commonly called sea stars, but scientists classify them separately. They are all in Kingdom Animalia. These marine animals have bony skeletons, but they do not have a backbone. They all belong to the Echinoderm phylum. The true sea star at top belongs to the class Asteroidea. The brittle star and basket star are similar to the true sea star, but they differ from it in important ways. They are classified into the class Ophiuroidea.

▶ How are these organisms alike? How are they different?

_____

_____

_____

_____

_____

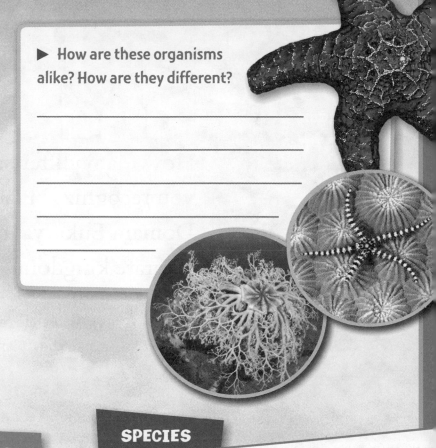

FAMILY

Orders can be further divided into families. Camels belong to the family Camelidae.

GENUS

A **genus** is a subdivision of a family. This camel belongs to the genus *Camelus.*

SPECIES

Finally, organisms are classified by species. **Species** are unique organisms. This camel belongs to the species *dromedarius.*

The two-part scientific name for the camel is *Camelus dromedarius.* As you can see, the scientific name is made of the genus and species names. The first letter of the genus name is always capitalized, but the species name is not. This two-part name is based on a system developed by the scientist Carolus Linnaeus in the 1700s.

© Houghton Mifflin Harcourt Publishing Company   (bg) ©PictureNet/Corbis; (tr) ©Stone Nature Photography/Alamy; (cl) ©WaterFrame/Alamy; (cr) ©cbimages/Alamy

Plants and Animals

How many different plants and animals can you recognize? Plants and animals are both in Domain Eukarya, but they are grouped into separate kingdoms.

Active Reading As you read these two pages, underline the parts of the text that explain how plants and animals are classified.

There are more than 320,000 species of plants. Plants are made up of many cells and use sunlight to make food. Some plants are very large, while other plants may be tiny. Scientists classify plants according to the structures they have and how they use those structures to live.

Some plants have vascular tissue. Vascular tissue consists of long, narrow tubes that transport materials throughout the plant. Other plants just absorb the materials they need, like a sponge absorbs water.

Plants are also classified by the way they reproduce. Some plants produce seeds in fruits, while others produce seeds in cones. Some plants don't produce seeds at all! All of these characteristics are used to classify plants.

This conifer is a vascular plant. It produces seeds on cones, can grow tall, and lives for many years.

Mosses do not have vascular tissue. They grow low to the ground and absorb nutrients in a sponge-like manner.

Some plants use flowers to reproduce. Flowering plants make up the largest number of species in Kingdom Plantae.

© Houghton Mifflin Harcourt Publishing Company (bg) ©PictureNet/Corbis; (l) ©Christian Kober/John Warburton-Lee Photography/Alamy; (br) ©C Squared Studios/Photodisc/Getty Images

© Houghton Mifflin Harcourt Publishing Company (bg) ©PictureNet/Corbis; (tl) Greg Pease/Getty Images; (c) ©Getty Images Royalty Free; (tr) ©D. Hurst/Alamy; (cr) ©Purestock/Alamy

Crabs are invertebrates, meaning they do not have backbones. They live on land and in water.

This frog is an amphibian. It begins life under water as a tadpole before growing into an adult frog that lives on land.

This lion is a mammal. Mammals have fur. When they are young, they drink milk from their mothers' bodies.

Birds have wings and feathers. Although a chicken cannot fly far, most other birds can.

Most animals are made of multiple cells and cannot make their own food. Animals are often divided into two main groups. Animals that have backbones are called vertebrates. Vertebrates include fish, birds, reptiles, amphibians, and mammals. Animals without backbones are invertebrates. Invertebrates include insects, worms, jellyfish, and sponges.

Vertebrates make up only about 5% of the animal population on Earth. Approximately 95% of Earth's animals are invertebrates!

Within these two main groups, animals are further classified according to their body structures, how they take in oxygen and digest food, and many other factors. What do you think some of these other factors could be?

Do the Math!
Use Fractions

Mammals account for about $\frac{1}{10}$ of all vertebrates. Birds account for about $\frac{1}{6}$ of all vertebrates. Together, what fraction of vertebrates is made up of mammals and birds?

_____

Fungi and Protists

Sometimes microscopic, sometimes huge, Fungi and Protista are kingdoms that we often overlook.

Active Reading As you read these two pages, draw a box around the sentences that explain how fungi and protists are classified.

Mushrooms are fungi. Sometimes, we see only part of a fungus. Did you know that some of the largest organisms on Earth are fungi? Some species are even bigger than a whale!

Mushrooms are a kind of fungus that may grow in soil. Although some mushrooms grow out of the ground, they are not plants. Fungi do not make food from sunlight. Instead, they feed on dead or decayed materials.

Yeasts are another type of fungus. Unlike mushrooms, yeasts are made up of only one cell. Scientists classify fungi according to their size, shape, and the way they reproduce.

▶ List two reasons why fungi are classified in a different kingdom from plants.

_____

_____

_____

_____

_____

_____

A single yeast cell can be seen only with a microscope.

The mold on this bread is a fungus. The mold fungus is decomposing the bread for energy.

© Houghton Mifflin Harcourt Publishing Company   (cq) ©PictureNet/Corbis; (t) ©C. Huetter/Arco Images GmbH/Alamy; (b) ©Eye of Science/Photo Researchers, Inc.

Protists

Kingdom Protista is very diverse.
How would you classify these protists?

The single-cell amoeba can form a structure that allows it to move or reach out to capture food.

This brown algae is large and looks similar to a plant. It lives in water and performs photosynthesis.

Euglena is a single-celled protist. Like plants, it has structures that allow it to make food from sunlight.

A paramecium moves using hair-like structures on the outside of its one-celled body. Movement allows it to sense and capture prey.

Kingdom Protista is probably the most diverse kingdom within Domain Eukarya. Protists may look or act like plants, fungi, or even animals! Most protists are made up of only one microscopic cell, but some kinds of protists live in large colonies that look like a single organism.

Protists have developed various ways to move. Some form structures they use to drag themselves across surfaces. Other protists have hair-like structures they use to move around in water. Many protists don't move at all.

Within Kingdom Protista, scientists have traditionally classified organisms according to whether they are most like plants, animals, or fungi. Plant-like protists use sunlight to make food. They are classified according to size and color. Animal-like protists are able to move and capture prey. Fungus-like protists grow and feed like fungi.

© Houghton Mifflin Harcourt Publishing Company (bg) ©PictureNet/Corbis; (l) ©Andrew Syred/Photo Researchers, Inc.; (cr) ©M. I. Walker/Photo Researchers, Inc.; (c) ©David Spears/Clouds Hill Imaging Ltd./Corbis; (t) ©Biophoto Associates/Photo Researchers, Inc.

Bacteria and Archaea

Did you know that bacteria are some of the simplest living organisms? While some types of bacteria are harmful, other types are quite helpful!

Active Reading As you read these two pages, draw boxes around words that signal contrasts.

There are more bacteria on Earth than any other living thing. Bacteria are found almost everywhere. They are microscopic and cover the surfaces of everything you see. They can live on humans and other organisms—and even inside them, too!

Bacteria can cause disease and pollute lakes and streams, but they can also be helpful. Bacteria are used to make foods such as yogurt and cheese. We even have bacteria in our bodies that help us digest food! Bacteria are classified according to their shape, size, how they get food, and whether or not they use oxygen.

Some of the foods that you may eat are made using bacteria.

The cyanobacteria in this stream are reproducing quickly, causing a bloom. In a bloom, all of the oxygen in the water may be used up, causing other organisms to die.

© Houghton Mifflin Harcourt Publishing Company · (b) ©RJH Catalog/Alamy; (inset) ©Manfred Kage/Peter Arnold, Inc./Alamy; (t) ©PictureNet/Corbis; (b) ©RJH Catalog/Alamy

Archaea are single-celled organisms similar to bacteria. However, the structures and genetic material of Archaea and bacteria are different, so they are classified in separate domains.

Archaea live in extreme environments and get energy from unusual resources. Some archaea are found in springs where temperatures are so high that nothing else can survive there. Some archaea get energy from ammonia or sulfur gas. Most archaea are classified according to their chemical structure or genetic material.

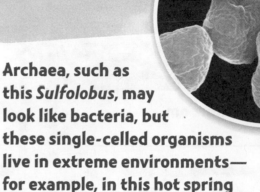

Archaea, such as this *Sulfolobus*, may look like bacteria, but these single-celled organisms live in extreme environments— for example, in this hot spring in Yellowstone National Park.

▶ Use the information in this lesson to fill out the table below.

Kingdom	Description of Kingdom	Example
		Canary
		Pine tree
Fungi		Bread mold
Protista		
Bacteria		

© Houghton Mifflin Harcourt Publishing Company   (bg) ©PictureNet/Corbis; (r) ©Eye of Science/Photo Researchers, Inc.; (l) ©Alan L. Detrick/Photo Researchers, Inc.

Sum It Up!

When you're done, use the answer key to check and revise your work.

Write the name of the kingdom to which each organism belongs.

mushroom

_____

moss

_____

cyanobacteria

_____

sea star

_____

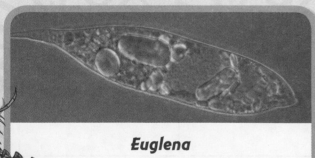

Euglena

_____

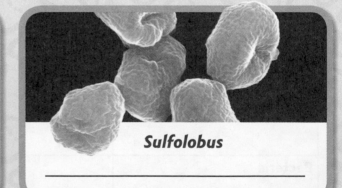

Sulfolobus

_____

© Houghton Mifflin Harcourt Publishing Company   (cr) ©C. Huetter/Arco Images GmbH/Alamy; (tl) ©C. Huetter/Arco Images GmbH/Alamy; (tr) ©Manfred Kage/Peter Arnold, Inc./Alamy; (bl) ©David Spears/Clouds Hill Imaging Ltd./Corbis; (cl) ©Manfred Kage/Peter Arnold, Inc./Alamy; (br) ©Eye of Science/Photo Researchers, Inc.

Answer Key: mushroom: Kingdom Fungi; moss: Kingdom Plantae; cyanobacteria: Kingdom Bacteria; sea star: Kingdom Animalia. *Euglena*: Kingdom Protista; *Sulfolobus*: Kingdom Archaea

 **Brain Check**

Name _____

Word Play

1 Use the clues to help you unscramble the words below.

1. nomaids   _____   The three broadest groups used for classification

2. gunif   _____   The kingdom that includes yeasts and mushrooms

3. iclsifastinoca   _____   The organization of living things into categories

4. espsice   _____   The name that identifies a unique organism

5. snuge   _____   The first part of the scientific name of an organism

6. stoprtia   _____   The kingdom that includes *Euglena*

7. minkdog   _____   The classification level that comes after domain

© Houghton Mifflin Harcourt Publishing Company

Apply Concepts

2 Explain how and why scientists classify organisms.

_____

_____

_____

_____

_____

_____

3 Draw an organism that would be classified as an animal.

4 Circle the organism that would be classified as a plant.

   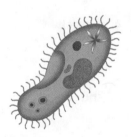

5 Explain why you chose the organism you circled. What characteristics would cause it to be classified this way?

_____

_____

_____

Take It Home!

Share what you have learned about classification with your family. Take a walk with an adult and name the kingdoms of the organisms you see.

© Houghton Mifflin Harcourt Publishing Company

Name _____

Essential Question

What Is a Dichotomous Key?

Set a Purpose
What will you learn from this investigation?

_____

_____

_____

Think About the Procedure
Why are the beans you are given different from one another?

_____

_____

_____

Record Your Data
In the space provided, make your dichotomous key using the bean characteristics you identified.

Draw Conclusions

Scientists classify and organize living things based on how they are similar or different from one another. Why is it important for scientists to use the same characteristics to classify living things?

_____

_____

_____

_____

Scientists must be very specific when describing living things. Why might scientists want to avoid using terms such as *small, big, heavy,* and *light* when classifying living things?

_____

_____

_____

_____

Analyze and Extend

1. Which characteristics did you use to classify the beans? Which characteristics did your classmates use?

_____

_____

_____

_____

2. Compare charts with a classmate. Was one chart easier to use than the other chart?

_____

_____

_____

_____

3. How might grouping and classifying things, rather than just describing them, make it easier for others to identify the things?

_____

_____

_____

_____

4. How was the dichotomous key you made to classify beans different from dichotomous keys scientists use to classify organisms?

_____

_____

_____

_____

5. What other questions would you like to ask about how scientists use dichotomous keys?

_____

_____

_____

_____

© Houghton Mifflin Harcourt Publishing Company

Essential Question

How Do Plants Grow and Reproduce?

Engage Your Brain!

Find the answer to the following question in this lesson and record it here.

How are plants different from each other, and how are they the same?

_____

_____

_____

_____

Active Reading

Lesson Vocabulary

List the terms. As you learn about each one, make notes in the Interactive Glossary.

_____ _____

_____ _____

_____ _____

Sequence

Many ideas in this lesson are connected by a sequence, or order, that describes the steps in a process. Active readers stay focused on sequence when they mark the transition from one step in a process to another step.

© Houghton Mifflin Harcourt Publishing Company (b) ©Michael Willis/Alamy

Tubes for Transport

Have you ever wondered why a giant tree and a tiny moss are so different in size? Vascular tissues that work like the veins in your body allow trees to reach towards the sky!

Active Reading As you read these two pages, circle words that describe a nonvascular plant, and underline words that describe a vascular plant.

Not all plants have vascular tissue. **Nonvascular plants**, such as mosses and liverworts, are the simplest plants. They are usually very small plants that grow in damp places. Since they lack vascular tissue, they cannot easily transport water from the ground up into the plant. This means that nonvascular plants almost never grow taller than 10 cm! So how do nonvascular plants move materials? Nonvascular plant parts absorb nutrients and water in the same way that a dry sponge absorbs water.

Nonvascular

These tiny liverwort plants are a kind of nonvascular plant. They grow in damp areas where it is easy to absorb nutrients and water.

A liverwort may look like other, larger plants, but it doesn't have true roots or leaves. Like other nonvascular plants, the liverwort doesn't transport materials using vascular tissue.

© Houghton Mifflin Harcourt Publishing Company   (r) ©Jon Silver/Alamy; (inset) ©Dr. Jeremy Burgess/Photo Researchers, Inc.

When you look at a very tall tree, you are looking at a vascular plant. If the tree takes in water from the soil with its roots, how does the water get to the leaves at the top? **Vascular plants** have vascular tissues that allow them to move water, nutrients, and sugars across long distances. Tiny tubes in vascular tissues move water and nutrients up a plant the same way that you pull up water when you drink through a straw. Most of the plants around us, including trees, grasses, and shrubs, are vascular plants.

Do the Math!
Find the Average

A grouping of moss plants has the following height measurements: 9 cm, 5 cm, 8 cm, 11 cm, and 7 cm. A grouping of pepper plants has the following height measurements: 55 cm, 65 cm, 48 cm, 52 cm, and 60 cm. Calculate the averages, and compare the heights of the vascular and nonvascular plants.

_____

_____

_____

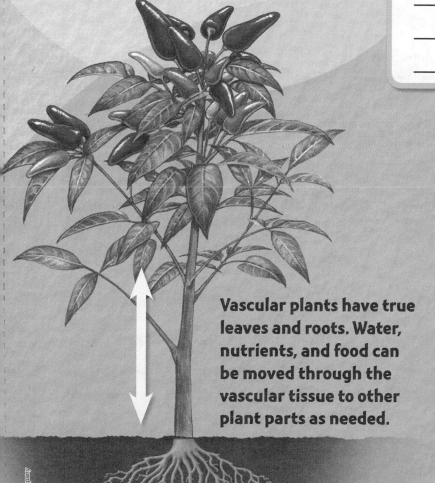

Vascular plants have true leaves and roots. Water, nutrients, and food can be moved through the vascular tissue to other plant parts as needed.

Vascular

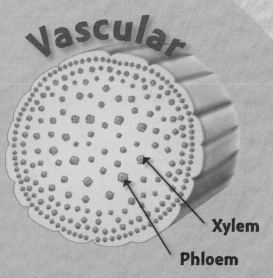

Xylem

Phloem

If you cut away a section of vascular tissue, you would see two kinds of smaller tubes. *Xylem* carries water and nutrients from the roots to all the other parts of the plant. *Phloem* carries sugar from the leaves to the rest of the plant.

© Houghton Mifflin Harcourt Publishing Company

No Seeds, Please!

Have you ever seen a fern? If so, you know they aren't tiny plants. Did you know that they started out no bigger than a tiny cell?

Active Reading As you read these two pages, write numbers next to steps to show the sequence of each life cycle.

A **spore** is a single reproductive cell that can grow into a whole new plant. Mosses, liverworts, and ferns are examples of plants that grow from spores. Mosses and liverworts are nonvascular plants, while a fern is a vascular plant. All three of these plants have two forms in their life cycles.

The thin stalk that develops from a fertilized egg is the less familiar form of the moss plant.

A capsule grows at the end of each stalk. Spores form inside the capsule. When the capsule opens, the spores shoot out.

The "leafy" form of the moss plant has male parts that produce sperm and female parts that produce eggs. During moist periods, the sperm swim to the eggs and fertilize them.

The green "leafy" form of moss is the most familiar form of the plant. Mosses don't have true leaves or roots. Instead, they have leaflike structures that make food and rootlike structures that anchor them to the ground.

Spores land on the ground and develop into threadlike plants. These form buds that become green "leafy" structures.

© Houghton Mifflin Harcourt Publishing Company

Like mosses, ferns also use spores to reproduce. If you look at a fern leaf, you will see many small, black or brown clusters that line the underside of the leaflets.

These clusters hold smaller pockets of spores. When the pockets burst, the spores are released.

The young fern grows into the large, upright fern plant, called the frond. This is the other form of the fern.

The heart-shaped structure of the plant releases sperm and egg cells. The sperm cells swim to the egg cells and fertilize them. The fertilized egg grows into a young fern.

Spores typically fall to the ground, where each spore may grow into the tiny, green, heart-shaped form of the fern plant. If you look closely, you can see this form of the plant, although it's very small.

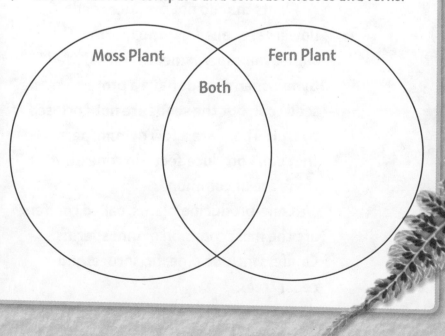

▶ Use the table to compare and contrast mosses and ferns.

Moss Plant

Fern Plant

Both

Reproductive spores form inside these clusters on the underside of the fern leaflets.

© Houghton Mifflin Harcourt Publishing Company   (br) ©Purestock/Carlos Adolfo Sastoque N/SuperStock

Seed Power!

You have probably seen many types of seeds, and even eaten some! How are seeds different from spores?

Active Reading As you read these two pages, circle the phrases that describe gymnosperms. Draw boxes around phrases that describe angiosperms.

These pinecones are part of a gymnosperm. This gymnosperm produces seeds on cones. The smaller male cones produce *pollen*. The larger female cones contain eggs within structures called *ovules*.

The fertilized ovule on each scale of a female pinecone becomes a seed.

Some plants grow from seeds instead of spores. Seeds have an advantage over spores for multiple reasons. Spores need to stay moist and sprout soon after being released, but seeds do not. A seed has a covering that protects it, enabling the seed to rest in an environment for years until conditions are right for sprouting. Scientists have grown plants from seeds that are hundreds, and even thousands, of years old!

Plants that do not produce seeds in flowers are called **gymnosperms**. The word *gymnosperm* means "naked seed." Gymnosperm seeds have a protective seed coat, but the seeds are not enclosed by fruit. There are a few gymnosperms that don't produce seeds in cones, but these are uncommon.

Cone-producing plants, called conifers, are the most common gymnosperms. Conifers include pine, fir, spruce, and cedar trees.

© Houghton Mifflin Harcourt Publishing Company (l) ©Walter H. Hodge/Peter Arnold, Inc./Alamy; (b) ©Peter Anderson/Dorling Kindersley/Getty Images

▶ The shapes below are an orange, a watermelon, and a green bean. Draw seeds for each one and explain why you drew them where you did.

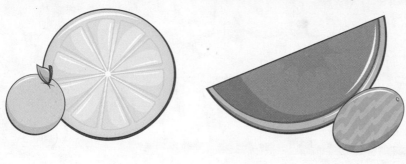

_____

_____

Gymnosperms aren't the only plants that produce seeds. **Angiosperms** are plants that produce seeds in flowers. More than 85% of the total species of plants on Earth are angiosperms. Think of the plants that grow near your school. Do you think that most of these are gymnosperms or angiosperms?

Some angiosperm seeds have an advantage over gymnosperm seeds. Since angiosperm seeds are often enclosed in a fruit, they are easily spread when animals eat the fruits. Gymnosperm seeds may also be spread by animals, but typically fall to the ground and grow where they land.

This pomegranate tree produces flowers. The flowers produce sperm and eggs that unite to become seeds within the fruit.

© Houghton Mifflin Harcourt Publishing Company   (bl) ©Artville/Getty Images; (br) ©Hanan Isachar/Alamy

From Flower to Fruit and Seed

Many angiosperms use flowers to reproduce. Do you know how flowers form fruit?

Active Reading As you read these two pages, circle the names of the parts of a flower.

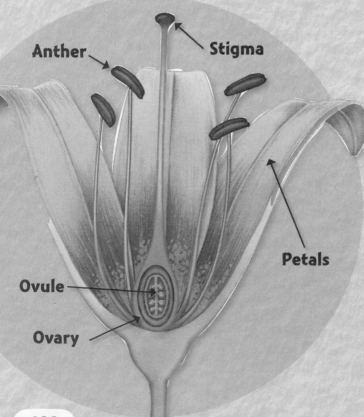

Anther

Stigma

Petals

Ovule

Ovary

Although you might think of flowers as big and colorful, many flowers are tiny and hard to spot. For example, did you know that grasses grow flowers? Oak trees and maple trees do, too!

Typical flowers have both male and female reproductive parts. A male part, the *anther*, produces pollen grains, which contain sperm. The female parts include the *stigma* and the *ovary*, which contains eggs in ovules.

Flowers that are colorful or fragrant produce sticky nectar that some animals eat. As an animal gathers nectar, pollen may stick to its body. As the animal moves from flower to flower, it transfers pollen to the stigmas of these flowers. This is called pollination.

After pollen lands on a stigma, sperm from the pollen move down to the ovules within the ovary. Fertilization occurs when a sperm cell unites with the egg inside each ovule. The ovules develop into seeds, and each ovule wall becomes a seed coat. The ovary surrounding the ovules becomes a fruit.

© Houghton Mifflin Harcourt Publishing Company (t) ©Juniors Bildarchiv/Alamy

▶ Write the sequence of events that occurs during pollination.

_____

_____

_____

_____

_____

Pumpkin Seed Development

Pollen enters the ovary of the flower and fertilizes eggs inside the ovules.

The ovary grows and the petals fall off. The ovules develop into seeds inside the ovary.

The outer layer of the ovary thickens to form a fruit around the seeds.

The mature pumpkin fruit is filled with seeds.

© Houghton Mifflin Harcourt Publishing Company (t) ©Thomas J. Peterson/Alamy; (c) ©John Kaprielian/Photo Researchers, Inc.; (br) ©John Kaprielian/Photo Researchers, Inc.

How Seeds Grow

Once a seed is released, it can sit and rest for a long time. But when conditions are right, look out! The seed sprouts and grows into a new plant.

Active Reading As you read these two pages, write numbers next to captions to show the order of events.

What happens to seeds when they are released in cold or dry weather? Seeds have a hard outer coat that protects them. The coat allows a seed to rest until the environment is right for growing. Many plant seeds rest during winter and then **germinate**, or start to grow, when the conditions are right in the spring and the ground becomes warm and moist.

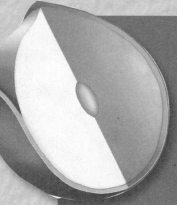

This avocado seed contains an embryo that will grow into a new plant. In avocados, the embryo is mostly made up of two *cotyledon*s. These embryonic leaves provide energy for the emerging plant. The embryo and cotyledons are surrounded by a protective seed coat.

plants not shown to scale

A dormant seed lies in the soil when the environment is not suitable for a plant to grow.

When conditions are right, the seed germinates. The embryo absorbs water and breaks through the seed coat. A stem grows upward and a root grows downward.

Cotyledons provide extra energy for growth. Roots grow denser.

© Houghton Mifflin Harcourt Publishing Company · HMH Credits

► List the sequence of events that occur as the avocado seed germinates.

Leaves mature and the plant starts absorbing more energy from sunlight.

The plant continues to grow as the shoot pushes upward.

The plant grows and matures until it produces flowers and fruit.

© Houghton Mifflin Harcourt Publishing Company   (t) ©Artville/Getty Images

Sum It Up!

When you're done, use the answer key to check and revise your work.

Write the term that matches each photo and caption.

1  _____

The type of plant that must grow in damp places

2  _____

The type of tissue that can transport materials throughout the plant

3  _____

The structure that contains spores in mosses

4  _____

The structure that produces seeds in angiosperms

5  _____

The structure that produces seeds in gymnosperms

6  _____

A reproductive structure that stays protected before germinating

Answer Key: 1. nonvascular 2. vascular 3. capsule 4. flower 5. cone 6. seed

© Houghton Mifflin Harcourt Publishing Company

 **Brain Check**

Name _____

Word Play

1. Use the words in the box to complete the puzzle.

Across

7. This becomes the seed on a cone scale or a flower

8. A plant that doesn't have true leaves or roots and doesn't grow tall

10. The male part of a flower

Down

1. A plant with tissue that can transport materials throughout the plant

2. What a plant does when it sprouts from a seed

3. A type of plant that produces flowers to make seeds

4. A reproductive structure that stays protected before germinating

5. Leaves that provide food for a germinating plant

6. A type of plant that produces seeds within a cone

9. A reproductive structure a fern grows from

| gymnosperm* | angiosperm* | germinates* | nonvascular* | vascular* |
| spore* | seed | anther | cotyledons | ovule |

* Key Lesson Vocabulary

© Houghton Mifflin Harcourt Publishing Company

Apply Concepts

2 Draw and label the sequence that shows how a flower produces a seed inside a fruit.

3 Circle the plant that will produce a seed inside a fruit.

4 Draw a picture of the underside of a fern leaflet, including the clusters. What do these clusters contain?

_____

5 Explain how you would tell the difference between a male cone and a female cone on a pine tree.

_____

_____

_____

_____

_____

Take It Home! Research a plant that you would like to grow. With an adult, plant a seed that will grow into your plant. Observe how it changes weekly.

© Houghton Mifflin Harcourt Publishing Company

How It Works:

Tracking Wildlife

Tracking animals helps scientists learn the animals' patterns of movement. Researchers fit animals with a variety of devices that send back information. Mammals often wear tracking collars. Toads can wear tracking belts. Fish can swallow tiny devices that work inside their bodies!

This lion is fitted with a GPS collar. Sometimes collars like these also have cameras that send back video.

Tracking devices are attached to marine animals with glue or suction cups. The collars send signals to GPS satellites, enabling scientists to locate and track the collars over time.

Troubleshooting

Describe how an animal's body, its movement, and its environment determine the design of a tracking device.

_____

_____

© Houghton Mifflin Harcourt Publishing Company (c) ©Lynda Richardson/Corbis; (t) ©Jeffrey W. Lang/Photo Researchers, Inc.; (l) ©Paul Sutherland/National Geographic/Getty Images; (l) ©O. Alamany & E. Vicens/Corbis

Animal tracking devices help scientists understand the behaviors of animals within their natural habitats.

Choose an animal. Draw a diagram of how a tracking device might be attached to the animal. Explain how the device is attached and what information it captures.

Research an animal species that has been studied using a tracking device. Which kind of device was used? What kind of data did it gather, and what did scientists learn about the species?

Build On It!

Rise to the engineering design challenge—complete **Make a Process: Mimicking an Adaptation** in the Inquiry Flipchart.

© Houghton Mifflin Harcourt Publishing Company   (b) ©Ann & Steve Toon/Photo Researchers, Inc.

Name _____

Essential Question

What Factors Affect Germination Rate?

Set a Purpose
Why is it important to know the factors that affect germination?

_____
_____
_____
_____

Think About the Procedure
Which two factors are you testing in this activity?

_____
_____
_____
_____
_____

Record Your Data
In the space below, make a table to record your observations.

© Houghton Mifflin Harcourt Publishing Company

Draw Conclusions

Which plants grew the most? Which plants grew the least?

_____

_____

_____

_____

How does light affect seed germination?

_____

_____

_____

_____

How does water affect seed germination?

_____

_____

_____

_____

Analyze and Extend

1. What other factor do you think might affect germination?

_____

_____

_____

2. How could you test this factor?

_____

_____

_____

_____

3. What other questions would you like to ask about germination rates?

_____

_____

_____

_____

4. Choose one question you wrote and investigate it. Write a summary of your investigation.

_____

_____

_____

_____

© Houghton Mifflin Harcourt Publishing Company

Essential Question

How Do Animals Grow and Reproduce?

Engage Your Brain!

Find the answers to the following questions in this lesson and record them here.

How are these organisms similar? How are they different?

_____

_____

_____

_____

_____

Active Reading

Lesson Vocabulary

List the terms. As you learn about each one, make notes in the Interactive Glossary.

_____ _____

_____

_____

_____

Main Ideas and Details

Detail sentences give information about a topic. The information may be examples, features, characteristics, or facts. Active readers stay focused on the topic when they ask, What fact or information does this sentence add to the topic?

© Houghton Mifflin Harcourt Publishing Company (bg) ©Heinrich van den Berg/Gallo Images/Getty Images

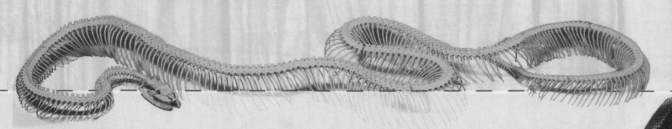

HAVE A BACKBONE?

How are birds and fish similar? They have backbones! What other animals have backbones?

Active Reading As you read this page, underline the main idea.

Animals differ so much that you may wonder what factors scientists could ever use to classify them. One of the major factors that scientists use when classifying animals is whether an animal has a backbone. **Vertebrates** are animals with backbones. Look at the different vertebrates on these pages. Find other factors that scientists may use to classify these animals.

Most backbones are made up of bones that are linked together, as you can see in the snake backbone above.

Fish are vertebrates that live in water. They use gills to take in oxygen present in water.

Frogs are amphibians. Amphibians are vertebrates with smooth skin. Most amphibians live part of their lives on land and part in water.

© Houghton Mifflin Harcourt Publishing Company (bg) ©Sanatan Kochar/Photodisc/Getty Images; (bg) ©Arville/Getty Images; (bl) ©Justus de Cuveland/imagebroker/Alamy; (t) ©Chris Parks/Image Quest Marine/Alamy; (t) ©Dan Herrick/iStockExclusive/Getty Images

A snake is a reptile. Reptiles are vertebrates with scaly skin. Most reptiles live on land and some live in water.

Because the bones are separate and linked, as opposed to one solid bone, backbones are flexible. Flexibility allows vertebrates to move easily.

Vertebrates can be grouped into five classes: mammals, birds, reptiles, amphibians, and fish. Even though most of the animals you can name are probably vertebrates, these animals make up only about 4.5% of all animal species!

Mammals are vertebrates that have hair or fur on their bodies. Young mammals drink milk from their mothers' bodies.

Draw a Vertebrate

This dog is a vertebrate. Draw in the body part that causes it to be classified in this way. What did you draw?

Birds are vertebrates with feathers and wings. Most birds can fly.

© Houghton Mifflin Harcourt Publishing Company (bl) ©Dan Herrick/iStock Exclusive/Getty Images; (l) ©Chris Parks/Image Quest Marine/Alamy Images; (b) ©Santosh Kochar/Alamy Images; (bg) ©Artville/Photodisc/Getty Images; (tr) ©Mike Lane/Alamy; (b) ©Juniors Bildarchiv/Alamy

Spider

"SPINELESS" INVERTEBRATES

About 95.5% of all animals lack backbones!
What kind of animals could these be?

Active Reading As you read these two pages, circle the clue words that signal a detail such as an example or an added fact.

Animals without backbones are **invertebrates**. Invertebrates vary from very simple sponges to complex insects. Invertebrates fill the coral reefs in the oceans and break down dead matter in soil. Some invertebrates even serve as food for humans!

The simplest invertebrates are corals, sponges, and jellyfish. You are probably familiar with earthworms. Earthworms are invertebrates that break down materials in soil.

Mollusks, such as the whelk, are more complex. Many mollusks have a shell that protects their soft bodies. Squid are mollusks that have internal shells. Octopi are mollusks that do not have shells at all.

Marine sponge

Whelk

© Houghton Mifflin Harcourt Publishing Company (bg) ©Santokh Kochar/Photodisc/Getty Images; (br) ©Frank Greenaway/Getty Images; (bl) ©Corbis; (t) ©littlebloke/Alamy; (inset) ©Paul Springett 04/Alamy

Do the Math!

Analyze Data

Number of Species of Some Invertebrates (estimated)	
Mollusks	85,000 species
Arachnids	102,000 species
Crustaceans	47,000 species
Insects	1,000,000 species

Use the table to answer the questions.

If you were to find an invertebrate, what type of invertebrate would it most likely be? Why?

_____

_____

_____

How many more species of this type are there than all of the other listed invertebrates combined?

_____

The reef lobster is a crustacean.

Echinoderms, such as sea urchins and sea stars, are invertebrates that live in salt water. When fully grown, they have body parts in multiples of five.

The largest group of invertebrates is the *arthropod* group. Arthropods have body parts in segments. The arthropod group includes crustaceans, spiders, and insects. *Crustaceans* have hard exterior shells and five pairs of jointed limbs. Spiders have two body segments and eight legs. Insects have antennae, jaws, and three body segments. There are more insect species on Earth than all other animal species combined.

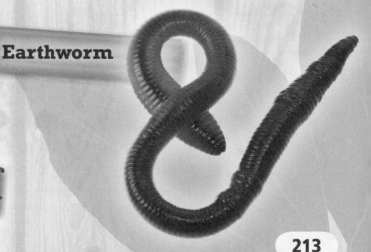

Earthworm

Sea urchin

© Houghton Mifflin Harcourt Publishing Company (bg) ©Santokh Kochar/Photodisc/Getty Images; (bg) ©Artville/Getty Images; (bg) ©Gary Bell/Corbis; (bl) ©Trevor Bonderud/All Canada Photos/Alamy; (br) ©Maximilian Weinzierl/Alamy; (c) ©Artville/Getty Images

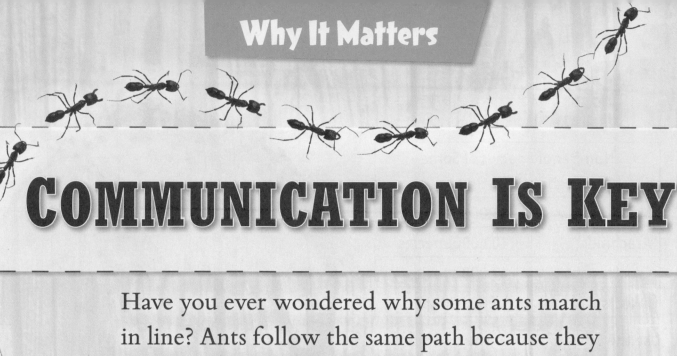

COMMUNICATION IS KEY

Have you ever wondered why some ants march in line? Ants follow the same path because they release chemical signals for other ants to follow.

How do you tell others that you are hungry? Maybe you use words. You may also communicate by making facial expressions or using gestures. Communication is as important to animals as it is to humans.

Many animals other than ants communicate using chemicals that animals can smell. Scents are useful in communicating danger or finding mates. Cats, dogs, and other animals use scents to mark boundaries.

Some animals communicate using visual cues. Cuttlefish change colors to send messages. Some animals use movement to send information. Japanese cranes dance to find a mate. Honeybees also perform a dance. The complicated wiggling honeybee dance tells the rest of the hive where food has been found.

These Japanese cranes communicate using movement. The dances are performed to attract a mate.

© Houghton Mifflin Harcourt Publishing Company (bg) ©Santokh Kochar/Photodisc/Getty Images; (tl) ©Anville/Getty Images; (b) ©Robert Pickett/Papilio/Alamy

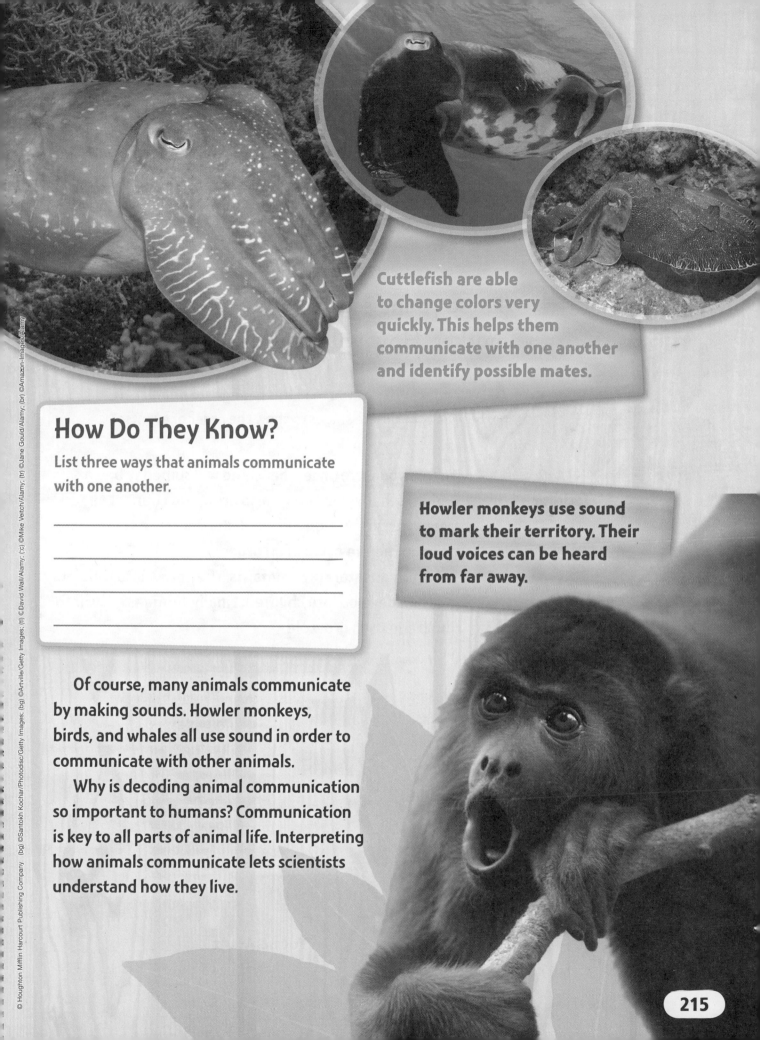

Cuttlefish are able to change colors very quickly. This helps them communicate with one another and identify possible mates.

How Do They Know?

List three ways that animals communicate with one another.

_____

_____

_____

_____

Howler monkeys use sound to mark their territory. Their loud voices can be heard from far away.

Of course, many animals communicate by making sounds. Howler monkeys, birds, and whales all use sound in order to communicate with other animals.

Why is decoding animal communication so important to humans? Communication is key to all parts of animal life. Interpreting how animals communicate lets scientists understand how they live.

© Houghton Mifflin Harcourt Publishing Company   (bg) ©Santokh Kochar/Photodisc/Getty Images; (bg) ©Artville/Getty Images; (tl) ©David Wall/Alamy; (c) ©Mike Veitch/Alamy; (tr) ©Jane Gould/Alamy; (br) ©Amazon-Images/Alamy

STAGES OF LIFE

Infant

Toddler

Child

Young Adult

These young scorpions are different from their mother. How will they change over time?

Active Reading As you read this page, write numbers next to the appropriate stages to show the order of events.

Just as you were once a baby and will someday be an adult, other living things also grow and change. All organisms go through different stages. These stages all make up the **life cycle** of an organism.

All humans start off as infants. They grow into toddlers and then develop into children. Finally, humans grow into adults and then grow old.

© Houghton Mifflin Harcourt Publishing Company (bg) ©Santokh Kochar/Photodisc/Getty Images; (bg) ©Artville/Getty Images; (tl) ©PhotoDisc/Getty Images; (cl) ©Rubberball Productions/Getty Images; (cl) ©PhotoDisc/Getty Images; (br) ©gulfimages/Getty Images; (tr) ©Scott Camazine/Alamy

Every life cycle begins with a fertilized egg. In some animals, like birds or reptiles, the egg may be enclosed in a hard or leathery protective shell, from which the young hatch. The eggs of most mammals develop inside the mothers' bodies. After a young organism develops from the egg, it will continue to grow.

The development of an organism can happen very quickly, or it may take many years. The organism grows larger and changes as it develops. When it is an adult, it is able to live on its own. Now the organism can reproduce, or make its own offspring. The organism will continue to age. Eventually, it dies.

From an egg to a hatchling, a duck changes as it grows.

Mature Adult

▶ Draw a line from the young stage of each animal to its adult stage.

kitten   goose
puppy   cat
colt   human adult
gosling   horse
human child   dog
chick   chicken

© Houghton Mifflin Harcourt Publishing Company (bg) ©Santokh Kochar/Photodisc/Getty Images; (bg) ©Arville/Getty Images; (b) ©Comstock/Getty Images; (t) ©Juniors Bildarchiv/Alamy; (tcr) ©Lee Bee/Alamy; (bcr) ©Juniors Bildarchiv/Alamy

IT'S TIME FOR A CHANGE

Some animals don't just get larger as they grow. An animal may change so much that at different stages it doesn't even look like the same organism!

Active Reading As you read these two pages, draw boxes around the clue words that signal things are being compared.

Some organisms completely change form as they grow. This process is called metamorphosis. Insects are the most common animals that undergo metamorphosis.

In **complete metamorphosis**, an insect, such as this ladybug, goes through four different stages in its life cycle.

1. The insect begins life as an egg.
2. The egg hatches to produce a *larva*. The larva eats and quickly grows in size.
3. A larva develops into a *pupa*. Because the pupa does not move, this is often called the "resting stage." Although it is not moving in the pupa stage, the insect's body is undergoing dramatic change.
4. The adult emerges from the pupa. The adult insect can fly and reproduce.

Complete Metamorphosis

egg

larva

pupa

adult

© Houghton Mifflin Harcourt Publishing Company   (bg) ©Santokh Kochar/Photodisc/Getty Images; (bg) ©Artville/Getty Images; (tr) ©Ed Reschke/Peter Arnold, Inc./Alamy; (tl) ©Michael Willis/Alamy; (tr) ©Ed Reschke/Peter Arnold, Inc./Alamy; (tl) ©Michael Willis/Alamy; (tr) ©Ed Reschke/Peter Arnold, Inc./Alamy; (bcl) ©Justus de Cuveland/Imagebroker/Alamy; (c) ©W. Holzenbecher/Arco Images GmbH/Alamy; (bch) ©Juniors Bildarchiv/Alamy; (b) ©Nature's Images/Photo Researchers, Inc.

Another type of metamorphosis that occurs in some insects is incomplete metamorphosis. **Incomplete metamorphosis** has three stages: the egg, the *nymph*, and the adult. The nymph stage looks like a smaller version of the adult, but a nymph cannot fly or reproduce. As the nymph grows, it *molts*, or sheds its hard outer shell. The nymph molts several times until it finally becomes an adult.

Metamorphosis is not limited to insects. Frogs also undergo metamorphosis as they go from egg to tadpole to adult. Can you think of any other animals that undergo metamorphosis?

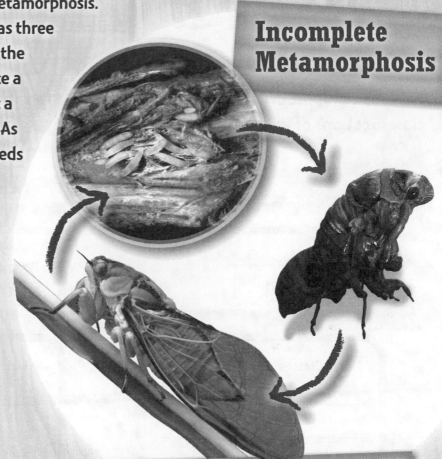

Incomplete Metamorphosis

The cicada goes through incomplete metamorphosis. A small nymph emerges from the egg. The nymph grows and molts until it becomes a mature adult.

Insect Life Cycles

You see an insect egg lying on a leaf. Which stage is next? Name or describe the stage you would expect to see come out from the egg if the insect undergoes:

a. incomplete metamorphosis:

_____

b. complete metamorphosis:

_____

© Houghton Mifflin Harcourt Publishing Company (bg) ©Santokh Kochar/Photodisc/Getty Images; (bg) ©Artville/Getty Images; (tc) ©James H. Robinson/Photo Researchers, Inc.; (cr) ©James L. Amos/Peter Arnold Inc./Alamy; (c) ©David Wall/Alamy; (b) ©Gregory Bergman/Alamy

When you're done, use the answer key to check and revise your work.

Fill in the graphic organizer below with information about the classifications of animals.

Animals

1. _____ have backbones.

2. _____ do not have backbones.

3. Five Classes

_____

_____

_____

_____

_____

4. Five Kinds

_____

_____

_____

_____

_____

Summarize

Fill in the boxes with the missing stages for both types of metamorphosis.

Incomplete metamorphosis

Egg → 5. _____ → Adult

Complete metamorphosis

Egg → 6. _____ → 7. _____ → Adult

220

Answer Key: 1. Vertebrates 2. Invertebrates 3. Answers may vary: reptiles, fish, mammals, birds, amphibians 4. arthropods, mollusks, echinoderms, sponges, worms 5. nymph 6. larva 7. pupa

© Houghton Mifflin Harcourt Publishing Company

Name _____

Word Play

1 Draw lines to match the definition to the word or phrase and then to the photo.

An animal with a backbone

mollusk

Shedding of a hard
outer skeleton during
incomplete metamorphosis

pupa

The stage an adult emerges
from during complete
metamorphosis

life cycle

An invertebrate that
uses a shell

molt

An invertebrate with
hard spines

vertebrate

The different stages
of development of
an organism

sea urchin

© Houghton Mifflin Harcourt Publishing Company (tc) ©Chris Parks/Image Quest Marine/Alamy; (bc) ©Frank Greenaway/Getty Images; (tcr) ©Trevor Bonderud/All Canada Photos/Alamy; (t) ©Scott Camazine/Alamy; (b) ©Nature's Images/Photo Researchers, Inc.; (bcr) ©James L. Amos/Peter Arnold, Inc./Alamy

Apply Concepts

2 Write a number below each picture to show the correct order of the ladybug life cycle.

_____ _____ _____ _____

3 Draw circles around the vertebrates. Draw boxes around the invertebrates.

4 Draw lines to match each vertebrate to the characteristics that describe it.

Vertebrate	Description
amphibian	scaly skin
bird	lives part of life in water and part on land
fish	body covered with feathers
mammal	lives and takes in oxygen under water
reptile	young drinks milk from mother

Take It Home!

Get a deck of cards and pair up with a family member. Create a code to communicate to your partner—without speaking—which card is chosen. Test your code by choosing cards and communicating.

© Houghton Mifflin Harcourt Publishing Company (cr) ©Maximilian Weinzierl/Alamy; (cr) ©Justus de Cuveland/imagebroker/Alamy; (tl) ©Nature's Images/Photo Researchers, Inc.; (c) ©Juniors Bildarchiv/Alamy; (tl) ©W. Holzenbecher/Arco Images/imagebroker/Alamy; (tcl) ©Justus de Cuveland/imagebroker/Alamy; (cl) ©Corbis; (bl) ©Dani Herrick/Stock Exclusive/Getty Images; (bc) ©Dan Herrick/iStock Exclusive/Getty Images; (bc) ©Juniors Bildarchiv/Alamy

Meet the Animal Activists

Lisa Stevens

Lisa Stevens is a zoologist. She has worked with animals for most of her life. Stevens manages the giant-panda exhibit at the National Zoo in Washington, D.C. As part of her job, she teaches people about this endangered species. When the panda cub Tai Shan was born at the National Zoo, Stevens took care of him. There are only 1,600 giant pandas living in the wild today. About 250 live in zoos around the world.

Raman Sukumar

Raman Sukumar grew up in India, where he loved studying nature. His grandmother called him *vanavasi*, an Indian name for "forest dweller." He has studied Asian elephants in the wild for more than 30 years. Sukumar wants to find a solution to the problem caused by people and elephants using the same land. He has taught many people why it is important to preserve the habitats of this endangered species.

© Houghton Mifflin Harcourt Publishing Company (tl) ©Jessie Cohen/Smithsonian's National Zoo/Handout/Reuters/Corbis; (br) ©Raman Sukumar; (cr) ©WILDLIFE GmbH/Alamy; (tr) ©Artville/Getty Images; (inset) ©Ian Dagnall/Alamy; (b) ©Mark Shenley/Alamy; © WILDLIFE GmbH/Alamy Images

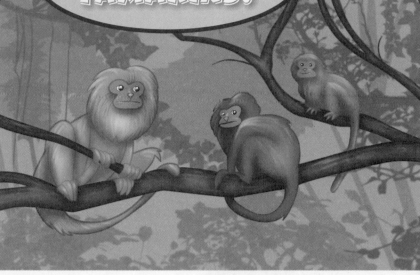

SAVE THE TAMARINS!

Golden lion tamarins are an endangered species. Read the story about the golden lion tamarin. Draw the missing pictures to complete the story.

Golden lion tamarins live in the rainforests of Brazil.

Logging and building have broken up the tamarins' habitat into small areas cut off from each other.

There are few golden lion tamarins left. There is little food and no place to roam.

Solution: People can set aside land as the tamarins' habitat.

Over time, the number of tamarins increases. They will have the food they need to live.

© Houghton Mifflin Harcourt Publishing Company   (t) ©Martin Bennett/Alamy; (b) ©Digital Vision/Getty Images

Essential Question

What Are Physical and Behavioral Adaptations?

Engage Your Brain!

Find the answer to the following question in this lesson and record it here.

Watch out! Don't get bitten by that... caterpillar? What type of adaptation does this caterpillar have?

_____

_____

_____

Active Reading

Lesson Vocabulary
List the terms. As you learn about each one, make notes in the Interactive Glossary.

_____

_____

Signal Words: Details
This lesson gives details about how living things are suited to where they live. Signal words link main topics to added details. *For example* and *for instance* are often used as signal words. Active readers look for signal words that link a topic to its details.

© Houghton Mifflin Harcourt Publishing Company (b) ©Stephen J. Krasemann/Photo Researchers, Inc.

Adaptations

Living things have many similarities. They also have many interesting differences.

Active Reading As you read this page, underline the definition of *adaptation*.

Deserts are home to many kinds of snakes. This is because snakes have characteristics that help them survive in a desert. For example, snakes have tough, scaly skin that keeps them from drying out.

A characteristic that helps a living thing survive is called an **adaptation**. Suppose an animal is born with a new characteristic. If this characteristic helps the animal survive, the animal is likely to reproduce and pass on the characteristic to its young. As long as the animal's habitat doesn't change, the young that have this characteristic are also likely to survive and reproduce. Over time, the adaptation becomes more common in the population. In this way, populations of plants and animals become adapted to their habitats.

These rabbits live in very different habitats. Because of this, they have different adaptations.

An arctic hare lives in a cold habitat. It has thick fur to keep it warm and small ears that prevent heat from being lost.

A jackrabbit lives in a hot habitat. Jackrabbits have large ears that help keep their blood cool.

© Houghton Mifflin Harcourt Publishing Company (tc) ©Cristina/Alamy; (tr) ©Visual&Written SL/Alamy; (b) ©Terry W. Eggers/Corbis

Ostriches, rheas, and emus all live on different continents. Even though they live very far from each other, they look almost the same! Their habitats are very similar, and so they share similar adaptations. These birds are all adapted for running fast. Ostriches are the fastest flightless birds on Earth. They can reach speeds of 72 km/hr (45 mi/hr)!

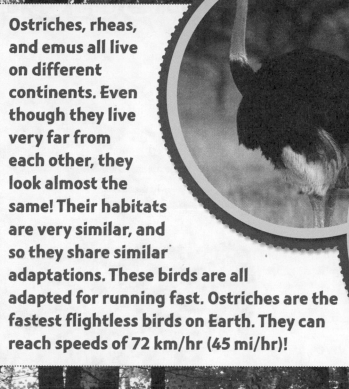

ostrich

emu

rhea

▶ Vines and trees are both plants, but they are very different from each other. What adaptations can you see in these plants, and how do you think these adaptations help them survive?

_____

_____

_____

_____

_____

_____

© Houghton Mifflin Harcourt Publishing Company (bg) ©Elipsa/Alamy; (cr) ©Arco Images GmbH/Alamy; (tl) ©Stephen J. Krasemann/Photo Researchers, Inc; (tr) ©De Agostini/Getty Images

Form and Function

Why can penguins live in the Antarctic while most other birds can't? They have a layer of blubber to keep them warm!

Active Reading As you read these two pages, underline the words and phrases that describe animal and plant adaptations.

Some adaptations are differences in the bodies of organisms. These are called physical adaptations. Organisms have physical adaptations that help them survive in different environments. When a plant or animal has a characteristic that enables it to survive in a way that other plants or animals cannot, the organism with the adaptation has an advantage. Consider how some of the organisms shown on these two pages are better able to survive in their environments than organisms that do not have these adaptations.

The eyes of this bird are covered with a thin, transparent eyelid that keeps the eye moist when the bird flies.

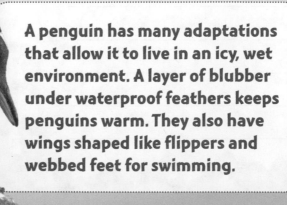

A penguin has many adaptations that allow it to live in an icy, wet environment. A layer of blubber under waterproof feathers keeps penguins warm. They also have wings shaped like flippers and webbed feet for swimming.

© Houghton Mifflin Harcourt Publishing Company (b) ©Gistimages/Alamy; (r) ©Frontline Photography/Alamy; (l) ©BA LaRue/Alamy; (r) ©Frontline Photography/Alamy (bg) ©Eastcott Momatiuk/Photodisc/Getty Images; (c) ©Eastcott Momatiuk/Photodisc/Getty Images; (b) ©Frontline Photography/Alamy

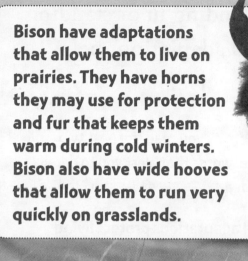

Bison have adaptations that allow them to live on prairies. They have horns they may use for protection and fur that keeps them warm during cold winters. Bison also have wide hooves that allow them to run very quickly on grasslands.

The sharp spines of a cactus are actually modified leaves. The spines have a small surface area that minimizes water loss. This cactus shown has a thick stem that holds water, which is another important adaptation in a dry desert environment.

▶ Choose an animal or imagine a new animal. Write a description of the environment in which the animal lives. Then describe the adaptations that allow the animal to live in that specific environment.

_____

_____

_____

_____

_____

_____

_____

© Houghton Mifflin Harcourt Publishing Company   (t) ©Eastcott Momatiuk/Photodisc/Getty Images; (b) ©Frontline Photography/Alamy

Eat or Be Eaten

Whether blending in or standing out, physical adaptations help organisms survive.

Active Reading As you read the next two pages, circle signal words that alert you to details about the main idea.

Some physical adaptations protect living things from being eaten. For example, roses have sharp thorns that help keep their stems from being eaten. Other physical adaptations help to keep an animal hidden. This type of adaptation is called *camouflage* [KAM•uh•flazh]. When green lizards hide in green grass, they are camouflaged.

Animals that hunt, such as eagles, have adaptations that help them catch food. Eagles have very good eyesight. They also have sharp claws on their feet, which they use to capture their food.

Many plants have adaptations that help spread their seeds. Some seeds can be carried by the wind. Other seeds are inside berries. When the berries are eaten, the seeds are carried to a new location.

Can you see the owl in this picture? The owl is camouflaged to look like bark.

The bright color of this rose attracts pollinators, but the thorns keep plant-eating animals away.

© Houghton Mifflin Harcourt Publishing Company (bg) ©David Stuckel/Alamy; (t) ©Adam Jones/Photo Researchers, Inc.; (b) ©Clive Boursnell/Getty Images

Catching Flies

Bright coloring on an animal is often a warning that the animal is dangerous. Many animals know that paper wasps, like the one shown below, have a painful sting. The black and yellow hoverfly doesn't have a stinger. It is completely harmless. But because the hoverfly looks like a wasp, animals will think twice before trying to eat it. This adaptation is called *mimicry*.

▶ Draw a line from the chameleon's tongue to the insect it would most likely eat.

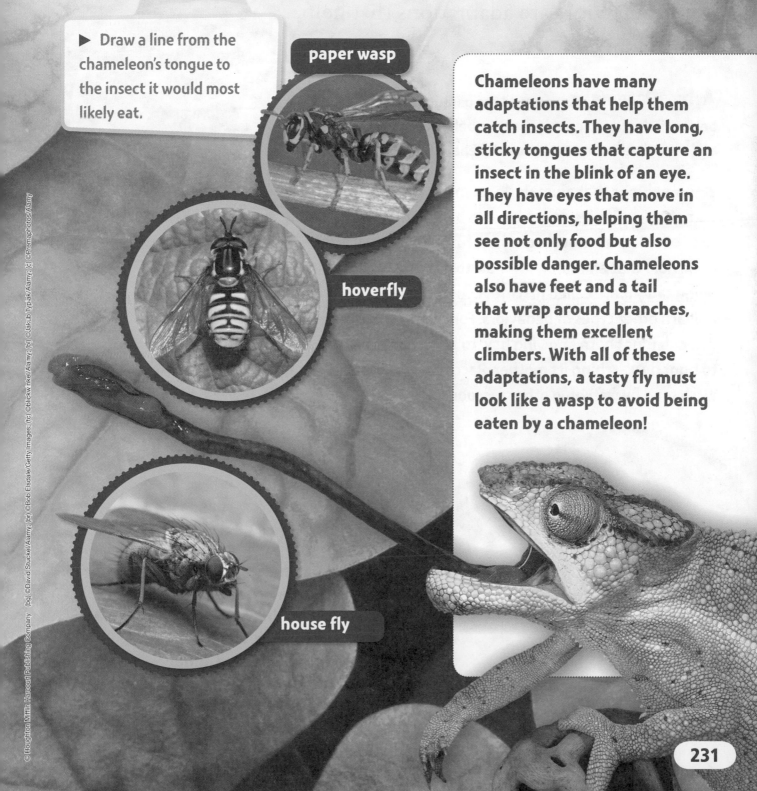

paper wasp

hoverfly

house fly

Chameleons have many adaptations that help them catch insects. They have long, sticky tongues that capture an insect in the blink of an eye. They have eyes that move in all directions, helping them see not only food but also possible danger. Chameleons also have feet and a tail that wrap around branches, making them excellent climbers. With all of these adaptations, a tasty fly must look like a wasp to avoid being eaten by a chameleon!

© Houghton Mifflin Harcourt Publishing Company   (bg) ©David Stuckel/Alamy; (br) ©Bob Eisdale/Getty Images; (tc) ©blickwinkel/Alamy; (b) ©Jakub Typiak/Alamy; (c) ©Premaphotos/Alamy

On Your Best Behavior

The way living things act is called behavior. Some behaviors are adaptations that help animals survive.

Active Reading As you read the paragraph below, circle examples of instinctive behavior and underline exampes of learned behavior.

Some things that animals do seem to come naturally. Babies do not have to be taught how to cry. Spiders are not taught how to spin webs. Behaviors that animals know how to do without being taught are called **instincts**. Animals have to learn other types of behaviors. For example, a lion cub is not born knowing how to hunt. It learns to hunt by watching its mother. Raccoons learn to wash food by watching other raccoons.

Some bats are *nocturnal*. This means they are active at night and sleep during the day. This allows bats to hunt insects that are active only at night.

Many animals have behaviors that help protect them from predators. When an octopus is frightened, it releases ink into the water. If the octopus is being attacked, the animal attacking it will not be able to see, and the octopus can escape.

232

© Houghton Mifflin Harcourt Publishing Company (bg) ©Kevin Shields/Alamy; (t) ©Richard Packwood/Getty Images; (b) ©Don Farrall/Getty Images

Each year, millions of snow geese migrate south in autumn and north in spring.

Some animals move to different locations at certain times of the year to find food, reproduce, or escape very cold weather. This instinctive behavior is called *migration*. Many birds, butterflies, and some bats migrate long distances.

Other animals hibernate. *Hibernation* is a long period of inactivity that is like sleeping. But hibernation is not the same as sleeping. When an animal hibernates, its body processes slow down and it stays inactive for months. Can you imagine taking a three-month nap?

The way that animals act toward other animals of the same type is called *social behavior*. Honeybees have very complex social behavior. They communicate using movements called the "waggle dance." A bee that finds food will return to the hive and do a waggle dance. The pattern of the dance gives other bees a lot of information! The dance communicates which way to go, how far away the food is, how much food there is, and even what kind of food it is!

Do the Math!

Interpret Data in a Bar Graph

Ground squirrels hibernate. They must eat a lot during the spring, summer, and fall to store up enough energy to survive hibernation. Study the graph below.

Ground Squirrel Body Mass

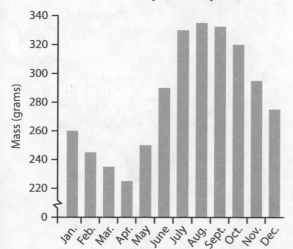

About how much mass does a ground squirrel have in March?

_____

During which month do ground squirrels start to hibernate? How do you know?

_____

_____

© Houghton Mifflin Harcourt Publishing Company (bkgd) ©Kevin Shields/Alamy; (t) ©Johann Schumacher/Alamy; (b) ©James Simon/Photo Researchers, Inc.

The Circle of Life

All living things grow and develop. The way that living things develop can be an adaptation.

Active Reading Circle two different examples of organisms whose life cycles keep adults and young from competing for food.

Living things go through stages of growth and development called a *life cycle*. A living thing's life cycle is related to its habitat. Because of this, differences in life cycles are a type of adaptation.

Most frogs are adapted to live near water. A frog's life cycle starts when its eggs are laid in water. When the eggs hatch, tadpoles emerge. Tadpoles live in water until they grow legs and lungs. At this point, they are frogs and ready to live on land. In places where water dries quickly, tadpoles develop more quickly. This variation in frog life cycles helps tadpoles survive.

Tadpoles and frogs live in different places, and eat different foods. This is another kind of adaptation. Frogs and tadpoles don't compete with each other for food, allowing for more frogs to survive. Many other organisms have similar adaptations. For example, caterpillars eat plant leaves and most butterflies sip nectar from flowers.

adult luna moth

luna moth caterpillar

salmon eggs

Adult salmon live in the ocean, which is a dangerous place for young salmon. Adults migrate from the ocean to shallow rivers to lay eggs. More young salmon are able to survive in rivers.

© Houghton Mifflin Harcourt Publishing Company   (bg) ©George H/H, Hsu/Corbis; (t) ©Snoobeard/Corbis; (c) ©James Urbach/SuperStock; (r) ©Corbis/SuperStock; (bd) ©Natural Visions/Alamy

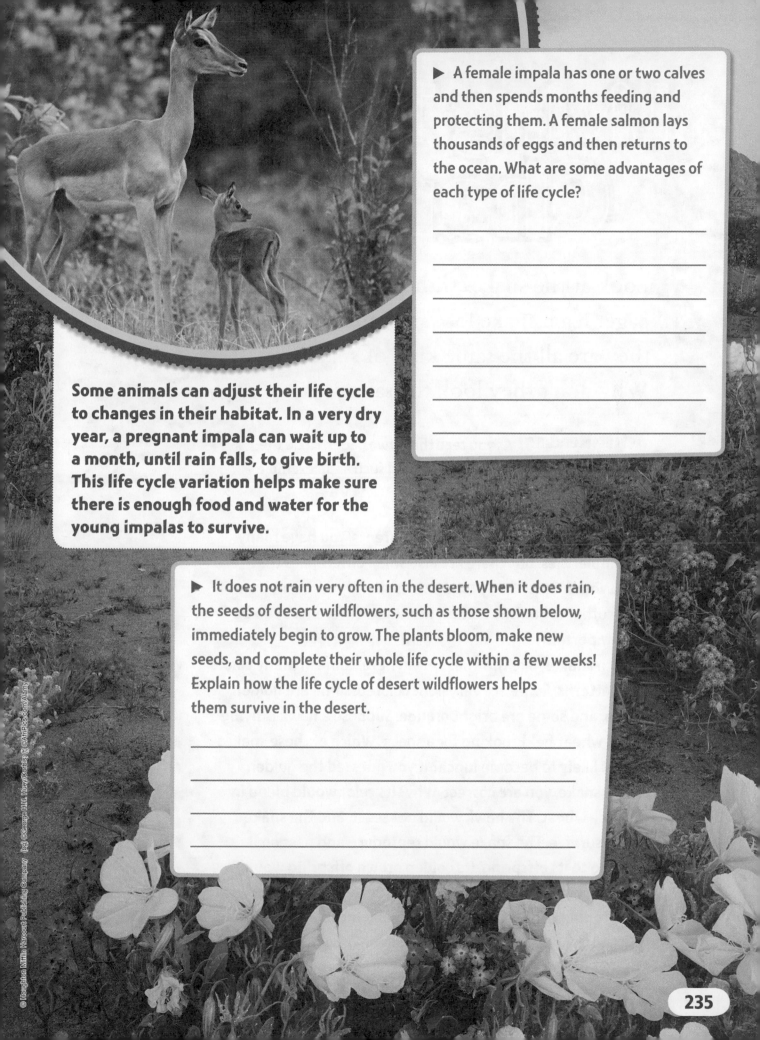

▶ A female impala has one or two calves and then spends months feeding and protecting them. A female salmon lays thousands of eggs and then returns to the ocean. What are some advantages of each type of life cycle?

_____

_____

_____

_____

_____

_____

Some animals can adjust their life cycle to changes in their habitat. In a very dry year, a pregnant impala can wait up to a month, until rain falls, to give birth. This life cycle variation helps make sure there is enough food and water for the young impalas to survive.

▶ It does not rain very often in the desert. When it does rain, the seeds of desert wildflowers, such as those shown below, immediately begin to grow. The plants bloom, make new seeds, and complete their whole life cycle within a few weeks! Explain how the life cycle of desert wildflowers helps them survive in the desert.

_____

_____

_____

_____

© Houghton Mifflin Harcourt Publishing Company (bg) ©George Hill; Corbis (t) ©AirPics.com/Alamy

Living Things Change

Look at the snakes slithering on this page. Each snake looks different, but they are all the same kind of snake. Why don't they look the same?

Active Reading As you read these two pages, circle the clue word or phrase that signals a detail such as an example or an added fact.

You don't look exactly like your parents. You have many similarities, but there are also small differences that make you unique. Every organism is slightly different from every other organism. Sometimes these differences can be very important.

Corn snakes, like the ones shown here, come in many colors and patterns. Some are very light colored, some are golden brown, and some are bright orange. Suppose a hawk is flying over a wheat field, looking for a snack. Which of these snakes is least likely to become lunch? If you guessed the golden brown snake, you are correct. Why? Its color would blend in with the wheat. The hawk would not see it, and the snake would survive. The snake would reproduce and pass on its coloring to its offspring. Its golden brown offspring would have a better chance of surviving in the wheat field and would also produce more offspring. Eventually, most of the snakes living in the wheat field would be golden brown.

© Houghton Mifflin Harcourt Publishing Company (bg) ©David Stuckel/Alamy; ©Dan Suzio/Photo Researchers, Inc.

Sometimes living things change because their environment changes. For example, bacteria have changed as a result of their changing environment. Since the discovery of antibiotics, people have learned how to kill bacteria. The first antibiotic, penicillin, saved many lives by killing bacteria that cause disease.

But in a very large population of bacteria, a few are not affected by penicillin. These bacteria survive and multiply. Over time, they produce large populations of bacteria that are not affected by penicillin.

Researchers have had to find new antibiotics to kill these bacteria. But, again, some bacteria are not killed. These bacteria continue to multiply.

While different types of antibiotics have been developed, bacteria have become resistant to many of them. Now there are bacteria that are resistant to almost all known types of antibiotics. These bacteria are extremely difficult to kill.

Do the Math!
Find Median and Mean

Length of Corn Snakes	
Snake 1	3.5 m
Snake 2	5.5 m
Snake 3	4.6 m
Snake 4	5.1 m
Snake 5	4.8 m
Snake 6	3.9 m
Snake 7	5.3 m

Adult corn snakes vary not only in color, but also in length. The table shows the lengths of several adult corn snakes. Study the data, and then answer the questions.

1. The median is the middle number of a data set when the numbers are placed in numerical order. Find the median of the data set. _____

2. The mean is the average of a data set. Find the mean of the data set. _____

Antibiotics in soaps and cleaners kill many bacteria. However, when not all of the bacteria are killed, the ones that survive multiply. Little by little, bacteria are becoming resistant to antibacterial soap and cleaners.

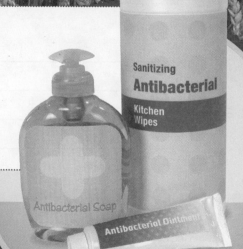

Sanitizing
Antibacterial
Kitchen Wipes

Antibacterial Soap

Antibacterial Ointment

© Houghton Mifflin Harcourt Publishing Company   (bc) ©David Steckel/Alamy (b) ©Stephen J. Krasemann/Photo Researchers, Inc

Sum It Up!

When you're done, use the answer key to check and revise your work.

The outline below is a summary of the lesson. Complete the outline.

Summarize

I. Instincts: A behavior that a living thing does without being taught to do.

   A. Example: _____

      _____

   B. Example: _____

      _____

II. Adaptations: A characteristic that helps a living thing survive is called an adaptation. Kinds of adaptations include:

   A. Physical Adaptations

     1. Example: _____

        _____

     2. Example: _____

        _____

   B. Behavioral Adaptations

     1. Example: _____

        _____

     2. Example: _____

        _____

   C. Life Cycle Adaptations

     1. Example: _____

        _____

     2. Example: _____

        _____

Answer Key: Your answers may vary. Sample answers: I.A. spiders spin webs I.B. babies cry II.A.1. camouflage II.A.2. thorns that keep plant-eating animals away II.B.1. migration II.B.2. hibernation II.C.1. controlling when offspring are born II.C.2. having young that don't eat the same food as adults

238

© Houghton Mifflin Harcourt Publishing Company (br) ©Stephen J. Krasemann/Photo Researchers, Inc.

Name _____

Word Play

1 Use words from the lesson to complete the puzzle.

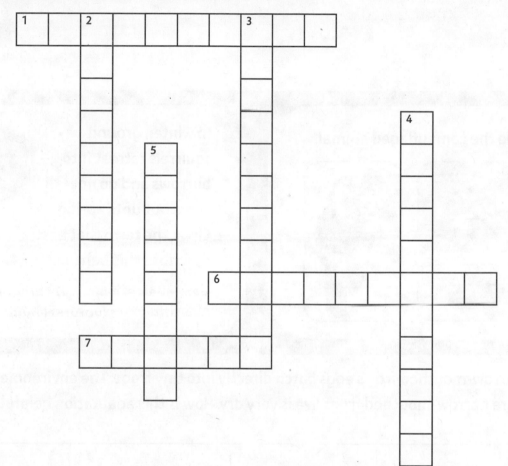

Across

1. What type of adaptation helps a living thing hide in its environment?

6. An animal that is active at night is described as being _____.

7. Stages that living things go through as they develop are called life _____.

Down

2. An example of _____ is birds flying south in winter.

3. What are characteristics that help an animal survive?

4. What behavior causes an animal to be inactive for a long period of time?

5. A behavior that an animal doesn't need to learn is a(n) _____.

© Houghton Mifflin Harcourt Publishing Company

Apply Concepts

2 Draw a picture of a cactus. Next to the cactus, draw a plant that is found in a non-desert environment. Label three adaptations that help the cactus plant survive in a desert.

3 Circle the camouflaged animal.

4 In winter, ground squirrels retreat into burrows and do not come out until spring. Circle the term that best describes this behavior.

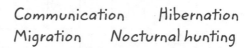

Communication   Hibernation

Migration   Nocturnal hunting

5 A narrow-mouthed frog's eggs hatch directly into tiny frogs. The environment where narrow-mouthed frogs live is very dry. How is this adaptation helpful?

_____

_____

_____

_____

Take It Home!

Go for a walk through your neighborhood or a local park with your family. Look at different plants and animals, and point out different adaptations that the plants or animals have.

240

© Houghton Mifflin Harcourt Publishing Company

Unit 4 Review

Vocabulary Review

Use the terms in the box to complete the sentences.

> adaptation
> classification
> dichotomous key
> germinates
> life cycle
> spore

1. A seed that begins to grow into a plant starts to sprout, or

   _____.

2. A single reproductive cell that can grow into a new plant is

   a(n) _____.

3. When scientists organize living things according to similar

   characteristics, they are using _____.

4. The different stages that an animal such as an insect
   goes through as it grows and reproduces is called

   its _____.

5. Any characteristic that helps an organism survive is considered

   to be a(n) _____.

6. A chart with many choices that guide you to the name
   of the organism or object you want to identify is called

   a(n) _____.

Science Concepts

Fill in the letter of the choice that best answers the question.

7. Ramon wants to classify an organism.
   The organism can be seen without a
   microscope. Its cells have cell walls
   but no chloroplasts. The organism gets
   food by breaking down dead organisms.
   Which kingdom does this organism likely
   belong to?

   (A) animal   (C) plant

   (B) fungi   (D) protist

8. During the life cycle of a plant, pollen
   comes in contact with the stigma and
   an embryo forms. What is the name of
   this process?

   (F) fertilization

   (G) germination

   (H) hibernation

   (I) migration

© Houghton Mifflin Harcourt Publishing Company   HMH Credits

Science Concepts

Fill in the letter of the choice that best answers the question.

9. Some plants have a structure like the one shown here.

What function is carried out by this structure?

(A) anchoring

(B) reproducing

(C) making food

(D) transporting water

10. The coloring of the rough green snake allows it to blend in with its background. What type of adaptation is the rough green snake's color?

(A) behavioral adaptation

(B) life-cycle adaptation

(C) physical adaptation

(D) reproductive adaptation

11. Animals can be classified as vertebrates or invertebrates. Which structure must be present in order for an animal to be classified as a vertebrate?

(A) a tail

(B) a brain

(C) a wing

(D) a backbone

12. Manuel did a science fair project on seed germination. Here is the procedure he followed:

Step 1: Place equal amounts of moist soil into two 1-gallon glass jars, and plant 10 radish seeds in each jar.

Step 2: Cover both jars.

Step 3: Place one jar in the refrigerator. Place the other jar in a dark closet.

Step 4: Observe both jars at the same time every day. Record any differences observed in the germination of the seeds.

What was the purpose of Manuel's project?

(A) to determine whether moisture affects germination

(B) to determine whether seeds need oxygen for germination

(C) to determine whether temperature affects germination

(D) to determine how long it takes different types of seeds to germinate

13. Vanessa is observing an organism undergoing metamorphosis. Which stage must she observe in order to conclude that the organism undergoes incomplete metamorphosis?

(A) adult

(B) larva

(C) nymph

(D) pupa

© Houghton Mifflin Harcourt Publishing Company   HMH Credits

14. The diagram below shows how an ant lion catches its food.

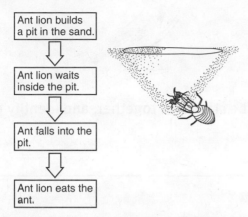

Ant lion builds a pit in the sand.
↓
Ant lion waits inside the pit.
↓
Ant falls into the pit.
↓
Ant lion eats the ant.

What does the diagram suggest about the ant lion?

(A) The ant lion is not adapted to its habitat.

(B) The ant lion has a diet of both plants and animals.

(C) The ant lion survives by hunting and chasing food.

(D) The ant lion has behavioral adaptations for its environment.

15. Alam is classifying organisms into different kingdoms. When he observes one group of organisms under a microscope, he sees that they are each made up of one cell with no cell wall. Which kingdom do these organisms **most likely** belong to?

(A) plant kingdom

(B) fungi kingdom

(C) animal kingdom

(D) bacteria kingdom

16. Scientists use classification to group living things. What is likely about living things that are placed in the same group?

(A) they are all the same age

(B) they are all the same color

(C) they are all the same size

(D) they all have similar characteristics

17. The picture below shows a structure found on one type of plant.

Which type of plant produces this structure?

(A) ferns

(B) mosses

(C) angiosperms

(D) gymnosperms

© Houghton Mifflin Harcourt Publishing Company HMH Credits

Apply Inquiry and Review the Big Idea

Write the answers to these questions.

18. These organisms are very different, and yet they are all classified in the same group.

Identify the two characteristics that allow them to be classified together, and identify the group to which they all belong.

_____

_____

_____

19. Lily wants to learn how changing the amount of water that she gives a pumpkin seed will affect its germination rate. List the steps she could take in a scientific experiment to determine whether water affects the seeds' germination.

_____

_____

_____

_____

20. A population of white rabbits lives in a snowy mountain environment. Hawks that fly high in the air hunt for the rabbits. Describe how the population of white rabbits might change if the climate of the mountain changed and the snow melted for a long period of time.

_____

_____

_____

_____

© Houghton Mifflin Harcourt Publishing Company   HMH Credits

Ecosystems

Big Idea

Ecosystems change over time, both naturally and as a result of human activity.

I Wonder Why

Sea turtles hatch in sand and make their way to the ocean. Why should sea turtle nests be protected? *Turn the page to find out.*

SAVE OUR SEA TURTLES

PROTECTED ENDANGERED SPECIES

NESTING SEASON MAY–OCTOBER
REPORT NESTING TURTLES

CLEARWATER
MARINE SCIENCE CENTER

© Houghton Mifflin Harcourt Publishing Company (inset) ©John Taylor/Alamy; (bg) ©Mark Conlin/Alamy; (border) ©NHPA/Age Fotostock

Here's Why Human activities, such as accidentally walking on nests, can harm turtle eggs. Turtle nests are protected so that the young turtles can safely hatch and reach the ocean.

In this unit, you will explore the Big Idea, the Essential Questions, and the Investigations on the Inquiry Flipchart.

SAVE OUR SEA TURTLES
PROTECTED ENDANGERED SPECIES
NESTING SEASON MAY–OCTOBER
REPORT NESTING TURTLES

CLEARWATER
MARINE SCIENCE CENTER

Levels of Inquiry Key ■ DIRECTED ■ GUIDED ■ INDEPENDENT

Track Your Progress

Big Idea Ecosystems change over time, both naturally and as a result of human activity.

Essential Questions

Now I Get the Big Idea!

Science Notebook

Before you begin each lesson, be sure to write your thoughts about the Essential Question.

Essential Question

What Is an Ecosystem?

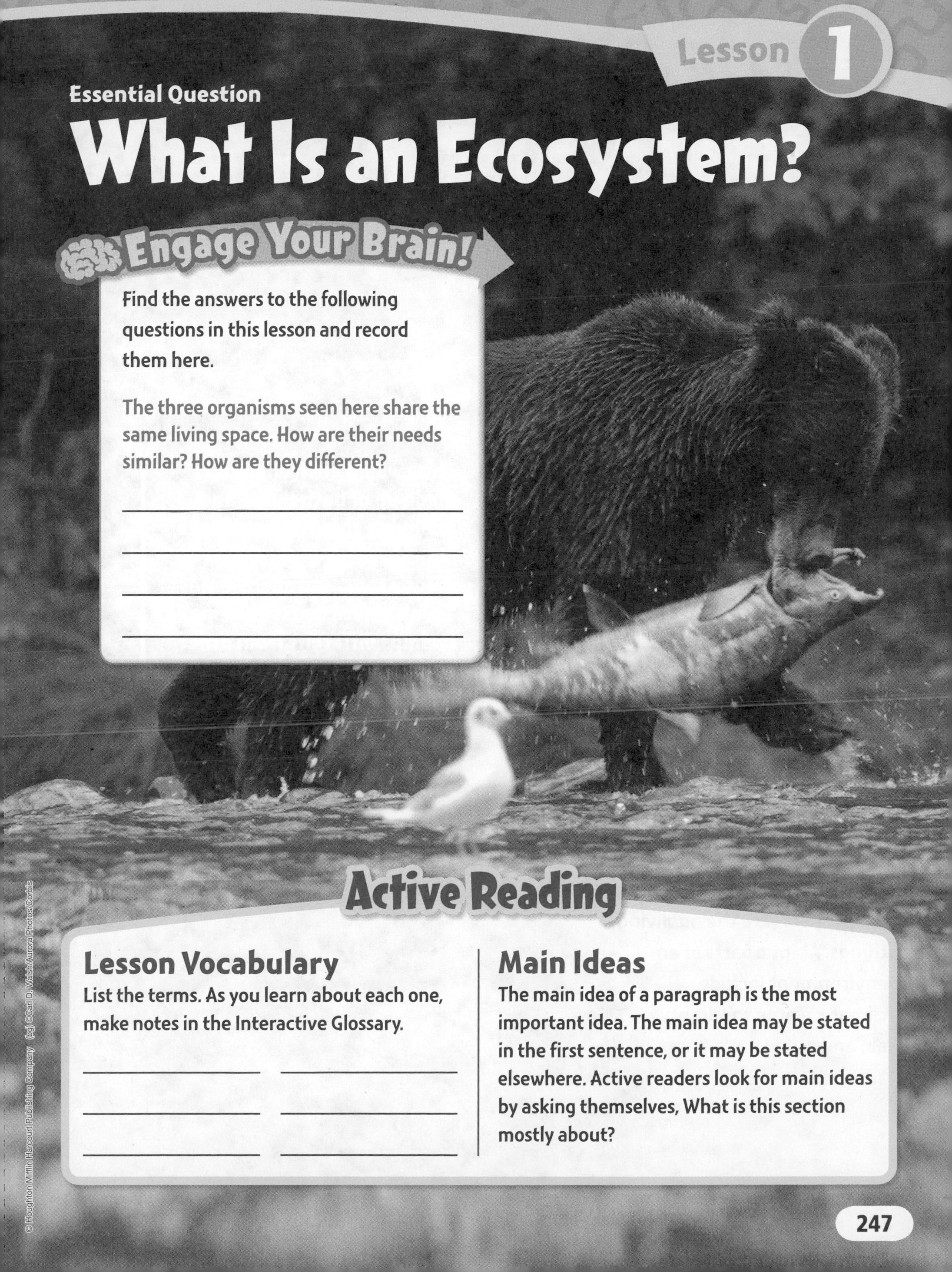

🧠 Engage Your Brain!

Find the answers to the following questions in this lesson and record them here.

The three organisms seen here share the same living space. How are their needs similar? How are they different?

_____

_____

_____

_____

Active Reading

Lesson Vocabulary
List the terms. As you learn about each one, make notes in the Interactive Glossary.

_____ _____

_____ _____

_____ _____

Main Ideas
The main idea of a paragraph is the most important idea. The main idea may be stated in the first sentence, or it may be stated elsewhere. Active readers look for main ideas by asking themselves, What is this section mostly about?

© Houghton Mifflin Harcourt Publishing Company (bg) ©Carl D. Walsh/Aurora Photos/Corbis

What Is an Ecosystem?

A frog that lives in a pond couldn't survive in a desert or on a mountaintop. Could you live in a swamp?

Active Reading As you read these two pages, **circle** the biotic parts of environments. Draw a box around each abiotic part.

An organism's **environment** is all the living and nonliving things that surround and affect the organism. You are surrounded by many things that make your environment suitable for you to live in. Would that be true if you lived in a swamp? Environments include biotic parts and abiotic parts. *Biotic* parts are the living things in an environment: plants, animals, and other organisms. *Abiotic* parts are the nonliving things. Abiotic parts of an environment include climate, water, soil, light, air, and nutrients.

This swamp environment is made up of both living and nonliving things. The climate, abundance of water, moist air, muddy soils, and shady areas are all abiotic parts that make swamps different from other environments.

© Houghton Mifflin Harcourt Publishing Company (bg) ©Mark Conlin/Alamy; (b) ©Dave Sherman/Alamy; (M) ©James Hager/Alamy

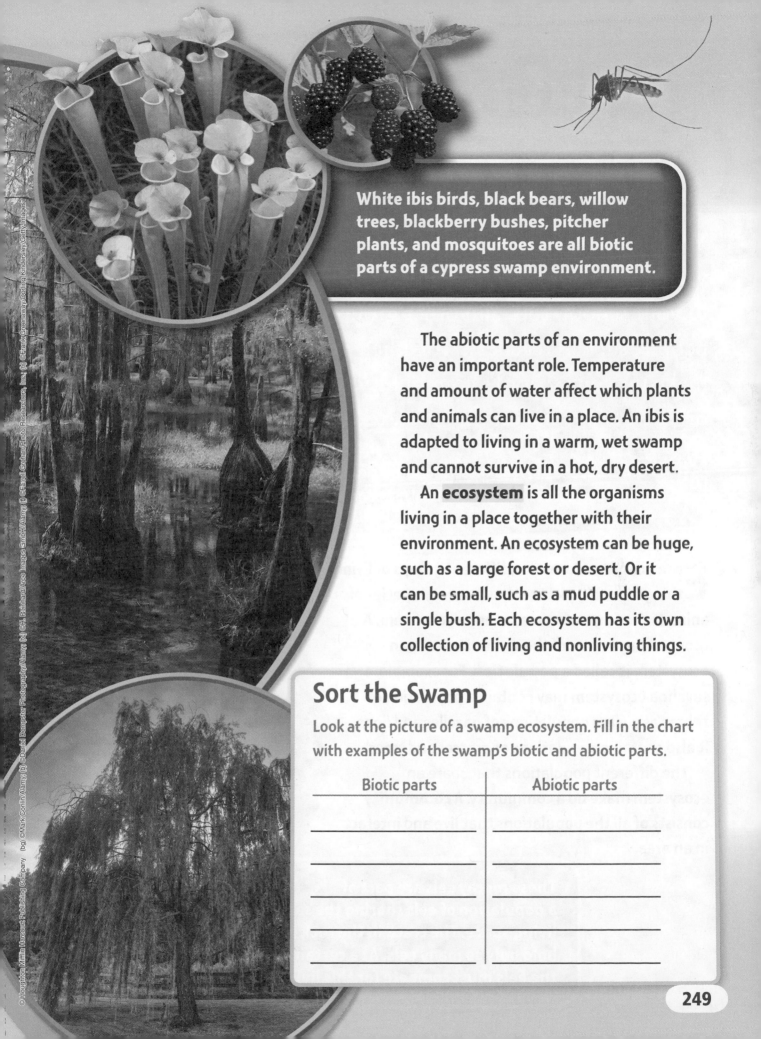

White ibis birds, black bears, willow trees, blackberry bushes, pitcher plants, and mosquitoes are all biotic parts of a cypress swamp environment.

The abiotic parts of an environment have an important role. Temperature and amount of water affect which plants and animals can live in a place. An ibis is adapted to living in a warm, wet swamp and cannot survive in a hot, dry desert.

An **ecosystem** is all the organisms living in a place together with their environment. An ecosystem can be huge, such as a large forest or desert. Or it can be small, such as a mud puddle or a single bush. Each ecosystem has its own collection of living and nonliving things.

Sort the Swamp

Look at the picture of a swamp ecosystem. Fill in the chart with examples of the swamp's biotic and abiotic parts.

Biotic parts	Abiotic parts

© Houghton Mifflin Harcourt Publishing Company   (bg) ©Mark Conlin/Alamy; (b) ©Daniel Dempster Photography/Alamy; (c) ©H. Reinhard/Arco Images GmbH/Alamy; (c) ©Farrell Grehan/Photo Researchers, Inc; (t) ©Frank Greenaway/Dorling Kindersley/Getty Images

Populations and Communities

You are part of a group of students in your classroom. There are other classes in your school, too, and other groups of people, such as teachers. Together, you make up your school's community. Other organisms live in communities, too.

Active Reading As you read these two pages, circle the two common, everyday words that have a special meaning in science.

Each ecosystem contains different groups of living things. The big picture shows several species of animals sharing water in a savanna ecosystem. A group of organisms of the same species in an ecosystem is called a **population**. For example, a savanna ecosystem may contain a population of zebras as well as populations of gazelles and lions. It also contains populations of grasses and trees.

The different populations that share an ecosystem make up a community. A **community** consists of all the populations that live and interact in an area.

These moray eels are part of a population of eels sharing the same living space. The crack in the rock will hold only so many eels. At a certain point the eels must compete for this living space.

© Houghton Mifflin Harcourt Publishing Company (t) ©Fernando Quevedo de Oliveira/Alamy; (b) ©Jeff Rotman/Alamy

These plants and animals are part of the community that lives in an ecosystem. Each population competes with other populations for the resources in the ecosystem.

In winter, a population of bison must work to find food. As resources become scarce, bison within the population compete with each other.

© Houghton Mifflin Harcourt Publishing Company (b) ©Jeff & Alexa Henry/Peter Arnold, Inc./Alamy; (t) ©Fernando Quevedo de Oliveira/Alamy

Do the Math!
Calculate Area

Bison graze on grass. It takes 5 acres of grass to feed 2 bison for a season. How much land would be needed to support 100 bison for a season?

Populations in every ecosystem need food, water, shelter, and space to live. The interaction between populations to meet needs is called *competition*. Populations that compete and obtain enough resources will survive. Those that cannot compete will not survive in the ecosystem. Because there is only enough food, water, shelter, and space to support a certain number of organisms, these resources are called *limiting factors*.

Competition also occurs within populations. The stronger individuals in a population are the ones that get the most food and take the best shelter for themselves. Weaker individuals may not survive.

Find Your Niche

Maybe you have to share your room, your clothes, or snacks with your family members. Organisms that live in the same ecosystem often compete for available resources.

Active Reading As you read these two pages, draw boxes around the clue words that compare and contrast habitat and niche.

An organism's **habitat** is the place where it lives within an ecosystem. Several populations often live in a single habitat. For example, barred owls and red-shouldered hawks live in habitats with woods, nearby open country, and bodies of water.

An organism's **niche** [NICH] is its complete role, or function, in its ecosystem. A niche is different from a habitat because it includes all the ways the organism survives. An organism's niche includes how it finds food as well as the climate it thrives in.

The panda has a narrow niche in terms of food. Its diet consists mainly of bamboo, so pandas cannot survive in habitats where bamboo does not grow.

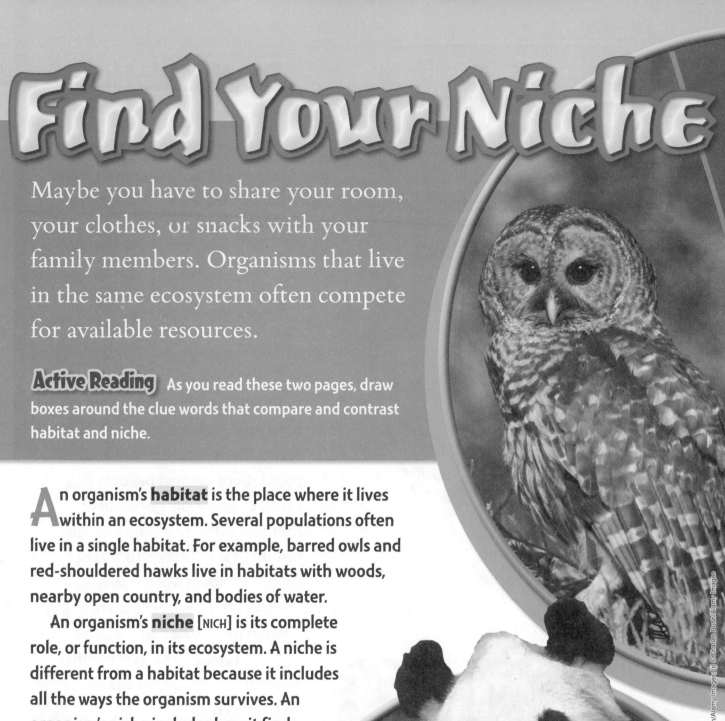

© Houghton Mifflin Harcourt Publishing Company · (b) ©Top-Pics TBK/Alamy; (t) ©Charles Bush/Alamy Images; (t) ©Charles Bush/Alamy Images

Red-shouldered hawks and barred owls share a habitat but have different niches. How is this so?

_____

_____

Every organism has a niche. Having different niches allows organisms to survive in the same habitat. When an organism has a very specific way of living, it has a narrow niche. For example, a bird that eats just one type of insect or lives only in one kind of tree has a narrow niche, while an animal that can eat many kinds of food has a broad niche. Organisms with a narrow niche tend to live in specific places, while those with a broad niche often move around large areas.

Populations can share a habitat but not the same niche. Red-shouldered hawks and barred owls, for example, share a habitat, but they have different niches. Hawks hunt by day and owls hunt at night, hunting different prey. If two populations of organisms share a niche, they must compete for resources.

Nice Niche

Suppose a bird is the only animal in a habitat that eats a certain type of berry. The berries are the bird's only food. Describe how this narrow niche could be both good and bad for the bird.

_____

_____

_____

_____

Sharks have a broad niche in terms of food. They are able to eat many different foods.

© Houghton Mifflin Harcourt Publishing Company (l) ©Joe Vogan/Alamy; (t) ©Charles Bush/Alamy; (b) ©WaterFrame/Alamy; (t) ©Joe Vogan/Alamy Images

Diversity

Suppose all the shelves in your grocery store held only one kind of food. You couldn't stay healthy for long. Ecosystems need diversity, too.

Active Reading As you read these two pages, draw a star next to the most important sentence.

This coral reef is a diverse ecosystem. Many populations live closely together here.

The word *diverse* means "different in kind." *Diversity* is the variety of different species that live in an ecosystem. An ecosystem that is diverse contains a lot of species. Ecosystems without much diversity are inhabited by only a few species.

Why is diversity important? All organisms rely on other organisms. Their relationships are connected in a large, complex web. The more types of organisms in an ecosystem, the larger the web, and the more resources available.

A rain forest is a diverse ecosystem. The warm temperatures and high rainfall support many different populations.

© Houghton Mifflin Harcourt Publishing Company   (b) ©Alan Pappe/RubberBall/Alamy; (t) ©Digital Vision/Getty Images

Why are some ecosystems very diverse while others have only a small number of species? Climate and location affect the amount and types of resources that are available for organisms. Locations of high diversity make a pattern on the map. In general, very diverse ecosystems such as coral reefs and rain forests are found near the equator. The farther away from the equator, the less diverse environments tend to be.

Other things can affect diversity as well. Humans can damage ecosystems and reduce the number of species living in them. Activities such as overhunting may lower the numbers of important species. In some areas, humans have destroyed forests or other environments in order to build cities and other structures. Species in those environments have lost their habitats, and diversity has decreased.

The cold arctic is a less diverse ecosystem. The polar bear is one of a small number of large organisms that can survive there.

Habitat Change

Describe how you think building a large shopping mall and parking lot might affect the diversity of a forest.

_____

_____

_____

_____

_____

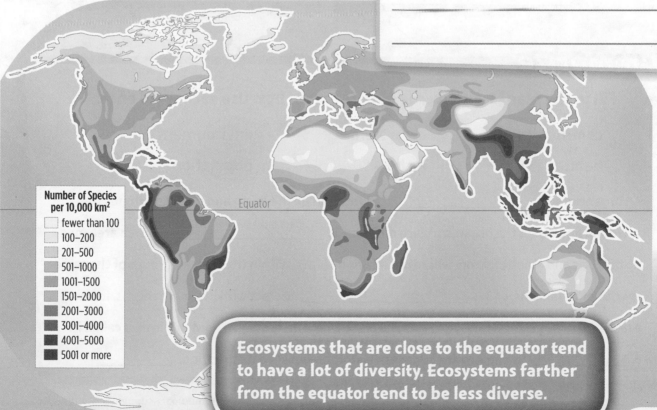

Number of Species per 10,000 km²
- fewer than 100
- 100–200
- 201–500
- 501–1000
- 1001–1500
- 1501–2000
- 2001–3000
- 3001–4000
- 4001–5000
- 5001 or more

Equator

Ecosystems that are close to the equator tend to have a lot of diversity. Ecosystems farther from the equator tend to be less diverse.

© Houghton Mifflin Harcourt Publishing Company   (t) ©Corbis

When you're done, use the answer key to check and revise your work.

1

The words in the ovals describe parts of a desert ecosystem. Draw lines to show whether each part is a *biotic* or *abiotic* part.

Cactus

Sandy soil

Biotic

Lizard

Rattlesnake

Little water

Sunlight

Abiotic

Summarize

2 Fill in the blanks with words from the word box. Use each word once.

| community | ecosystem | environment |
| habitat | niche | population |

An organism's 1._____ includes all the living and nonliving things that

surround and affect the organism. Each different 2._____ is an area made

up of biotic and abiotic factors where organisms interact. Within these areas, groups of the same

species of organisms, or 3._____, interact with other organisms, forming

a large 4._____. The place where an organism normally lives is called its

5._____. The way the organism lives there is called its specific 6._____.

© Houghton Mifflin Harcourt Publishing Company

Answer Key: Biotic: Cactus, Rattlesnake, Lizard; Abiotic: Sunlight, Sandy soil, Little water; 1. environment 2. ecosystem 3. populations 4. community 5. habitat 6. niche

Name _____

Word Play

1 Use the words in the box to complete the puzzle.

Across

3. The average weather in an area over time

5. The variety of species in an ecosystem

6. Nonliving

Down

1. Living

2. The struggle for resources in an ecosystem

4. The type of factor that determines the size of a population

- abiotic
- biotic
- climate
- competition
- diversity
- limiting

Use the three across words to write a sentence.

_____

_____

_____

_____

© Houghton Mifflin Harcourt Publishing Company   (b) ©Dave Sherman/Alamy

Apply Concepts

2 Draw an organism and its habitat.

3 List three abiotic factors that are in your environment right now.

_____

_____

_____

4 Explain why two species of organisms can share a habitat but not a niche.

_____

_____

_____

5 Draw a line from the organism to the ecosystem it would most likely live in.

1. A warm, wet swamp

2. A grassy prairie

3. A snowy arctic ocean area

Take It Home!

Your neighborhood is an environment that supports plants and animals. With your family, list as many organisms living in your neighborhood as you can. Compare lists with your classmates.

© Houghton Mifflin Harcourt Publishing Company   (cr) ©Farrell Grehan/Photo Researchers, Inc.; (b) ©Jeff & Alexa Henry/Peter Arnold, Inc./Alamy; (t) ©Corbis

Quest for the Serpent Eagle

africa

Jane Juniper is a wildlife surveyor. She is deep in the forest of Madagascar, an island off the coast of Africa, observing birds.

What's that sound? Jane hears a loud, screeching bird call that she never expected to hear. It sounds like... But could it be?

Jane tiptoes quietly through the forest, searching the trees for movement. There!

Jane stands perfectly still. The bird has a dark back and a striped chest. It has yellow eyes, and sharp talons. But it's not supposed to exist!

Jane Juniper has studied all about African birds. It takes her just a moment to be sure. But she is still amazed! With her camera she collects evidence of her find.

Jane Juniper, wildlife surveyor, found a bird that was thought to be extinct—a Madagascar Serpent Eagle!

© Houghton Mifflin Harcourt Publishing Company

Now You Be the Surveyor

Imagine you're a wildlife surveyor. Survey the forest below. Write the kinds of animals you find and the number of each kind.

_____   _____

_____   _____

_____   _____

_____   _____

© Houghton Mifflin Harcourt Publishing Company

Name _____

Essential Question

What Makes Up a Land Ecosystem?

Set a Purpose
What do you think you will learn in this activity?

_____

_____

_____

_____

Think About the Procedure
Why do you think your sample site should have a variety of plants and soil coverings?

_____

_____

_____

_____

Why did you measure and mark your sample area?

_____

_____

_____

_____

Record Your Data
In the space below, make a table to record the different living things found in your sample site and their role in the ecosystem.

Draw Conclusions

How did you determine the role that each living thing played?

_____

_____

_____

_____

_____

Compare your results with the results of other groups. Explain any differences or similarities.

_____

_____

_____

_____

_____

Analyze and Extend

1. What kind of living things did you find in your sample area?

_____

_____

2. Which role in the ecosystem had the greatest amount of living things?

_____

_____

_____

3. Which role in the ecosystem had the greatest variety of living things?

_____

_____

_____

4. In the space below, draw a picture of your sample area. Make sure to include an example of a producer and a consumer that you found living in it.

5. Think of other questions you would like to ask about how living things interact in the ecosystem.

_____

_____

_____

_____

_____

© Houghton Mifflin Harcourt Publishing Company

Essential Question

How Do Environmental Changes Affect Organisms?

Find the answer to the following question in this lesson and record it here.

A forest fire can change a landscape in a matter of minutes! Trees are burned, and animals run for shelter. How could a forest fire be a good thing?

_____

_____

_____

Active Reading

Lesson Vocabulary

List the terms. As you learn about each one, make notes in the Interactive Glossary.

_____

_____

Compare and Contrast

Many ideas in this lesson are connected because they explain comparisons and contrasts—how things are alike and different. Active readers stay focused on comparisons and contrasts when they ask themselves, How are these things alike? How are they different?

© Houghton Mifflin Harcourt Publishing Company   (bg) ©Mario Graz/epa/Corbis

Change Comes Naturally

All environments change over time. Some changes happen slowly, while others occur quickly.

Active Reading As you read these two pages, draw a box around events that change the environment rapidly. Draw a circle around events that change the environment slowly.

Over hundreds of thousands of years, mountains weather and erode. Rivers cut canyons into rock and change course through valleys and plains. Gradual changes like these affect the organisms that live in environments.

Weather patterns change over time as well. Like changes to the land, *climate changes* affect organisms. Throughout Earth's history, the average temperature has gone up and down many times.

An ice age happens when Earth's temperatures are colder than normal for a very long time. Large areas of land are covered with ice for thousands of years. During warmer climate cycles, ice melts and uncovers land.

During the last ice age, ice nearly 4 km thick covered much of North America. Because the ice held so much frozen water, the level of the oceans dropped and coastlines changed.

PACIFIC OCEAN

ATLANTIC OCEAN

© Houghton Mifflin Harcourt Publishing Company

Do the Math!
Interpret a Graph

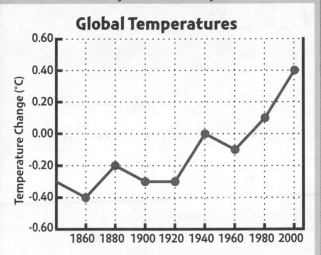

Global Temperatures

The graph shows average temperatures on Earth over time. Use the graph to describe temperature trends between 1900 and 2000.

_____

_____

_____

_____

Volcanic eruptions can quickly change the environment. Centuries of forest growth and the wildlife that live in it can be destroyed within hours.

Earth is now in a warming cycle. Many scientists think this warming trend will continue and is in part linked to human activities. It is unclear how warming might affect the planet as a whole. As some areas become warmer, the organisms that inhabit those areas will move, adapt to the change, or disappear.

Many things can happen to change environments quickly as well. Heavy storms can cause floods that wash away land. Mudslides can destroy years of plant growth in minutes. Volcanic eruptions can be destructive, but they can also form entirely new land that will eventually be inhabited by plants and animals and become an ecosystem.

A _drought_ occurs when little rain falls. Without water, plants and animals will disappear.

© Houghton Mifflin Harcourt Publishing Company   (t) ©Frithjof Hirdes/Corbis; (br) ©Mark Pearson/Alamy

Next, Please!

Ecosystems change all the time, but the changes are often so slow that they are hard to notice.

Active Reading As you read these two pages, write numbers next to appropriate sentences to show the order of events.

The picture below shows how bare rock can change into an ecosystem filled with living things. The gradual change of organisms in an ecosystem is called **succession**. *Primary succession* begins on bare rock, such as after a volcano erupts. Dust settles in cracks in the rocks. The first organisms to colonize are called pioneer species. Lichens are common pioneers. They break down the rock as they grow, producing soil. When they die, their litter decays, adding nutrients to the soil.

As soil develops, plants can begin to grow. Mosses flourish, and they help produce more soil. The soil becomes thicker, and bigger plants take hold. Eventually, trees grow. A mature, stable community establishes itself.

It can take hundreds of years for a stable community to establish itself. Where water is plentiful, succession can happen more quickly. Even mature, stable communities continue to change.

© Houghton Mifflin Harcourt Publishing Company

Secondary succession occurs where an ecosystem has been disturbed, but soil is still present. Areas burned by forest fires undergo secondary succession. Secondary succession occurs more quickly than primary succession. The existing soil usually contains seeds and roots that sprout and grow after the fire is over. The first plants to grow tend to be hardy shrubs and grasses. Gradually, larger plants colonize the burned area. Animals also return. Eventually a stable ecological community re-establishes itself.

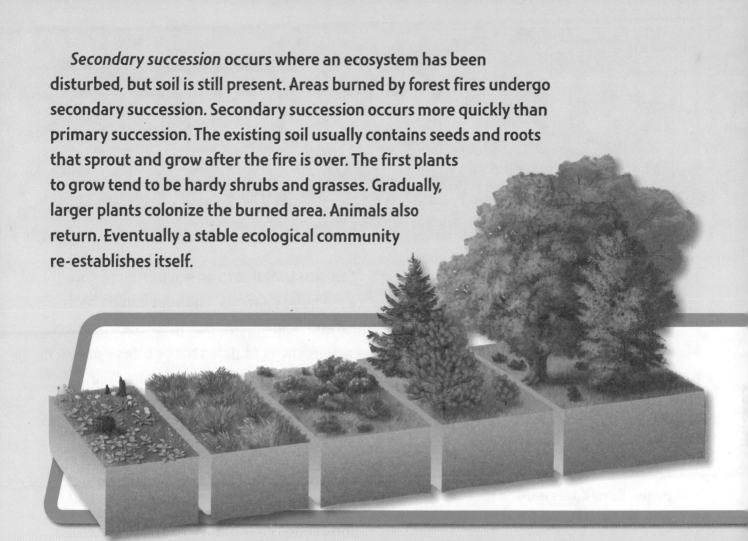

About Time

An area with no plants or animals returns to a grassy plain within a year. What kind of succession has occurred? Explain your answer.

_____

_____

_____

© Houghton Mifflin Harcourt Publishing Company   (b) ©Jurgen Vogt/Getty Images

For Better or Worse

Living things change the places where they live. Is this a good thing or a bad thing? It depends on your point of view!

Active Reading As you read these two pages, draw boxes around clue words that signal examples.

Organisms that live in an environment can cause huge changes. Changes can be both harmful and helpful. For example, when beavers make a dam, they cut down many trees—trees that provide food and shelter for other living things. In addition, the dam slows the flow of water, which affects animals that rely on faster-flowing water to live. On the other hand, the dams produce wetlands, which provide homes for other organisms.

Sometimes changes harm an ecosystem. They can even harm humans. When large numbers of algae in bodies of water reproduce rapidly, the algae release large amounts of harmful chemicals into the water and cause oxygen levels to drop. The resulting condition is known as red tide, which can kill fish and other wildlife and can poison people. When beaches experience red tides, officials post signs warning people to stay out of the water.

The algae that make up a red tide release harmful chemicals and use up oxygen that fish need to breathe.

© Houghton Mifflin Harcourt Publishing Company   (b) ©Don Paulson/SuperStock/Corbis

Beavers change their environment by building dams across streams. The dams cause flowing water to back up and form ponds. These changes create environments where new plants and animals can establish themselves.

Contrast

Describe a way that the activities of beavers can be helpful to an ecosystem. Then describe one way in which their activities can be harmful.

Helpful	Harmful
_____	_____
_____	_____
_____	_____

Goats, sheep, and other grazing animals remove grass and other plants from an environment. When too many animals graze in an area, they eat grass faster than it can grow back.

© Houghton Mifflin Harcourt Publishing Company (t) ©Paul Souders/Digital Vision/Getty Images; (tl) Beaver Dam: © David Hosking/Pho o Researchers, Inc.; (b) ©Mark Boulton/Photo Researchers, Inc.

Invasive Species

You may have seen a movie where space aliens invaded Earth. Invasions happen on Earth every day! Here's what happens when a new species moves into an environment.

Active Reading As you read these two pages, draw boxes around clue words or phrases that signal a main idea.

Sometimes the population of a species grows quickly after it is introduced into a new environment. This type of organism is called an *invasive species*. Invasive species take food and space away from *native species*, the organisms already living in an ecosystem. The factors that limit the growth of native species, such as predators, pests, and diseases, do not affect invasive species. The two species compete for resources. If no other species in the ecosystem can use the invasive species for food, there is no limit to its expansion. Invasive species often threaten less competitive organisms that have lived in an environment for a long time.

Populations of native harvester ants have been destroyed as invasive fire ants moved into harvester ant habitats and successfully competed with them for resources.

Zebra mussels are invasive to North America. They were accidentally carried into the Great Lakes in the hulls of ocean-going ships. Zebra mussels now grow in such large populations that they totally cover surfaces, block water outlets, and clog pipes in the lakes they have invaded.

© Houghton Mifflin Harcourt Publishing Company (bg) ©James H. Robinson/Photo Researchers, Inc; (t) ©Ed Reschke/Peter Arnold, Inc./Alamy

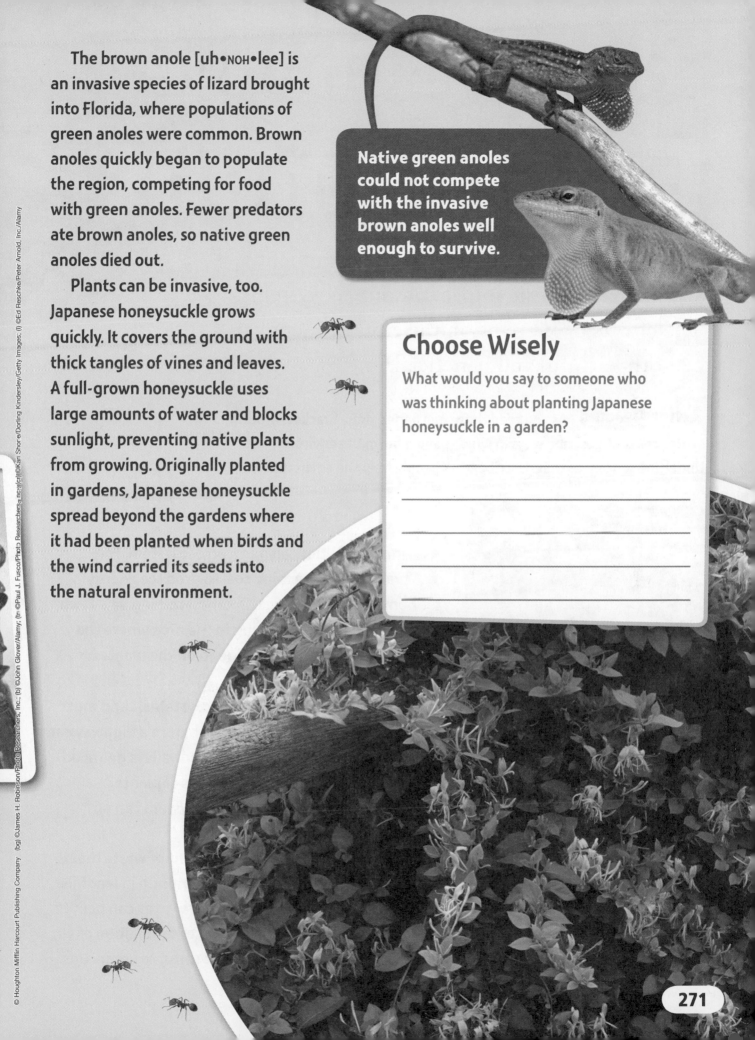

The brown anole [uh•NOH•lee] is an invasive species of lizard brought into Florida, where populations of green anoles were common. Brown anoles quickly began to populate the region, competing for food with green anoles. Fewer predators ate brown anoles, so native green anoles died out.

Plants can be invasive, too. Japanese honeysuckle grows quickly. It covers the ground with thick tangles of vines and leaves. A full-grown honeysuckle uses large amounts of water and blocks sunlight, preventing native plants from growing. Originally planted in gardens, Japanese honeysuckle spread beyond the gardens where it had been planted when birds and the wind carried its seeds into the natural environment.

Native green anoles could not compete with the invasive brown anoles well enough to survive.

Choose Wisely

What would you say to someone who was thinking about planting Japanese honeysuckle in a garden?

_____

_____

_____

_____

_____

© Houghton Mifflin Harcourt Publishing Company (bg) ©James H. Robinson/Photo Researchers, Inc.; (b) ©John Glover/Alamy; (tr) ©Paul J. Fusco/Photo Researchers, Inc; (cr) ©Kari Shore/Doring Kindersley/Getty Images; (l) ©Ed Reschke/Peter Arnold, Inc./Alamy

Humans Change the Environment

Humans are not outside of the environment, and we have a large impact on our ecosystems. The effects of humans on the environment can be both harmful and beneficial.

Active Reading As you read these two pages, draw brackets around sentences that describe ways in which people harm the environment. Underline sentences that describe ways people help the environment.

Human activities can harm an ecosystem. For example, people mine coal to produce energy for homes and businesses. Open-pit mining, as shown here, kills all the plants living in the area where the mine is dug. Animals that depend on the plants for food must move.

Highways can also disrupt ecosystems. Land must be cleared of plants and animals before a highway can be built. Often hills get leveled and valleys get filled in, blocking streams. Communities of plants and animals that lived in the ecosystem can no longer survive.

Humans produce a large amount of waste that is disposed of as trash. Most trash ends up in landfills. If landfills are not built properly, wastes can pollute soil and water. *Pollution* is the contamination of air, water, or soil by substances harmful to organisms.

© Houghton Mifflin Harcourt Publishing Company (bg) ©Colin Anderson/Photographer's Choice/Getty Images; (cl) ©rshantz/Alamy; (bl) ©rshantz/Alamy; (t) ©Inga Spence/Photo Researchers, Inc.

Not all changes caused by humans are harmful. People work to protect their environment and to protect organisms from harm as a result of ecosystem change. Protecting ecosystems and the organisms living in them is called *conservation*.

People try to restore habitats and repair damaged ecosystems by replanting trees and cleaning up pollution. People also remove invasive plants and animals so native organisms can survive.

In addition, people try to help organisms affected by natural disasters. People care for animals injured or orphaned by these disasters.

What Can You Do to Help?

In the space below, list things that you can do to help the environment. Include things you already do and what you would like to do in the future.

_____

_____

© Houghton Mifflin Harcourt Publishing Company (bg) ©Colin Anderson/Photographer's Choice/Getty Images; (t) ©Inga Spence/Photo Researchers, Inc.; (c) ©Peter Denren/Getty Images; (tr) ©Tim Pannell/Corbis

Gone!

Some living things change when their environment changes. Some living things move to new places. Others do not survive.

Millions of years ago, Earth was covered with giant reptiles. Now most of those reptiles are extinct. **Extinction** happens when all the members of a certain species die. Giant reptiles, such as the *Tyrannosaurus rex* shown here, lived in a time in which Earth was warm. Over time, the environment cooled, and many of the reptiles could not survive.

Golden toads were once numerous in a part of the mountainous tropical forest of Costa Rica. Scientists think a period of drought that dried up the pools where the toads laid their eggs and where tadpoles matured caused a rapid population decline. The drought also allowed a fungus that harmed the toads to spread. Golden toads have not been seen since 1989 and are thought to be extinct.

© Houghton Mifflin Harcourt Publishing Company (t) ©PjrIdcks/Alamy; (b) ©Fred Grover Jr./Alamy

The Tasmanian wolf lived in Australia and New Guinea. Ranchers believed the wolves killed sheep and cattle, but this was never proven. The Tasmanian wolf was hunted to extinction by the 1930s.

The dodo bird lived on an island in the Indian Ocean. Around 1600, people arrived on the island. They hunted the birds for food. They cut down the island's forests to make room for houses. Invasive species, such as cats and pigs brought by people, destroyed the dodo birds' nests. Within 80 years, dodo birds were extinct.

Time Traveler

If you could go back to the island of the dodo birds in 1600, what advice could you give to help conserve dodo birds?

_____

_____

_____

_____

_____

Today, people work to conserve habitats and protect organisms from extinction. Even so, many organisms are in danger of becoming extinct. As these organisms' environments continue to change, some will adapt, some will move, and some will not survive.

© Houghton Mifflin Harcourt Publishing Company   (tl) ©AFP/Getty Images; (tr) ©Peter Arnold, Inc./Alamy; (l) ©Getty Images

When you're done, use the answer key to check and revise your work.

Read the summary statements below. Each one is incorrect. Rewrite the part of the summary in blue so it is correct.

1

1. Pollution is all the living and nonliving things that affect an organism's life.

   _____

2. A natural event that causes the environment to change slowly is an earthquake.

   _____

3. People can help conserve habitats by mining, building landfills, and cutting down forests.

   _____

   _____

4. Protecting ecosystems is an example of extinction. _____

2 **The idea web below summarizes the lesson. Complete the web. Start with number 5.**

A gradual buildup of organisms in an environment that consists of bare rock is called 7. _____ succession.

A gradual buildup of organisms in an environment that has soil is called 8. _____ succession.

An environment can change 5. _____ or 6. _____.

A(n) 9. _____ is any nonnative plant or animal that takes over an environment.

An environment can be changed suddenly by a natural event such as a 10. _____
_____.

Answer Key: 1. any harmful substance that gets into the environment 2. ice age 3. replanting forests, cleaning up garbage, and removing invasive plants and animals 4. conservation 5. slowly 6. quickly 7. primary 8. secondary 9. invasive species 10. flood, earthquake, or volcano eruption

© Houghton Mifflin Harcourt Publishing Company

Name _____

Word Play

1 Use the clues to unscramble the words below.

1. `iavinvse` __ __ __ __ __ __ __ __ : A nonnative animal that moves into a new place

2. `ecnntavosroi` __ __ __ __ __ __ __ __ __ __ __ __ : Protecting ecosystems and the organisms living in them

3. `nlpituloo` __ __ __ __ __ __ __ __ __ : Litter on the ground or harmful chemicals in the water

4. `tgurhdo` __ __ __ __ __ __ __ : Occurs when no rain falls for a long period of time

5. `consisuces` __ __ __ __ __ __ __ __ __ __ : The gradual change and buildup of organisms in an environment

6. `galea` __ __ __ __ __ : Organism that causes red tide when present in large numbers

7. `vebera` __ __ __ __ __ __ : Can be helpful or harmful, depending on point of view

8. `lonea` __ __ __ __ __ : Brown lizard that has invaded some areas of Florida

9. `vmetneonrin` __ __ __ __ __ __ __ __ __ __ __ : Everything around an organism, such as other organisms, air, water, and land

10. `txoniecnit` __ __ __ __ __ __ __ __ __ __ : Happened to dodo birds and Tasmanian wolves

11. `navoolc` __ __ __ __ __ __ __ : Can cause long-term environmental change by blowing dust and gases into the sky

Bonus: What kind of dinosaur accidentally smashes everything in its path?

_____   _____

© Houghton Mifflin Harcourt Publishing Company

Apply Concepts

2 Label each picture as a change caused by people, animals, or a natural event.

_____ _____ _____

_____ _____ _____

3 Name four invasive species and describe their effect on ecosystems.

_____

_____

_____

_____

_____

_____

_____

_____

_____

_____

4 Draw one circle around animals that became extinct because of natural events. Draw two circles around animals that became extinct because of human activities.

© Houghton Mifflin Harcourt Publishing Company

5 In the first box below, draw a landscape that includes a river. In the second box, draw how the same landscape might look after a flood. Include captions explaining how the environment changed.

_____   _____
_____   _____

6 Fill in the graphic organizer below to describe how beavers change the environment. The first box is already completed.

Beavers build a dam in a stream.

↓

_____
_____

↓

_____
_____

© Houghton Mifflin Harcourt Publishing Company

Describe a way that people might be able to solve each environmental problem listed below.

7 Coal mining can harm habitats and cause pollution.

_____

_____

_____

8 Building a new highway destroys habitats and can lead to soil erosion.

_____

_____

_____

9 Waste from garbage in landfills can enter the ground and pollute soil and water.

_____

_____

10 Imagine that an orange tree frog eats only a certain type of small blue fly. A giant red fly starts moving into the tree frog's ecosystem. The red fly eats all the blue fly's food. In the space below, draw a flow chart that shows what might happen to the frog.

Bonus: How might orange frogs change because of the red fly? _____

_____

Take It Home!

Share what you have learned about conservation with your family.
Come up with at least four ways to help conserve resources at home.
Carry out your family's plan, and report the results to the class.

© Houghton Mifflin Harcourt Publishing Company

S.T.E.M.
Engineering & Technology

Terrarium

How It Works:
Life in a Box

In what way are an aquarium, a terrarium, and the International Space Station the same? They are all artificial environments. In each contained space, different parts of the environment must be controlled to make it possible for organisms to live there. Some of these parts include light, heat, water, and oxygen.

Aquarium

Troubleshooting

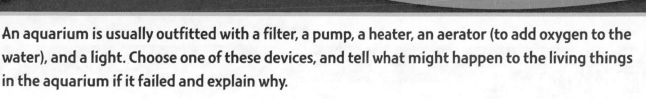

An aquarium is usually outfitted with a filter, a pump, a heater, an aerator (to add oxygen to the water), and a light. Choose one of these devices, and tell what might happen to the living things in the aquarium if it failed and explain why.

_____

_____

Artificial environments must have all of the things that the organisms living inside them need.

Draw an organism in an artificial environment. Explain how the environment is designed to supply what the organism needs.

Research Biosphere 2. What is it?

_____

_____

What was one problem people living in such a closed system would have?

_____

_____

How could they solve it?

_____

_____

Biosphere 2

Build On It!

Rise to the engineering design challenge — complete **Design It: Mobile Ecosystems Lab** in the Inquiry Flipchart.

© Houghton Mifflin Harcourt Publishing Company   (b) © Joe Sohm/Visions of America, LLC/Alamy

Name _____

Essential Question

How Does Drought Affect Plants?

Set a Purpose
What will you better understand about plants after doing this experiment?

_____

_____

_____

State Your Hypothesis
Write your hypothesis, or testable statement.

_____

_____

_____

Think About the Procedure
What parts of your experiment stay the same for each test group?

_____

_____

_____

What part of the experiment did you change?

_____

_____

_____

Record Your Data
Record your observations in the table below.

Plant Observations	
Cup A	
Cup B	
Cup C	
Cup D	
Cup E	

© Houghton Mifflin Harcourt Publishing Company

Draw Conclusions

Was your hypothesis supported? Why or why not?

_____

_____

_____

_____

What conclusions can you draw from this investigation?

_____

_____

_____

_____

Analyze and Extend

1. What natural conditions did Cup A and Cup E represent?

_____

_____

_____

2. Did the plants in the cups that got the most water do the best? What can you infer based on your results?

_____

_____

_____

3. Suppose you are studying pea plants. You find that half of the individual pea plants are able to survive in mild drought conditions. Why might this data be imporant?

_____

_____

_____

_____

4. How would you set up an experiment to test the following hypothesis: The amount of fertilizer does not affect how quickly plants grow. Draw and label a picture that shows your setup.

5. Think of other questions you would like to ask about how environmental conditions affect plants.

_____

_____

_____

_____

© Houghton Mifflin Harcourt Publishing Company

Unit 5 Review

Vocabulary Review

Use the terms in the box to complete the sentences.

> community
> ecosystem
> environment
> extinction
> habitat
> niche
> population
> succession

1. A community of organisms and the environment in which they live is called a(n) _____.

2. A scientist would look at a group of rabbits that live in a meadow and call them a(n) _____.

3. All of the living and nonliving things that surround you make up your _____.

4. A scientist who is describing the place where an organism lives is defining the organism's _____.

5. The role a plant or animal plays in its habitat is its _____.

6. The disappearance of an entire species of organisms is known as _____.

7. The gradual change of organisms in an ecosystem that follows an event such as a volcanic eruption is called _____.

8. A group of plants and animals that live in the same area and interact with each other is called a(n) _____.

© Houghton Mifflin Harcourt Publishing Company HMH Credits

Science Concepts

Fill in the letter of the choice that best answers the question.

9. The organisms that live around a pond interact with biotic and abiotic factors. Which of the following is a biotic factor of the pond environment?

(A) cattail plants

(B) muddy soil

(C) slowly flowing water

(D) warm temperature

10. A coral reef has many different kinds of species. An area near the arctic has few species. Which term describes the variety of species that live in an ecosystem?

(A) community   (C) niche

(B) diversity   (D) population

11. In a science experiment, soil was placed in four different beakers. The diagram below shows the conditions of the soil for each beaker.

A   B   C   D

Which of the beakers models drought conditions?

(A) Beaker A   (C) Beaker C

(B) Beaker B   (D) Beaker D

12. Alejandra wants to identify an ecosystem to research. She starts by looking at the globe below.

Where on the globe should she look to identify the most areas with high biodiversity?

(A) near water

(B) near mountains

(C) near the equator

(D) near the north or south pole

13. A volcano erupts and covers the ground with lava that hardens into rock. As primary succession begins, which organism is likely to be the **first** to populate the area?

(A) birds   (C) lichens

(B) snakes   (D) bears

14. Sometimes a species that is introduced to an area grows quickly and crowds out organisms that were already living there. What is this introduced species called?

(A) a native species

(B) a protected species

(C) an invasive species

(D) a beneficial species

© Houghton Mifflin Harcourt Publishing Company HMH Credits

15. A new shopping center was built on a vacant lot. The table shows the numbers of plants before and after construction.

Plants	Before	After
flowers	500	1,000
grass	1,000	0
shrubs	260	50
trees	26	3

Which of these statements is **true** based on these data?

(A) Humans did not change the environment.

(B) There were fewer total plants before the shopping center was built.

(C) There were more kinds of plants before the shopping center was built.

(D) There were more kinds of plants after the shopping center was built.

16. The picture below shows organisms that live in a land ecosystem.

Which organism is the producer?

(A) organism 1

(B) organism 2

(C) organism 3

(D) organism 4

17. A farmer plants corn every year. One year, the farm experiences a drought and receives less rainfall than is normal during the growing season. Which of the following is the **most** likely result?

(A) The corn plants will not grow at all.

(B) The corn plants will be taller than usual.

(C) The corn plants will be shorter than usual.

(D) The corn plants will grow the same as usual.

18. Tropical rainforests are ecosystems that have a great deal of diversity. Many different organisms live there because of the abundance of resources. Which factors affect the amount of resources and the diversity of an ecosystem?

(A) age and altitude

(B) motion and humans

(C) climate and location

(D) minerals and sunshine

19. Which of the following things signals that an ecosystem has become a stable community after years of succession?

(A) moss

(B) rocks

(C) soil

(D) trees

© Houghton Mifflin Harcourt Publishing Company   HMH Credits

Apply Inquiry and Review the Big Idea

Write the answers to these questions.

20. Leo is exploring a small creek near his home. Identify two biotic and two abiotic factors that the frogs living in the creek are likely to interact with.

_____

_____

_____

21. Eli's class takes a field trip to a grassy meadow. He sees several field mice scurrying through the grass. He records ways that the mice both <u>use</u> resources and <u>are</u> resources in the meadow. What is it likely that Eli recorded?

a. How mice use resources: _____

_____

b. How mice are resources: _____

_____

22. The graphic below shows the changes that occurred after a forest fire removed all the trees from a mountain meadow, leaving barren soil.

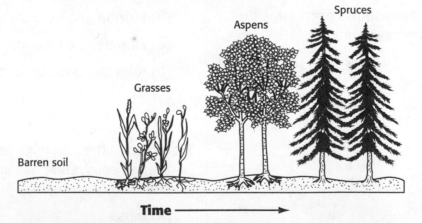

Describe what occurred at the different stages. Include how these changes affected the other organisms that live in the ecosystem.

_____

_____

© Houghton Mifflin Harcourt Publishing Company HMH Credits

Energy and Ecosystems

© Houghton Mifflin Harcourt Publishing Company (bg) ©Accent Alaska/Alamy; (inset) ©Francois Gohier/Ardea London Ltd.; (border) ©NHPA/Age Fotostock

Big Idea

Living things interact with one another in ecosystems. Energy flows from the sun to plants to animals.

I Wonder Why

Polar bears and gray whales live in the Arctic. Polar bears eat seals and fish. Why are polar bears eating a whale? *Turn the page to find out.*

Here's why While polar bears are mainly carnivores that hunt seals and fish for food, they will also scavenge the meat of dead whales that they find.

In this unit, you will explore the Big Idea, the Essential Questions, and the Investigations on the Inquiry Flipchart.

Levels of Inquiry Key ■ DIRECTED ■ GUIDED ■ INDEPENDENT

Track Your Progress

Big Idea Living things interact with one another in ecosystems. Energy flows from the sun to plants to animals.

Essential Questions

Now I Get the Big Idea!

Science Notebook

Before you begin each lesson, be sure to write your thoughts about the Essential Question.

© Houghton Mifflin Harcourt Publishing Company (tc) ©Accent Alaska/Alamy; (inset) ©Francois Gohier/Ardea London Ltd; (border) ©NDisc/Age Fotostock

Essential Question

What Are Roles of Organisms in Ecosystems?

Engage Your Brain!

Find the answer to the following question in the lesson and record it here.

Giraffes eat tree leaves to get the energy they need to live and grow. Where do trees get their energy?

_____

_____

_____

_____

Active Reading

Lesson Vocabulary

List the terms. As you learn about each one, make notes in the Interactive Glossary.

_____ _____

_____ _____

_____ _____

Signal Words: Details

Signal words show connections between ideas. *For example* and *for instance* signal examples of an idea. *Also* and *in fact* signal added facts. Active readers remember what they read because they are alert to signal words that identify examples and facts about a topic.

© Houghton Mifflin Harcourt Publishing Company (bg) ©Westend61 GmbH/Alamy

Green Machines

You know that animals depend on plants for food. Did you know that animals depend on the oxygen plants produce, too?

Active Reading As you read, underline three things plants need in order to make their own food.

The movement of gases back and forth between plants and animals is called the carbon dioxide–oxygen cycle.

The Carbon Dioxide–Oxygen Cycle

Plants use carbon dioxide to make the food that most living things need to live.

1. Plants take in carbon dioxide. Plants need carbon dioxide and energy from sunlight to make sugars they use for food. As a byproduct, plants give off oxygen.

2. When animals breathe in they take in oxygen. When animals breathe out, they give off carbon dioxide.

3. Most plants take in some oxygen. Plants use oxygen to process the sugars they make. As plants do so, they give off carbon dioxide.

© Houghton Mifflin Harcourt Publishing Company

Chloroplast

Photosynthesis

1. Carbon dioxide enters a plant through tiny holes in its leaves.

2. Water from the soil enters the plant through its roots.

3. Chloroplasts inside cells found in leaves and other green parts of the plant capture energy from sunlight.

4. Chlorophyll helps change carbon dioxide, water, and solar energy into sugar and oxygen.

The process by which plants and plantlike organisms make food is **photosynthesis** [foh•toh•SIN•thuh•sis]. Photosynthesis takes place with the help of a green molecule called **chlorophyll** [KLAWR•uh•fil]. Chlorophyll is found in structures within a plant's cell called chloroplasts. During photosynthesis, plants use the energy in sunlight to change water and carbon dioxide into sugars and oxygen. The oxygen is released from tiny holes called stomata on the plants' leaves. All of the oxygen we breathe comes from plants and plantlike organisms.

The Carbon Dioxide-Oxygen Cycle

Write the missing terms to complete the cycle.

carbon dioxide

give off

used by

_____

_____

used by

give off

oxygen

© Houghton Mifflin Harcourt Publishing Company

Eat Your Vegetables!

Have you ever heard these words? You may think that you can live without plants. But even if you skip the spinach, you still depend on plants for food.

Active Reading As you read these two pages, circle the clue words or phrases that signal a detail such as an example or an added fact.

All organisms need energy to live and grow. That energy comes from food. **Producers** are organisms that make their own food. Plants are producers. Tiny plantlike organisms called phytoplankton that live in oceans and other bodies of water are also producers.

This hippopotamus is a consumer that eats plants.

© Houghton Mifflin Harcourt Publishing Company (bg) ©XiFiPics.com/Alamy (l) ©mediacolor's/Alamy

Humans are consumers. Most people eat both producers and other consumers.

Squirrels are consumers that eat mostly producers.

Organisms that cannot make their own food are called **consumers**. Consumers eat other living things in order to get the energy they need to live and grow. Some consumers eat only plants. Some eat only animals. Others eat both plants and animals.

No matter what kind of consumer an organism is, it cannot survive without producers. For example, mice and rabbits eat only plants. Hawks eat the mice and rabbits. If there were no plants, then the mice and rabbits would die. The hawks that eat the mice and rabbits would also die. Living things depend on the food made by plants.

Consumer or Producer?

Write which are producers and consumers.

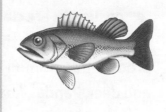

_____ _____

_____ _____

_____ _____

© Houghton Mifflin Harcourt Publishing Company (bg) ©AflPics.com/Alamy; (tr) ©Jerzy Kanarek/Alamy

You Are What You Eat

Some people eat only foods made from plants. Others eat a mix of meat and plant foods. Just like people, different kinds of consumers eat different types of food.

Active Reading As you read this page and the next, underline the definitions of herbivore, carnivore, and omnivore.

Consumers are classified into three main groups based on what they eat. *Herbivores* eat only producers. Common herbivores are mice, rabbits, and deer. Pandas, koalas, elephants, and most insects, including butterflies, are also herbivores.

Meat-eating consumers are called *carnivores*. When you think of a carnivore, you might think of the lion shown here. But not all carnivores are mammals. Penguins are birds that eat only fish. Ladybugs are beetles that eat other insects.

This snake is a carnivore. It eats other animals for food.

Lions are carnivores that eat other animals such as zebras and antelopes.

© Houghton Mifflin Harcourt Publishing Company (t) ©Justin Peach/Image Quest Marine/Alamy (b) ©WILDLIFE GmbH/Alamy (t) ©Lawren Lu/Cutcaster.com

Consumers that eat both plants and animals are called *omnivores*. Forest-dwelling box turtles, for example, eat strawberries, blackberries, and mushrooms. The box turtles also eat insects and spiders.

Carnivores and omnivores that hunt and eat other animals are also called *predators*. The animals that predators hunt are called *prey*. The numbers of predators and prey are linked. As a predator population increases, it consumes more and more prey. Eventually the predators consume so much prey that the prey animals become scarce. The predators have trouble finding food. Some predators may move away. Others die. With fewer predators to eat them, prey animals have a chance to increase in number again.

A toucan is an omnivore. It will eat fruit, insects, snakes, and just about anything else it can find.

Do the Math!
Interpret a Line Graph

The graph shows the number of lynx and snowshoe hares in an area over time.

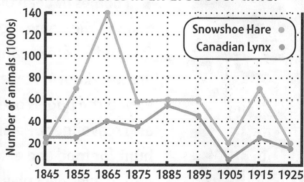

How many hare and lynx were there?

	in 1865	in 1905
hare	_____	_____
lynx	_____	_____

What do you notice about the relationship of predators to prey?

_____

_____

_____

Break It Down, Clean It Up

Just as garbage collectors remove the garbage people throw away, nature has its own cleanup crew.

Active Reading As you read these two pages, underline the main roles of scavengers and decomposers.

Have you ever thought about what happens to the bodies of dead plants and animals? When plants and animals die, some organisms in the environment eat them for food. These organisms are called *scavengers*. Vultures are well-known scavengers. These birds are famous for eating the bodies of dead animals. Some carnivores are also scavengers. Polar bears, sharks, and leopards both hunt for food and eat dead animals that they find. Scavengers play an important role in cleaning up the environment.

Millipedes are scavengers. They eat dead plant matter that they find in the soil.

Crabs scavenge algae, fungus, and decaying matter from the ocean floor.

© Houghton Mifflin Harcourt Publishing Company (l) ©Eureka/Alamy; (c) ©Justin Lewis/UpperCut Images/Alamy; (t) ©Bernd Zoller/imagebroker/Alamy

Many vultures don't have feathers on their heads. This helps these birds keep clean when they stick their heads inside the dead animals they scavenge.

▶ Explain what you think an ecosystem would look like without scavengers and decomposers.

_____

_____

_____

_____

_____

_____

_____

Scavengers aren't the only living things that clean up dead organisms. **Decomposers** are organisms that break down, or decompose, wastes and the remains of dead organisms. This process returns nutrients to the soil, air, and water. Bacteria are microscopic decomposers that use chemicals called enzymes [EHN•zymz] to break down the last remains of plants and animals and animal wastes. In so doing, they obtain the energy they need to carry out their life processes.

Fungi are decomposers that release enzymes. These enzymes break down dead matter, releasing nutrients that enrich the soil.

© Houghton Mifflin Harcourt Publishing Company   (bg) ©Justin Lewis/UpperCut Images/Alamy; (t) ©Bernd Zoller/imagebroker/Alamy; (cr) ©imagebroker/Alamy

A Starring Role

Every organism plays an important part in its ecosystem.

Scientists study living things in their environment to better understand how these organisms relate to one another. Some species cannot survive if their habitat changes even in small ways. Tiger salamanders, for example, live in wetlands. Scientists know that if the number of salamanders in a wetland goes down, it is a sign that the wetland has been polluted or damaged .

Some species, such as the Bengal tiger of South Asia, are in danger of dying out. Governments work to protect these species as well as their habitats. When a species' habitat is protected, all the organisms within it are protected, too. Kelp forests are rich ocean habitats where many fish have their young. Kelp forests are found throughout the world in cold, coastal waters. Protecting these forests helps protect the organisms that depend on them, in the same way that protecting the animals that live in the kelp forests helps protect the forests themselves.

▶ Think of a species that is common in your area. What might happen if this species suddenly disappeared?

_____

_____

_____

_____

_____

Tiger salamander

© Houghton Mifflin Harcourt Publishing Company (bg) ©Mark Conlin/Alamy (b) ©Michelle Gilders/Alamy

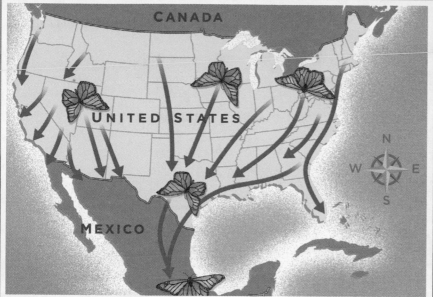

Monarch butterflies migrate south to warm climates for the winter. Over their lifetime, monarchs live in many different ecosystems. Conservationists have worked to protect the areas where these insects live. Doing so also protects other organisms that share the same area with the monarchs.

Sea turtles eat small animals that they find floating in seaweed. Conservationists have focused on protecting sea turtles. That in turn helps protect both their habitats and the organisms that live there.

Sea urchins feed on kelp. If there are too many urchins, they can completely destroy the forest. Sea otters eat sea urchins and help keep kelp beds healthy.

© Houghton Mifflin Harcourt Publishing Company (l) ©Mark Conlin/Alamy (b) ©Marvin Dembinsky Photo Associates/Alamy, (r) ©Richard Ellis/Getty Images; (bg) ©Mark Conlin/Alamy

Sum It Up!

When you're done, use the answer key to check and revise your work.

Match each picture to its description.

1

2

3

A Omnivores are consumers that eat both plants and animals.

B Carnivores and omnivores that hunt and eat other animals are also called predators.

C Plants make food through the process of photosynthesis.

Summarize

The idea web below summarizes the lesson. Complete the web.

Roles of Organisms

A 4. _____ makes food for itself and other animals.

Bacteria are 5. _____ that break down dead matter and wastes.

Carnivores are consumers that 7. _____ .

The number of predators tends to rise when there is a rise in the number of 6. _____ .

Answer Key: 1. C 2. B 3. A 4. producer 5. decomposers 6. prey 7. eat other animals

© Houghton Mifflin Harcourt Publishing Company

Word Play

1 Unscramble each group of letters to spell an important term from the lesson. Use the clues to help you.

Name _____

1. breehivor

_ _ _ _ _ _ _ _ _

An animal that eats only producers

2. toradrep

_ _ _ _ _ _ _ _

A living thing that hunts and eats other animals

3. reyp

_ _ _ _

An animal that is hunted by other animals

4. pocodemser

_ _ _ _ _ _ _ _ _ _

An organism that breaks down wastes and plant and animal remains and returns their nutrients to the soil

5. evormoni

_ _ _ _ _ _ _ _

An animal that eats plants and other animals

6. vengescra

_ _ _ _ _ _ _ _ _

An organism that eats dead plants or animals

7. clyophohlrl

_ _ _ _ _ _ _ _ _ _ _

A green molecule that enables plants to turn water, carbon dioxide, and sunlight into sugars

8. rumcosne

_ _ _ _ _ _ _ _

An organism that cannot make its own food

Bonus: List five omnivores.

_____

_____

_____

_____

© Houghton Mifflin Harcourt Publishing Company

Apply Concepts

2 Complete the sentences to identify two roles of decomposers in an ecosystem.

a. Decomposers break down the remains of _____ and the wastes of _____.

b. Decomposers return _____ to the soil.

3 All scavengers are consumers, but not all consumers are scavengers. True or false?

_____

Explain your answer.

_____

_____

_____

_____

4 Circle the activity that occurs when plants make sugars for food.

Plants take in oxygen and give off carbon dioxide.

Animals take in oxygen and give off carbon dioxide.

Plants take in carbon dioxide and give off oxygen.

5 Label the consumers and producers.

_____ _____ _____ _____

Take It Home! List all the plants and animals your family eats today in a two-column chart. Don't forget to count the plant materials that make up bread and pasta! Are the members of your family herbivores, carnivores, or omnivores?

© Houghton Mifflin Harcourt Publishing Company

Meet the Environment Detectives

Erika Zavaleta

Erika Zavaleta is an ecologist in California. She studies the links between the environment and people. Cities grow and climates change. These changes make it hard for some plants and animals to survive. Part of Erika Zavaleta's job is figuring out good ways for people, plants, and animals to live in harmony.

Recently, Erika Zavaleta has studied oak trees. Fires and other disasters can kill a whole forest of these trees. She is studying the best ways to help new trees grow after such a disaster.

Peter & Rosemary Grant

Peter and Rosemary Grant study animal adaptation. On the Galápagos Islands off the coast of South America, they study how birds called finches change over time. They are most interested in changes in the birds' beaks. The Grants have found that beak shape and size change when the environment changes.

During severe droughts many birds die of starvation. When the only seeds remaining on the ground are large, hard seeds, only the birds with the biggest beaks can crack them. They survive and the small-beaked birds die. The next year, the big-beaked birds produce big-beaked young like themselves.

© Houghton Mifflin Harcourt Publishing Company (bkg) ©Danita Delimont/Alamy (t) ©Ambient Images Inc./Alamy (b) ©Frans Lanting/Corbis

305

Now You Look For Clues

Answer the questions below about the scientists you just read about.

What kind of problems in the environment does Erika Zavaleta study?

_____

_____

_____

_____

What measurements do you think the Grants made as part of their studies?

_____

_____

_____

_____

What have these scientists learned about plant and animal adaptation?

_____

_____

_____

_____

_____

© Houghton Mifflin Harcourt Publishing Company   (bkgd) ©GIPhotostock/Photo Researchers, Inc.; (ladybug) ©Alamy

How Does Energy Move Through Ecosystems?

🧠 Engage Your Brain!

Find the answer to the following question in the lesson and record it here.

There are many kinds of animals at this watering hole. Why aren't they running away from each other?

_____

_____

_____

_____

Active Reading

Lesson Vocabulary
List the terms. As you learn about each one, make notes in the Interactive Glossary.

_____

_____

_____

Using Diagrams
Diagrams add information to text that appears on the page with them. Active readers pause their reading to review diagrams and decide how the information in them adds to what is provided in the running text.

© Houghton Mifflin Harcourt Publishing Company   (c) ©Clem Haagner/Photo Researchers, Inc.

Food Chains

From producers to consumers to decomposers, the food chain never stops.

Active Reading As you read these two pages, underline all the important members of a food chain.

Tundra Food Chain

The tundra is the coldest, driest ecosystem on Earth. Short summers mean little plant life grows here. Many animals either migrate or hibernate during the long, cold winters.

Reindeer moss uses energy from the sun to make and store sugars. Producers, such as reindeer moss, form the base of tundra food chains.

Caribou are first-level consumers. These herbivores eat reindeer moss and other producers to get energy for their life functions.

Wolves are second-level consumers. They are predators. Animals, such as caribou, are their prey.

© Houghton Mifflin Harcourt Publishing Company (bg) ©Hickwinkel/Alamy; (t) ©JCHIRO/Getty Images; (l) ©Patrick Owen Photography/Alamy; (c) ©Steve Allen Travel Photography/Alamy; (r) ©Roy Corral/Getty Images

The transfer of food energy from one organism to the next in an ecological community is called a **food chain**. Almost every food chain begins when producers capture energy from the sun. Through photosynthesis, producers convert this light energy into chemical energy in sugars, which they use for food. Food not used for life processes is stored in the tissues of the producers and then passed on to herbivores that eat the producers. Herbivores are first-level consumers.

Next in the food chain are carnivores and omnivores, the second-level consumers. Second-level consumers eat herbivores and receive the food energy stored in their bodies. Third-level consumers eat second-level consumers. Scavengers may be second- or third-level consumers, as they eat organisms that have died.

Decomposers are the final link in any food chain. They get energy as they break down the remains of dead plants and animals and return nutrients to the soil.

▶ Number the pictures to show their position in a food chain.

Scavengers, such as this Arctic gull, feed on the dead bodies of caribou, wolves, and other animals. Fungi and bacteria do the final cleanup work as they decompose the final remains of tundra organisms.

© Houghton Mifflin Harcourt Publishing Company (tc) ©Birgit Koch/imagebroker/Alamy; (l) ©C. Huetter/Arco Images GmbH/Alamy; (c) ©blickwinkel/Alamy;

Food Webs

Like a spiderweb held together by many connecting threads, the paths in a food web show the feeding relationships among species in a community.

Active Reading As you read, underline the information that helps you understand the food web diagram.

You don't eat just one kind of food, and neither do organisms in food chains. Each consumer has a variety of choices when it comes to its next meal. A **food web** shows how food chains overlap. In other words, it shows what eats what. Look at the forest food web on the next page. Both the mouse and the insect eat parts of the pine tree or its seeds. A snake can eat a mouse or a salamander. All of these living things eventually become food for decomposers. Decomposers return nutrients to soil. These nutrients, in turn, are used by producers to make food.

Arrows in the web point in the direction that energy moves. Find the acorns and the mouse. Which way does the arrow point?

It points from the acorns to the mouse. Energy moves from producer to consumer when the mouse eats the acorns.

Predators limit the number of animals below them in a food web. If snakes were removed from this forest food web, the number of mice would increase. More mice mean that more plants would be eaten. Eventually, the mice might run out of food and begin to die off. This would affect the hawks and other living things that eat mice. All of the organisms in a food web are interdependent.

▶ In the forest food web, trace two overlapping food chains that include the snake. Make the path of each food chain a different color.

© Houghton Mifflin Harcourt Publishing Company

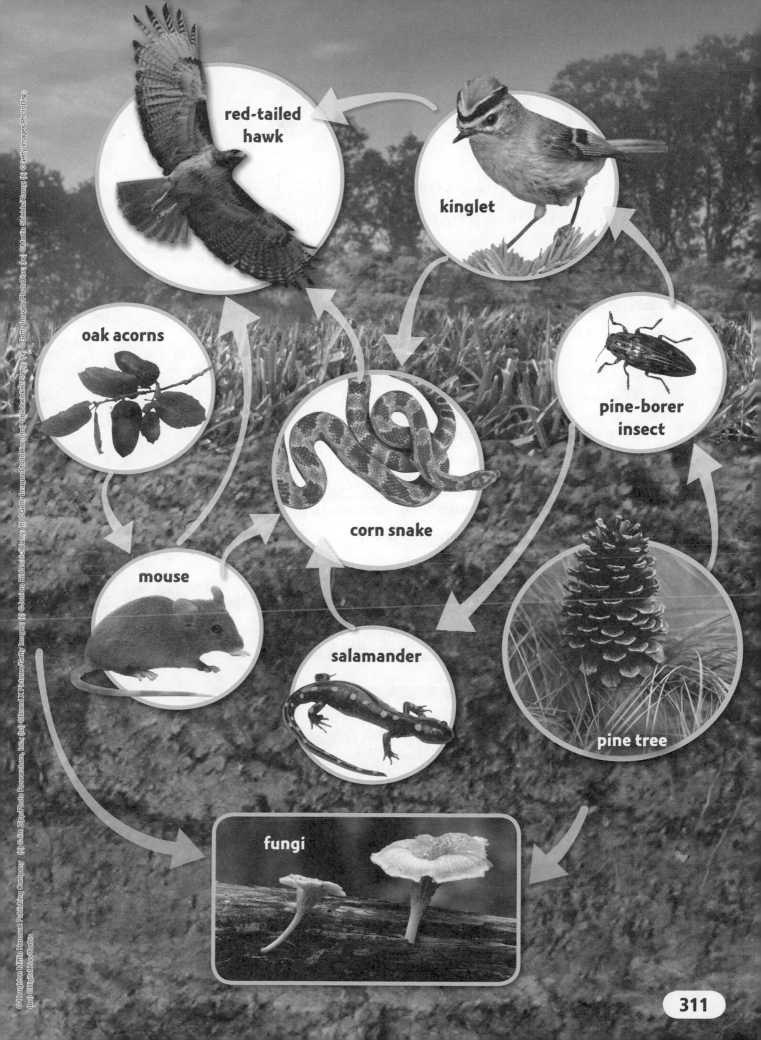

red-tailed hawk

kinglet

oak acorns

pine-borer insect

corn snake

mouse

salamander

pine tree

fungi

© Houghton Mifflin Harcourt Publishing Company (t) ©Jim Zipp/Photo Researchers, Inc.; (cl) ©Brand X Pictures/Getty Images; (c) ©Juniors Bildarchiv/Alamy; (tl) ©Getty Images/PhotoDisc; (l) ©Getty Images/PhotoDisc; (bc) ©Martin Shields/Alamy; (b) ©Getty Images/PhotoDisc; (cr) ©Chickwinkel/Alamy; (br) ©Digital Zoo/Corbis

At the Top

It takes a lot of grass to support a hawk at the top of a food chain. Although hawks don't eat grass, the energy they use comes from the grass at the bottom.

Active Reading As you read, circle the lesson vocabulary each time it is used.

An **energy pyramid** shows how much energy passes from one organism to another up a food chain. The organisms in a layer of the pyramid feed on those in a lower layer. Because it takes many producers to support a smaller number of consumers, producers in the bottom layer are the most numerous group.

Third-level consumers like the leopard seal, a predator at the top of this energy pyramid, have the least amount of energy available to them. That is why their population is small.

Second-level consumers, such as octopuses and salmon, feed on first-level consumers below them in the pyramid. Because less energy is available to them, they are fewer.

Krill, clams, and herring are first-level consumers. They consume phytoplankton. Some first-level consumers eat millions of tiny phytoplankton every day.

Producers called phytoplankton are the base of this ocean energy pyramid.

© Houghton Mifflin Harcourt Publishing Company (cs) ©WaterFrame/Alamy

Do the Math!
Calculate Units

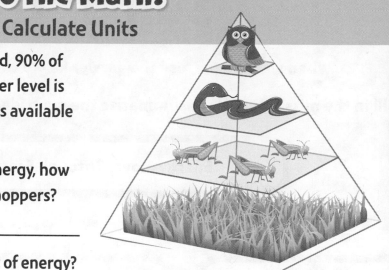

At each level of an energy pyramid, 90% of the energy received from the lower level is used for life processes. Only 10% is available to be passed upward.

If the grasses have 100 units of energy, how much can be passed to the grasshoppers?

_____

Why do the snakes only get 1 unit of energy?

_____

_____

BONUS How much energy is available to the owls that eat the snakes? Show your work.

_____

Environmental changes can affect energy flow in an energy pyramid. Suppose the number of salmon is reduced because of overfishing. Seals that eat the salmon may go hungry. They may even starve. Without salmon to eat them, the krill population could increase at a rapid rate. Such a large number of krill could then eat up its own food source as well as that of other species. One change in the flow of energy through an ecosystem affects every species in the ecosystem. Whatever happens at one level affects the energy available in the rest of the pyramid.

© Houghton Mifflin Harcourt Publishing Company (bg) ©WaterFrame/Alamy

Sum It Up!

When you're done, use the answer key to check and revise your work.

Fill in the missing words to summarize the main ideas of the lesson.

Energy Moves Through Ecosystems

Food Chains

The first organisms in a food chain are

1. _____.

Herbivores are the

2. _____-level consumers, and

3. _____

and 4. _____ are the second- and third-level consumers.

5. _____ are the final organisms in all food chains. They recycle materials by breaking down plant and animal remains, thereby returning nutrients to the environment.

Food Webs

A food web shows how food chains

6. _____.

Arrows show the direction of

7. _____ transfer through the web.

Energy Pyramids

Most of the energy in an ecosystem is present in the

8. _____.

At each level, organisms use

9. _____ percent of the available energy for life processes. Only

10. _____ percent of the energy is passed from one level to the next level above.

314

Answer Key: 1. producers 2. first 3. carnivores 4. omnivores 5. Decomposers 6. overlap 7. energy 8. producers 9. 90 10. 10

© Houghton Mifflin Harcourt Publishing Company

Name _____

Word Play

1 Unscramble the terms. The first letter of each term is in the center of the target. Use the definitions to help you.

1.  _____ A diagram that shows overlapping food chains (2 words)

2. 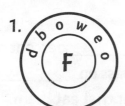 _____ Plants and some plantlike microorganisms

3. 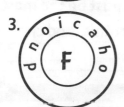 _____ A single path that shows how food energy moves from one organism to the next in an ecosystem (2 words)

4.  _____ Animals that eat plants and animals

5. 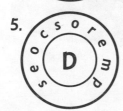 _____ Organisms that break down the nutrient remains of dead things

6.  _____ A diagram that shows how energy is used, stored, and passed on in each level of a food chain (2 words)

© Houghton Mifflin Harcourt Publishing Company

Apply Concepts

2 This food chain is scrambled. Rewrite the links in the correct order.

hawk ➡ bacteria ➡ corn ➡ mouse

_____ ➡ _____ ➡ _____ ➡ _____

3 Complete the facts about the energy pyramid below.

wolves

deer

shrubs

a. The shrubs use _____ percent of their energy and pass on _____ percent to the deer that eat them.

b. Which organisms get the least amount of energy?

_____

c. Which organisms must be the most plentiful to support this food chain?

_____

4 Many food chains used the sun's energy to produce the food in this sandwich. The cheese came from milk from a cow that ate grass that took energy from the sun, for example. Fill in the other chains.

sun _____ ➡ you

sun _____ ➡ you

sun _____ ➡ you

© Houghton Mifflin Harcourt Publishing Company

5 Label the role of each organism. Some have more than one role.
Use these terms: *producer, herbivore, carnivore, first-level consumer, second-level consumer, decomposer.*

_____   _____   _____   _____

_____   _____   _____   _____

6 A drought has affected an ecosystem. Many plants have died for lack of water. What do you think will happen to the other organisms in the area?

_____

_____

_____

_____

_____

_____

_____

_____

_____

© Houghton Mifflin Harcourt Publishing Company

7

Draw arrows to show what the hawk would eat.

Identify one complete food chain in this food web in the correct order.

_____

_____

Explain what might happen if the grass in this food web were to disappear.

_____

_____

_____

_____

Take It Home!

At your next meal, make a game with your family to identify the food chains that led to the different foods you are eating. What is the longest chain? The shortest chain?

© Houghton Mifflin Harcourt Publishing Company

Designing a New Dog

People modify animals for a variety of reasons. Selective breeding is the process of breeding animals so their offspring inherit certain desired traits. People have selectively bred dogs for many centuries. Now there are more than 200 breeds of dogs, each with its own characteristics.

The dog's primary ancestor is the wolf.

It's uncertain whether ancient people started keeping dogs for companionship or as work animals. But we know dogs and people have shared a bond for thousands of years.

Working dogs were historically bred to do certain jobs, such as hunt, haul things, or herd livestock.

Today dogs are bred mainly for companionship and sport.

Critical Thinking

How has selective breeding of dogs changed over time?

_____

_____

_____

© Houghton Mifflin Harcourt Publishing Company (cr) ©Roman/The Bridgeman Art Library/Getty Images (bl) ©Bkmedia.de/Alamy (cl) ©Corbis (bl) ©Kristine Jackson/Flickr/Getty Images (c) ©David Shaw/Alamy Images (t) ©Robert Adrian Hillman/Alamy

S.T.E.M.

continued

In nature, an animal's environment determines whether it survives to breed successfully. People control the environments of the dogs they breed, so people can choose to keep traits that might not have been passed on in nature.

Draw a dog that might lead a visually impaired person.

How do this dog's physical and behavioral characteristics help it do its job?

_____

_____

Draw a dog that might help to locate people after an earthquake.

How do this dog's physical features help it do its job?

_____

_____

Dogs have been bred for many reasons. What kind of new dog breed would you like to develop? What traits would your new dog need? What skills would you teach it?

_____

_____

Build On It!

Rise to the engineering design challenge—complete **Improvise It: Measuring Decomposer Activity** in the Inquiry Flipchart.

© Houghton Mifflin Harcourt Publishing Company   (t) ©Hans Stod日yto/Getty Images; (t) ©Robert Adrian Hillman/Alamy

Name _____

Essential Question

What Role Do Decomposers Play?

Set a Purpose

How do you think decomposers change materials?

_____

_____

_____

_____

Write a statement summarizing how you think mold changes the food it grows on.

_____

_____

_____

_____

Think About the Procedure

What are different observations you can make about the appearance of the bread?

_____

_____

_____

Why do we spray one of the bread slices with water and not the other?

_____

_____

_____

Record Your Data

In the space below, make a table in which you record your observations.

© Houghton Mifflin Harcourt Publishing Company

Draw Conclusions

In the space below, draw a picture of the appearance of breads *A* and *B* during the last day of your investigation.

Did your observations indicate that mold is a decomposer? Explain.

Analyze and Extend

1. **How did the mold change the bread?**

2. **Where do you think mold gets its nutrients from?**

3. **Did spraying the bread with water have any effect on how fast the mold grew? Explain.**

4. **What do you think would happen to the bread if you continued to let the mold grow on it?**

5. **Use your observations to describe the role of decomposers in the environment.**

6. **Think of other questions you would like to ask about decomposers.**

© Houghton Mifflin Harcourt Publishing Company

Name _____

Vocabulary Review

Use the terms in the box to complete the sentences.

> chlorophyll
> consumers
> decomposers
> energy pyramid
> food chain
> food web
> photosynthesis
> producers

1. A diagram that shows that energy is lost at each level in a food chain is called a(n) _____.

2. Organisms that break down wastes and the remains of dead organisms are called _____.

3. Organisms that do not make their own food are called _____.

4. A network of overlapping food chains is called a(n) _____.

5. Organisms that make their own food are called _____.

6. Most plants contain a green, food-producing molecule called _____.

7. The transfer of food energy from one organism to the next is called a(n) _____.

8. Plants make their own food through a process called _____.

© Houghton Mifflin Harcourt Publishing Company   HMH Credits

Science Concepts

Fill in the letter of the choice that best answers the question.

9. Renata was studying mountain lions like this one.

She made a list of the ways she could classify this animal. Which is Renata's correct list?

Ⓐ omnivore, prey, consumer

Ⓑ carnivore, predator, consumer

Ⓒ herbivore, predator, producer

Ⓓ carnivore, prey, consumer

10. Marc gets a pet rabbit for his birthday. He looks online and learns that rabbits are herbivores. Which of the following foods might he feed his new pet?

Ⓐ lettuce

Ⓑ bacteria

Ⓒ meat scraps

Ⓓ dead insects

11. Which of these is the final link in every food chain?

Ⓐ producers

Ⓑ decomposers

Ⓒ first-level consumers

Ⓓ second-level consumers

12. This diagram shows the movement of food energy through an ecosystem.

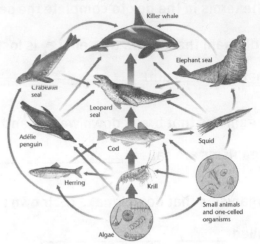

Which statement is the **best** description of this diagram?

Ⓐ It is an energy pyramid.

Ⓑ It is a forest food chain.

Ⓒ It is an ocean food web.

Ⓓ It is a chart of third-level consumers.

13. Which is the initial source of energy in most ecosystems?

Ⓐ sunlight

Ⓑ decomposers

Ⓒ nutrients in soil

Ⓓ oxygen in the air

14. Pablo has a hamburger and a salad for lunch. What does this tell you about him?

Ⓐ He is a producer.

Ⓑ He is a scavenger.

Ⓒ He is a herbivore.

Ⓓ He is an omnivore.

© Houghton Mifflin Harcourt Publishing Company   HMH Credits

15. Plants and animals are interdependent. Plants rely on animals to produce carbon dioxide. What do plants produce for animals?

Ⓐ food and oxygen

Ⓑ sunshine and rain

Ⓒ carbon dioxide and food

Ⓓ herbivores and carnivores

16. An ecosystem includes this food chain.

pine seed → mouse → snake → hawk

What would happen if all the mice died from a disease?

Ⓐ The snakes would eat pine seeds instead of mice.

Ⓑ The producers would stop making food.

Ⓒ The population of snakes would increase.

Ⓓ The population of snakes would decrease.

17. A shark is preparing to eat a fish swimming in front of it. What is the **best** way to describe these two animals?

Ⓐ predator and prey

Ⓑ producer and consumer

Ⓒ herbivore and omnivore

Ⓓ scavenger and producer

18. Some animals are known for their specific food-gathering behaviors. Vultures are examples of which of the following?

Ⓐ predator

Ⓒ scavenger

Ⓑ producer

Ⓓ decomposer

19. Halie is doing a report on photosynthesis. She draws a diagram to represent the materials used by plants to make food and the byproducts that this process produces. Which is the correct diagram?

Ⓐ sunlight + carbon dioxide + water → sugar + oxygen

Ⓑ sunlight + oxygen + water → sugar + carbon dioxide

Ⓒ sunlight + carbon dioxide + sugar → water + oxygen

Ⓓ sunlight + oxygen + sugar → carbon dioxide + water

20. Terrell notices that a tree in his backyard has fungi growing on one side. What is the role of fungi, and what are these organisms doing?

Ⓐ Fungi are producers. They are making their own food.

Ⓑ Fungi are scavengers. They are eating the dead parts of the tree.

Ⓒ Fungi are producers. They are providing the tree with food.

Ⓓ Fungi are decomposers. They are decomposing a part of the tree.

© Houghton Mifflin Harcourt Publishing Company   HMH Credits

Apply Inquiry and Review the Big Idea

Write the answers to these questions.

21. This diagram shows various organisms that live in the same ecosystem.

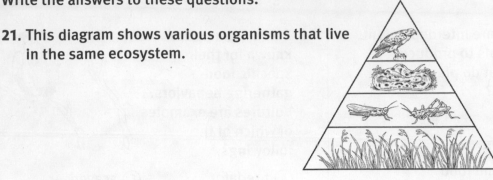

a. What is this diagram called, and what is its purpose? _____

_____

b. Describe a food-chain relationship between the four organisms shown. _____

_____

c. Suppose all the organisms on the third level died out. What would be the effect on the organisms on the levels above and below? _____

_____

_____

22. This diagram shows the carbon dioxide–oxygen cycle.

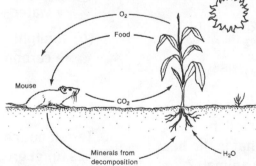

Explain the cycle, the gases involved, how they are used, and how they move in the cycle.

a. Plants in sunlight: _____

_____

b. Animals at any time: _____

_____

c. Plants at any time: _____

_____

© Houghton Mifflin Harcourt Publishing Company HMH Credits

Natural Resources

Big Idea

Natural resources are essential to life and must be used with care.

I Wonder Why

Rice can be grown almost anywhere, even on steep hills. Why do people build terraces on which to grow rice? *Turn the page to find out.*

© Houghton Mifflin Harcourt Publishing Company   (bg) ©Keren Su/China Span/Alamy; (inset) ©JTB Photo Communications, Inc./Alamy; (border) ©NDisc/Age Fotestock

Here's why Rice fields are kept very wet after they are planted. The water makes sure that only the strongest plants survive. Terraces allow farmers to flood the fields and use fewer chemicals to control weeds.

In this unit, you will explore the Big Idea, the Essential Questions, and the Investigations on the Inquiry Flipchart.

Levels of Inquiry Key ■ DIRECTED ■ GUIDED ■ INDEPENDENT

Big Idea Natural resources are essential to life and must be used with care.

Essential Questions

Now I Get the Big Idea!

Science Notebook

Before you begin each lesson, be sure to write your thoughts about the Essential Question.

© Houghton Mifflin Harcourt Publishing Company (b) ©Karen Su/China Span/Alamy (inset) ©JTB Photo Communications, Inc./Alamy (border) ©NDisc/Age Fotostock

Essential Question

How Do People Use Resources?

Engage Your Brain!

As you read the lesson, look for the answer to the following question and record it here.

What types of resources do you see here? Which type is more easily replaced?

_____

_____

_____

_____

_____

Active Reading

Lesson Vocabulary

List the terms. As you learn about each one, make notes in the Interactive Glossary.

_____

_____

_____

_____

Compare and Contrast

In this lesson, you'll read about renewable and nonrenewable resources. As you read about resources, ask yourself how they are alike and different. Active readers stay focused on comparisons and contrasts when they ask themselves, How are these things alike? How are they different?

© Houghton Mifflin Harcourt Publishing Company

Natural Resources

Water, wind, sunshine, soil, coal—these may not seem to have much in common. However, they are *all* natural resources. Every living thing uses natural resources each day.

Wind, or moving air, is a renewable energy resource. Wind turns this turbine to produce electricity.

Active Reading As you read these two pages, draw boxes around the names of the two kinds of resources that are being compared.

Did you use water this morning when you brushed your teeth? Did you eat some fruit with your breakfast? If you did, then you used a natural resource! A **natural resource** is anything useful or necessary for living beings that occurs naturally on Earth. Human beings depend on natural resources all the time. You use many of them without even thinking about it.

Scientists classify resources into two groups. **Renewable resources** are resources that nature can replace when they are used. New trees grow to replace trees that get cut down. The water cycle constantly replaces water. Air, plants, animals, wind, and sunlight are other renewable resources.

Farmers use natural resources such as soil, air, water, and sunlight to produce food.

© Houghton Mifflin Harcourt Publishing Company   (t) ©Corbis; (b) ©David Frazier/Corbis

Know Your Resources

Identify each resource as renewable or nonrenewable. Explain your answer.

_____   _____   _____   _____

_____   _____   _____   _____

Nonrenewable resources are resources that nature cannot replace after they are used. Someday they may disappear completely. Minerals and soil are nonrenewable resources. If used carefully, soil can last a long time, but if it is destroyed, it cannot be replaced.

Fossil fuels are also nonrenewable resources. A fossil fuel is an energy source formed deep inside Earth from the remains of organisms that lived long ago. Coal, natural gas, and oil are fossil fuels. Most of the energy we use comes from fossil fuels. Fossil fuels not only power cars and trucks;

they are burned in many energy stations to produce electricity.

Natural resources are used to make products of all sorts. Every product you use started out as a natural resource.

Some oil is pumped from deep below the ocean floor.

© Houghton Mifflin Harcourt Publishing Company (b) ©David Frazier/Corbis; (br) ©Kim Steele/Getty Images

Resources on the Move

OIL

The United States and many other countries produce oil. Tanker ships and pipelines move oil to places where it is needed.

Where do natural resources come from? Some occur near where you live. Other resources occur in other parts of the world and are transported long distances to get to the places where they are used.

Active Reading As you read these pages, find and underline the definitions of *import* and *export*.

Wyoming is tops for coal production. Coal is mainly used to generate electricity.

Iowa grows about 18 percent of the corn in the U.S. Corn is now used to make a fossil-fuel alternative.

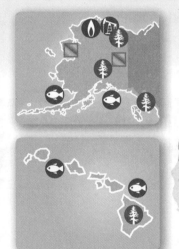

	Farming		Fishing
	Ranching		Gold
	Coal		Granite
	Copper		Hydroelectric
	Iron ore		Oil
	Limestone		Silver
	Logging		Uranium
	Natural Gas		

Where's the beef? You can find a lot of it in Texas! 17 percent of beef cattle in the U.S. are raised there.

Next time you enjoy your favorite rice cereal, think of Arkansas. This is where nearly half of all rice is grown in the U.S.

© Houghton Mifflin Harcourt Publishing Company   (tl) ©artpartner-images/Alamy

Have you ever visited a farmers' market? Local farmers bring their goods to the market soon after crops are harvested or products are made. Customers come to the market to buy fresh goods that are produced nearby. Goods sold at a farmers' market only travel short distances between where they are produced and where they are sold.

Most natural resources travel long distances between the places where they occur and the places where they are needed. For example, the United States uses more oil than it produces. The United States must import oil. An *import* is something brought into a country to be sold or traded. Other countries produce more oil than they use. These countries can sell the extra oil they produce. They export some of it to the United States. An *export* is something sent out of a country to be sold or traded.

Most imported oil arrives in the United States on huge tanker ships. These ships can carry large quantities of the natural resource. When the oil arrives in the United States, it is converted into fuel and other products. These products are carried around the country in pipelines and on trains and tanker trucks.

Huge oil tankers move large amounts of oil across long distances.

Do the Math!
Interpret a Circle Graph

This graph shows the amount of oil produced in different parts of the world. Each section shows production in one region. Label each section with the correct region and percentage.

- Middle East: 30%
- North America: 20%
- Eurasia (former Soviet Union): 15%
- Central and South America: 10%
- Asia and Oceania: 10%
- Africa: 10%
- Europe: 5%

©Houghton Mifflin Harcourt Publishing Company (b) ©Richard Sheppard/Alamy

Using Resources at Home

You use natural resources all day every day—without even realizing it!

When you wake up in the morning, what do you do? You may eat breakfast, brush your teeth, and listen to the radio.

Each of these activities uses natural resources. The food that you eat and the water you use are renewable resources. Your radio uses electricity that may have been generated from the nonrenewable resource coal. The metals, plastics, and other materials the radio is made of also come from nonrenewable resources.

People do not use most natural resources in their original form. Although you can eat some fruits and vegetables just as they are picked, most foods are cooked. Every product you use was made from one or more natural resources. For example, the paper you use to print your homework probably comes from trees. What about the plastic fork you used to eat lunch? Plastic can be made from oil. How many ways can you find resources being used in this home?

© Houghton Mifflin Harcourt Publishing Company

Water-saving products such as a drip irrigation system can help your family use less water.

A computer runs on electricity. Electrical energy is often generated in energy stations by the burning of coal. The computer itself is made of minerals and plastic.

In the bathroom, you use water to keep clean. You also use electricity to run appliances.

Name That Resource

Pick a room in your home. Describe how natural resources are used in that room.

_____

_____

_____

_____

_____

_____

© Houghton Mifflin Harcourt Publishing Company

What's That Smell?

Smog, trash, and dirty water are ways our use of natural resources can harm the environment.

Active Reading As you read these pages, draw a circle around the definition of *pollution*.

Smoke from resources burned by factories contributes to air pollution.

Cities and homes often draw water from underground. Waste from human activities can pollute underground water sources.

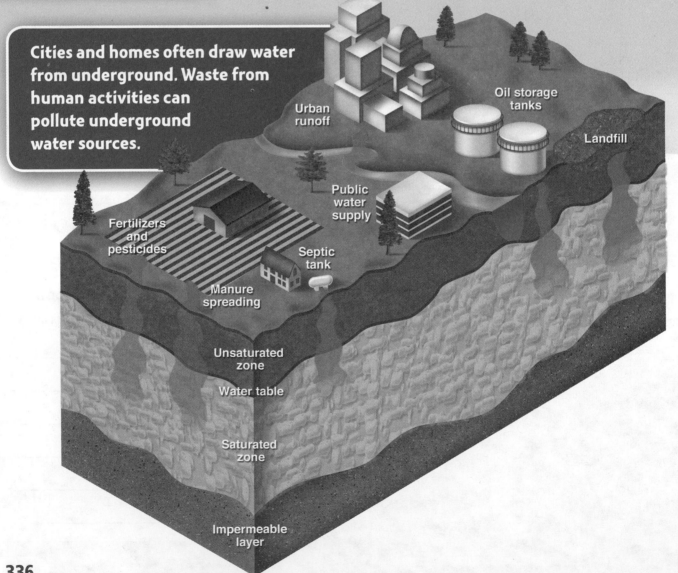

Urban runoff

Oil storage tanks

Landfill

Fertilizers and pesticides

Public water supply

Septic tank

Manure spreading

Unsaturated zone

Water table

Saturated zone

Impermeable layer

© Houghton Mifflin Harcourt Publishing Company (t) ©James Schwabel/Alamy

© Houghton Mifflin Harcourt Publishing Company   (tl) ©Daniel Dempster Photography/Alamy

Natural resources help people do and make many things, but the use of natural resources can also cause pollution. **Pollution** is the contamination of air, water, or soil by materials that are harmful to living things. Air, water, and soil are some of the most important natural resources.

Most air pollution comes from the burning of fossil fuels. Cars and trucks are the greatest source of air pollution, but many factories and energy stations also pollute. Air pollution can harm the health of people, plants, and animals.

Water can become polluted when trash, eroded soil, or chemicals from manufacturing, farming, and landfills get into rivers, lakes, and oceans. These pollutants can also enter groundwater. Water pollution harms organisms, including people, that need water to live.

Soil can be polluted, too. Chemicals leaking from storage sites or runoff from roads and parking lots can soak into soils, making them unusable for growing crops.

Pollution Affects Earth

Write two types of pollution in the *Effect* box. In the *Cause* box, explain the cause of each.

Cause	Effect

Sum It Up!

When you're done, use the answer key to check and revise your work.

Read the summary statements. Then draw a line to match each statement with the appropriate picture.

1 Renewable resources are resources that nature can replace after they are used.

2 Some renewable resources can be used to generate electrical energy.

3 Natural resources can be imported and exported throughout the world.

4 Pollution occurs when waste and chemicals harm land, air, and water.

Summarize

Fill in the Venn diagram by writing the correct number of each item in the appropriate category.

5. Natural resources

6. Air

7. Water

8. Soil

9. Fossil fuels

10. Minerals

11. Plants

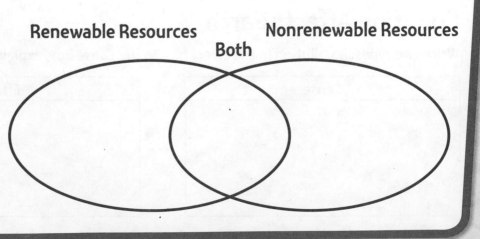

Renewable Resources   Both   Nonrenewable Resources

© Houghton Mifflin Harcourt Publishing Company

Answer Key: 1. (farm) **2.** (wind turbines) **3.** (cargo ship) **4.** (factory)
Venn diagram: Renewable Resources—6, 7, 11; **Both**—5; **Nonrenewable Resources**—8, 9, 10

Name _____

Word Play

1 Use the words in the box to complete each sentence. Then unscramble the circled letters to solve the riddle at the bottom.

chemicals	food	landfills	nonrenewable
replaced	pollution*	resource	wind

*Key Lesson Vocabulary

1. Renewable resources include air, water, sunlight, and ◯ _ ◯ _ .

2. Minerals are a _ _ _ _ _ _ ◯ _ _ _ _ _ resource because minerals cannot be replaced after they are used.

3. _ _ _ _ _ _ _ _ ◯ used on farms can pollute lakes and rivers.

4. A natural _ _ ◯ _ _ _ _ _ is something useful to living things that occurs naturally on Earth.

5. Some turbines use _ ◯ _ _ to generate electrical energy.

6. Renewable resources can be _ _ _ ◯ _ _ _ _ by nature.

7. Smog is a form of air _ _ ◯ _ ◯ _ _ _ caused by the burning of fossil fuels.

8. Much of the trash that humans generate ends up in _ _ _ _ ◯ _ _ _ .

What do dinosaurs use to run their cars?

_ _ _ _ _ _ _ _ _ _ !

© Houghton Mifflin Harcourt Publishing Company

Apply Concepts

2 Circle the renewable resource.

3 Draw an example of a resource you use every day. Then tell the kind of resource it is and how you use it.

_____

_____

_____

_____

_____

_____

4 Explain why people are researching ways to use fuels made from plants to power cars.

_____

_____

_____

_____

_____

_____

5 Draw a picture that shows land, air, or water pollution. Label the source of the pollution.

Take It Home! Even though renewable resources will not run out, they can run short. Make a list of all the ways you use water in one day. Think of three ways that you could use less water. Share your results with your family.

© Houghton Mifflin Harcourt Publishing Company

How It Works:

Getting to Oil

Oil forms deep below Earth's surface. To get oil, you have to drill a well. Then you need a pump to draw the oil up to the surface. Oil wells are drilled both on land and underwater into the ocean floor. Underwater drilling must be done carefully. Pipes to carry the oil must be in place before the well is drilled, or else the oil will escape into the water.

Prime Mover

Pump Jack

Offshore oil rigs operate from a platform in the ocean.

Pump Barrel

Oil Zone

Critical Thinking

Is it more difficult to pump oil from a well on dry land or an underwater well? Why?

_____

_____

_____

© Houghton Mifflin Harcourt Publishing Company   (j) ©Doug Menuez/Photodisc/Getty Images

Drilling an oil well and pumping oil out of it are two different jobs. Both must be done carefully so that oil does not spill into the environment.

Find out more about the oil drilling process. Draw a diagram that shows what happens below the surface, either on land or at sea. Label the parts.

What technology allows these workers to produce a drill long enough to reach the oil? Do more research to find out.

_____

_____

_____

Build On It!

Rise to the engineering design challenge—complete **Solve It: Separating Waste Materials** in the Inquiry Flipchart.

© Houghton Mifflin Harcourt Publishing Company   (t) ©Sebastian Brussels/Alamy (b) ©Horizon International Images Limited/Alamy

How Do People Conserve Resources?

Engage Your Brain!

As you read the lesson, look for the answer to the following question and record it here.

Which of the 3 Rs did the artist use when making this sculpture?

_____

_____

_____

_____

Active Reading

Lesson Vocabulary
List the term. As you learn about the term, make notes in the Interactive Glossary.

_____

_____

_____

_____

Main Idea and Details
The main idea of a paragraph is the most important idea. The main idea may be stated in the first sentence of a paragraph, or it may be stated somewhere else. Active readers look for main ideas by asking themselves, What is this paragraph mostly about?

© Houghton Mifflin Harcourt Publishing Company (t) ©Frank/Focus/Alamy

It's Cool to Conserve

People in the United States throw away millions of tons of trash every year. Landfills are overflowing. What can *you* do to help keep our Earth clean?

Active Reading As you read this page, draw a box around problems that are caused by too much trash. Underline the solutions.

These chairs were made from reused snow skis.

Using your own bag over and over saves resources and reduces trash.

You probably don't think about where trash goes after it is picked up from the curb. The truth is that trash is a big problem in our country. There is too much trash, and not enough places to put it. Garbage that is not disposed of properly pollutes natural resources—especially soil and water. So conservation is more important than ever. **Conservation** is using resources carefully and not wasting them. The 3 Rs—reducing, reusing, and recycling—help conserve our natural resources.

All of these items can be recycled. Next time you want to throw something away, check to see if you can recycle it instead.

344

© Houghton Mifflin Harcourt Publishing Company (cl) ©Jeffrey Coolidge/Photodisc/Getty Images; (t) ©Steve Skjold/Alamy; (cr) ©S. Meltzer/PhotoLink/Getty Images

To *reduce* means to use less. When you reduce the amount of waste you make, less of it ends up buried in landfills or burned in incinerators. Try using the same cloth shopping bag instead of a new plastic or paper bag every time you go to the grocery store. Use washable rags instead of paper towels to mop up messes.

You can *reuse* an item by turning it into something else. That old tire? It would make a great tree swing! Your brother's old T-shirts? Tear them into strips and use them to wash the car. Reusing takes time and creativity.

A *recycled* product is one made from materials recovered from thrown-away items by reprocessing them. Your backpack could be made from recycled plastic bottles! Car bumpers, park benches, and carpeting are just a few other products that can be made from recycled materials.

Don't Throw It Away!

Could you recycle or reuse the items below? Explain your ideas.

_____

_____

_____

_____

_____

At a recycling center, discarded items are sorted for reprocessing.

© Houghton Mifflin Harcourt Publishing Company   (b) ©Monty Rakusen/Getty Images; (tl) ©Steve Skjold/Alamy

It's Not Just Dirt!

Soil is one of the world's most valuable natural resources. What can we do to protect it?

Active Reading As you read these two pages, draw one line under each main idea and two lines under each supporting detail.

Dirt. You track it in on your feet. You may have played in it as a child. Why is it important to conserve dirt? Dirt, or soil, contains nutrients that plants need in order to grow. Most of our food comes from crops that grow in soil. Animals also depend on soil to provide the food they eat. Many organisms, such as earthworms, live in soil.

Natural events can cause soil to dry out, strip it of nutrients, and carry it away. Pollution, deforestation, road construction, and land development are some ways that humans harm soil.

Contour plowing follows the natural curves of the land, preventing soil from washing away in heavy rains.

Hydroponics

Intercropping

© Houghton Mifflin Harcourt Publishing Company (t) ©Nigel Cattlin/Alamy; (b) ©Timothy Hearsum/The Image Bank/Getty Images; (c) ©Scott Sinkler/AgStock Images/Corbis

People have developed ways to help conserve soil. Some farmers rotate crops, or plant a different crop every other year. For example, one year a farmer may plant corn. Corn removes nitrogen from soils. The next year, the farmer plants soybeans. These plants return nitrogen to the soil.

Intercropping is the planting of more than one crop in the same field at the same time. The crops protect each other from insects and disease. They also protect the soil from erosion.

Did you know you can grow plants *without* soil? Using hydroponics, people can grow certain plants in water or another material, such as sand or gravel. Hydroponics actually conserves water and soil and uses less space than traditional farming.

Crop rotation with corn and soybeans

Soil Smarts

Pick a type of soil conservation. Fill in the chart.

Type of Soil Conservation	Draw It or Describe It	Tell How It Helps
_____ _____		_____ _____ _____ _____ _____ _____

© Houghton Mifflin Harcourt Publishing Company   (t) ©Nigel Cattlin/Alamy; (bl) ©Timothy Hearsum/The Image Bank/Getty Images; (t) ©Torras Johanson/Alamy; (c) ©Nigel Cattlin/Alamy

Wonderful Water

Think of all the ways you use water. Scientists estimate that every person in the United States uses about 380 L (100 gal) of water every day. That's about 1,600 glasses of water!

Active Reading As you read these pages, underline the definition of *xeric landscaping*.

It's easy to take water for granted. After all, water's almost always there when you need it! Water is a renewable resource, but only some of it is available for use. It is important to keep an eye on how much water we use to make sure we always have enough.

Water conservation can start at home. Fixing a leaky faucet that drips at the rate of one drop per second can save more than 31 L (8 gal) of water every day! Do you have a garden that needs watering regularly? Your family can collect rainwater in a barrel or use a drip irrigation system. Drip irrigation slowly delivers water right to a plant's roots, so water is not lost due to evaporation or runoff.

Turning off the water when you brush your teeth can save about 11 L (3 gal) of water per day.

© Houghton Mifflin Harcourt Publishing Company (b) ©Jeffrey Van Daele/Alamy

Rain barrel

One method of gardening that helps conserve water in areas with little rainfall is xeric landscaping. Xeric landscaping is using native plants that match the natural growing conditions of an area. The result is—you guessed it!—less water is needed to keep plants alive. People who live in desert regions and plant desert plants in their yards do not have to waste water on thirsty lawns.

Xeric landscaping can reduce watering by 50 to 75 percent.

Do the Math!
Solve Real-World Problems

Items such as low-flow shower heads, low-flush toilets, and front-loading washing machines can help reduce water use. Use the data to complete the chart and find out just how much water can be saved.

	Traditional (water use in gal)	Water-Saving (water use in gal)	Water savings in one day	Water savings in one week
Shower head (assume 2 showers per day)	70 gal per shower (10-minute shower)	25 gal per shower (10-minute shower)		
Toilet (assume 10 flushes per day)	5 gal per flush	2 gal per flush		
Washing machine (assume 1 load per day)	40 gal per full load	20 gal per full load		

© Houghton Mifflin Harcourt Publishing Company (tl) ©Wayne Hutchinson/Alamy; (tr) ©Jerry Pavia/Red Cover/Alamy b) ©Jeffrey Van Daele/Alamy;

Who Turned Out the Lights?

Every time you ride in a car or bus, turn on a light, work on your computer, or turn on the heat on a cold day, natural resources go to work for you!

Active Reading As you read these pages, draw a box around the name of each natural resource that provides energy. Then underline the energy it provides.

_____
_____
_____

Electricity and heat are forms of energy that you use in your home. Energy doesn't just appear out of nowhere, though. Fossil fuels—coal, natural gas, and oil—help provide that energy. These resources are limited and burning them causes pollution, so using less both conserves them and helps clean the environment.

You have probably seen those new, bumpy light bulbs. They are called LEDs, or light-emitting diodes. LEDs use about a tenth of the electricity that regular bulbs use, and they last more than 40 times longer. Changing the bulbs in your home is an easy was to conserve energy. It can help your family save money, too!

How Can We Help?

Each picture on these pages shows a way to conserve energy. On the lines by the picture, tell how the item reduces energy use.

These turbines change the energy of moving air into electricity.

© Houghton Mifflin Harcourt Publishing Company (t) ©Clément Philippe/Arterra Picture Library/Alamy; (b) ©Haenel/Premium Stock Photography GmbH/Alamy

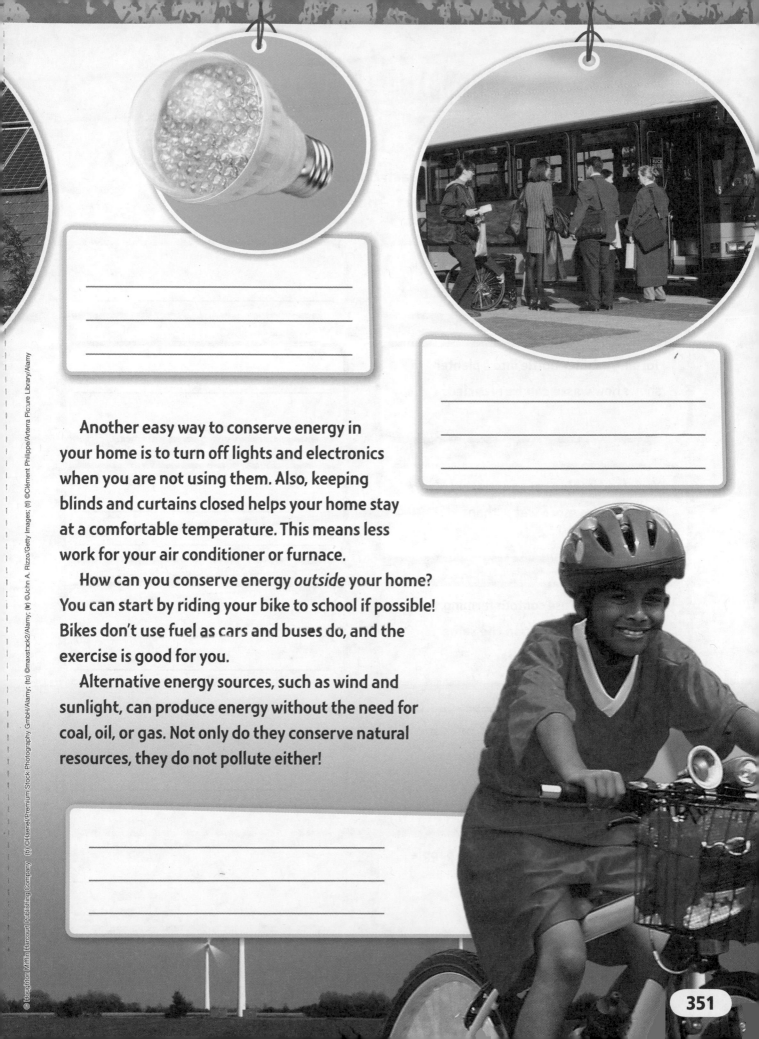

Another easy way to conserve energy in your home is to turn off lights and electronics when you are not using them. Also, keeping blinds and curtains closed helps your home stay at a comfortable temperature. This means less work for your air conditioner or furnace.

How can you conserve energy *outside* your home? You can start by riding your bike to school if possible! Bikes don't use fuel as cars and buses do, and the exercise is good for you.

Alternative energy sources, such as wind and sunlight, can produce energy without the need for coal, oil, or gas. Not only do they conserve natural resources, they do not pollute either!

© Houghton Mifflin Harcourt Publishing Company   (b) ©Haenel/Premium Stock Photography GmbH/Alamy; (tr) ©John A. Rizzo/Getty Images; (tl) ©Clément Phillipe/Arterra Picture Library/Alamy

When you're done, use the answer key to check and revise your work.

Read the summary statements below. Each one is incorrect.
Change the part of the summary in blue to make it correct.

1 When we conserve resources, we use more of them.

_____

2 Turning a 2-liter bottle into a planter shows how waste can be recycled.

_____

_____

3 Xeric landscaping uses nonnative plants that require more water than other plants.

_____

_____

4 When farmers use contour farming, they plant a different crop in the same location every other year.

_____

_____

5 To conserve energy resources, put your computer to "sleep" when you are not using it.

_____

_____

6 Water is a renewable resource, so people can use as much as they want.

_____

_____

Answer Key: 1. use less of them 2. waste can be reused 3. native plants that require less water 4. crops in rows that follow the contour of the land 5. turn your computer off 6. but we still need to conserve it

© Houghton Mifflin Harcourt Publishing Company

Word Play

Name _____

1 Unscramble the word to complete each sentence. The letter in the center is the first letter of the word.

e c l y c d e
R

_____

When something is _____, it is processed and then used to make something else.

a r s e o v i o n t n
C

_____

_____ is using natural resources wisely and not wasting them.

d e e c u
R

_____

When you _____ waste, you decrease the amount you make.

n r f u t o o
C

_____

_____ farming is the planting of crops along the natural curves and slopes of land.

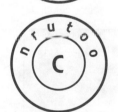
e s e u
R

_____

To _____ an item means using it again rather than throwing it away.

© Houghton Mifflin Harcourt Publishing Company

Apply Concepts

2 List two ways people can conserve water. For one answer, think of an example that is *not* in the text.

_____
_____
_____
_____
_____
_____
_____
_____
_____

3 Draw a room in your home. Label three ways you could conserve energy or water there.

4 Tell what is being conserved in each picture.

_____ _____ _____

Take It Home!

Share with your family what you have learned about conservation. Come up with ways you can conserve resources at home. After you carry out your family's plan, report on the results to the class.

354

© Houghton Mifflin Harcourt Publishing Company

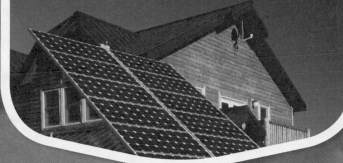

10
Things You Should Know About
Alternative Energy Engineers

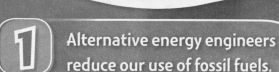

1. Alternative energy engineers reduce our use of fossil fuels.

2. They use renewable resources as energy sources.

3. They convert the sun's energy into heat and electrical energy.

4. They find the best ways to convert the wind's energy into heat and electrical energy.

5. They find ways to use plants such as corn for fuel.

6. They weigh the pros and cons of each kind of energy.

7. They replace old methods with new technologies that are better for the environment.

8. They share their research results with other scientists.

9. They look for new ideas that have not yet been explored.

10. They try to save Earth's resources, using them wisely.

© Houghton Mifflin Harcourt Publishing Company   (t) ©Russell Illig/Getty Images; (br) ©Volker Steger/Photo Researchers, Inc.; (bg) ©Comstock/Getty Images

Alternative Energy Debate

Electric cars may save money on fuel, but they cost more to buy. Two students are texting the pros and cons of using an electric car. Fill in the reasons for and against alternative energy.

They're great. One drawback, though, is

_____

_____

_____

Great car! Electric cars are a great idea because

_____

_____

_____

Another thing that is a challenge is

_____

_____

_____

but the technologies get better every day!

That's true, but a good thing is

_____

_____

_____

© Houghton Mifflin Harcourt Publishing Company (bl) ©R. Cox/Alamy; (br) ©John James/Alamy; (bg) ©Comstock/Getty Images

Name _____

Essential Question

How Can We Conserve Resources?

Set a Purpose
What will you learn from this investigation?

_____

_____

_____

Think About the Procedure
Why do you think starch is added to the pulp mixture?

_____

_____

_____

Why is it important to squeeze out the extra water?

_____

_____

_____

_____

Record Your Data
In the space below, describe the physical characteristics of the paper you made.

© Houghton Mifflin Harcourt Publishing Company   HMH Credits

Draw Conclusions

Some of the paper you use now has been recycled from old paper. Draw conclusions about why people might choose to make paper from waste material instead of directly from trees.

_____

_____

_____

_____

Analyze and Extend

1. Just as scientists do, you made a model to see how something might work on a larger scale. Using what you learned, suggest ways recycled paper might be made in a large factory.

    _____

    _____

    _____

    _____

2. How does the paper you made compare to the paper you use in school?

    _____

    _____

    _____

    _____

    _____

3. How does recycling paper help the environment and living things?

    _____

    _____

    _____

    _____

    _____

    _____

4. What are some other ways scrap paper could be recycled?

    _____

    _____

    _____

    _____

5. How would you change your paper if you were to make it again?

    _____

    _____

    _____

    _____

    _____

© Houghton Mifflin Harcourt Publishing Company   HMH Credits

Unit 7 Review

Name _____

Vocabulary Review

Use the terms in the box to complete the sentences.

> conservation
> nonrenewable resource
> pollution
> recycle
> renewable resource
> reuse

1. The process of preserving and protecting an ecosystem or resource is _____.

2. A resource that nature can replace if the resource is used is called a(n) _____.

3. You can paint an old glass bottle and turn it into a vase to _____ it.

4. Any waste product or contamination that harms or dirties an ecosystem and harms organisms is _____.

5. A resource that nature cannot replace once it is used up is called a(n) _____.

6. Reusing the material from a product to make something else after the product has served its original purpose is a way to _____ that material and conserve resources.

Science Concepts

Fill in the letter of the choice that best answers the question.

7. Where Amar lives, the weather is sunny much of the year. What could Amar's family use to generate electricity without burning fossil fuels?

   (A) drip irrigation

   (B) wind turbine

   (C) solar panel

   (D) LED bulbs

8. Air, water, plants, and wood are some natural resources that humans use. Which of the following statements best describes all natural resources?

   (A) They occur naturally.

   (B) They will never run out.

   (C) They are manufactured by humans.

   (D) They can be used only in their original form.

© Houghton Mifflin Harcourt Publishing Company   HMH Credits

Science Concepts

Fill in the letter of the choice that best answers the question.

9. You see this symbol on the bottom of a plastic container. What does it tell you about the container?

(A) It cannot be reused or recycled.

(B) It contains recycled materials.

(C) It cannot be reused.

(D) It can be recycled.

10. A farmer wants to protect his crops from insects and disease. He also wants to reduce soil erosion. Which soil conservation method should he use?

(A) crop rotation

(B) hydroponics

(C) intercropping

(D) contour farming

11. Jonah saw several of these objects in a field while on a trip with his family.

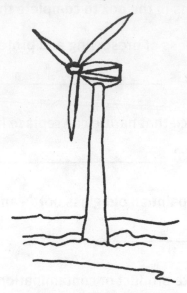

What natural resource does this object use to generate electricity?

(A) moving air

(B) burning oil

(C) burning coal

(D) sunlight

12. Luisa wants to help her family conserve water. She has made a list of ideas. Which of Luisa's ideas would **best** help her family save water?

(A) Take baths instead of showers.

(B) Turn off the water while brushing teeth.

(C) Run only small loads in the washing machine.

(D) Run the dishwasher when it is half full.

© Houghton Mifflin Harcourt Publishing Company   HMH Credits

13. A farmer has used contour plowing to prepare a field before planting a crop in it.

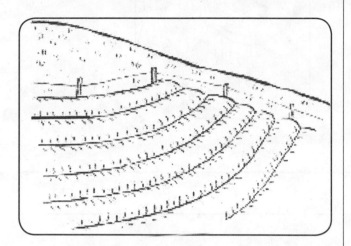

How does this type of plowing help protect soil?

Ⓐ It guards against insects.

Ⓑ It uses very little water.

Ⓒ It prevents disease.

Ⓓ It prevents erosion.

14. A country produces more coal than it needs. What will the country most likely do?

Ⓐ It will save the coal.

Ⓑ It will export the coal.

Ⓒ It will import more coal.

Ⓓ It will stop producing coal.

15. Andrea does the activities shown below every morning.

Which three natural resources do these activities use?

Ⓐ oil, plants, coal

Ⓑ air, sunlight, wind

Ⓒ wood, animals, oil

Ⓓ water, food, fossil fuels

16. Jake made the poster shown here.

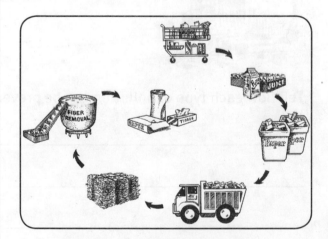

What would be the **best** title for his poster?

Ⓐ Reusing Paper Reduces Wastes

Ⓑ Dump Trucks Use Fossil Fuels

Ⓒ Recycling Paper Helps Conserve Resources

Ⓓ Grocery Shopping Takes a Lot of Time

© Houghton Mifflin Harcourt Publishing Company   HMH Credits

Apply Inquiry and Review the Big Idea

Write the answers to these questions.

17. Manuel's neighbor put an old tire out with the trash. Manuel found the tire and made the object in the picture. How many of the three Rs did Manuel apply? Explain your answer.

_____

_____

_____

18. The pictures below show two types of pollution.

Tell how each type of pollution can be prevented.

_____

_____

_____

19. A farmer is having trouble keeping nutrients in her soil. As a result, her crops are growing poorly. Even so, she wants to keep her use of chemical fertilizers to a minimum. What advice would you give the farmer as she plans next year's crops? Explain your answer.

_____

_____

_____

© Houghton Mifflin Harcourt Publishing Company   HMH Credits

Interactive Glossary

As you learn about each term, add notes, drawings, or sentences in the extra space. This will help you remember what the terms mean. Here are some examples.

Fungi [FUHN•jeye] A kingdom of organisms that have a nucleus and get nutrients by decomposing other organisms

A mushroom is from the kingdom Fungi.

physical change [FIHZ•i•kuhl CHAYNJ] Change in the size, shape, or state of matter with no new substance being formed

When I cut paper, the paper has a physical change.

Glossary Pronunciation Key

With every glossary term, there is also a phonetic respelling. A phonetic respelling writes the word the way it sounds, which can help you pronounce new or unfamiliar words. Use this key to help you understand the respellings.

Sound	As in	Phonetic Respelling	Sound	As in	Phonetic Respelling
a	bat	(BAT)	oh	over	(OH•ver)
ah	lock	(LAHK)	oo	pool	(POOL)
air	rare	(RAIR)	ow	out	(OWT)
ar	argue	(AR•gyoo)	oy	foil	(FOYL)
aw	law	(LAW)	s	cell	(SEL)
ay	face	(FAYS)		sit	(SIT)
ch	chapel	(CHAP•uhl)	sh	sheep	(SHEEP)
e	test	(TEST)	th	that	(THAT)
	metric	(MEH•trik)		thin	(THIN)
ee	eat	(EET)	u	pull	(PUL)
	feet	(FEET)	uh	medal	(MED•uhl)
	ski	(SKEE)		talent	(TAL•uhnt)
er	paper	(PAY•per)		pencil	(PEN•suhl)
	fern	(FERN)		onion	(UHN•yuhn)
eye	idea	(eye•DEE•uh)		playful	(PLAY•fuhl)
i	bit	(BIT)		dull	(DUHL)
ing	going	(GOH•ing)	y	yes	(YES)
k	card	(KARD)		ripe	(RYP)
	kite	(KYT)	z	bags	(BAGZ)
ngk	bank	(BANGK)	zh	treasure	(TREZH•er)

© Houghton Mifflin Harcourt Publishing Company   HMH credits

Interactive Glossary

abyssal plain [uh•BIS•uhl PLAYN] The vast floor of the deep ocean (p. 496)

accurate [AK•yuh•ruht] In measurements, very close to the actual size or value (p. 49)

adaptation [ad•uhp•TAY•shuhn] A trait or characteristic that helps an organism survive (p. 226)

amplitude [AM•pluh•tood] A measure of the amount of energy in a wave (p. 653)

angiosperm [AN•jee•oh•sperm] A flowering vascular plant whose seeds are surrounded by a fruit (p. 197)

asteroid [AS•tuh•royd] A chunk of rock or iron less than 1,000 km (621 mi) in diameter that orbits the sun (p. 548)

astronomy [uh•STRAHN•uh•mee] The study of objects in space and their properties (p. 562)

atom [AT•uhm] The smallest unit into which an element can be divided and still retain all the properties of that element (p. 630)

© Houghton Mifflin Harcourt Publishing Company   HMH Credits

atomic theory [uh•TAHM•ik THEE•uh•ree] A scientific explanation of the structure of atoms and how they interact with other atoms (p. 630)

biotechnology [by•oh•tek•NAHL•uh•jee] A product of technology used to benefit organisms and the environment (p.89)

B

balance [BAL•uhns] A tool used to measure the amount of matter in an object, which is the object's mass (p. 46)

bladder [BLAD•er] Organ in the excretory system that stores and releases urine (p. 159)

balanced forces [BAL•uhnst FAWRS•iz] Forces that cancel each other out because they are equal in size and opposite in direction (p. 704)

bones [BOHNZ] Hard organs that have a spongy layer inside and that may help support the body or protect other organs (p. 140)

brain [BRAYN] The organ in the human body that processes information (p. 128)

bioengineering [by•oh•en•juh•NIR•ing] The application of the engineering design process to living things (p. 88)

© Houghton Mifflin Harcourt Publishing Company   HMH credits

Interactive Glossary

C

cast [KAST] A model of an organism, formed when sediment fills a mold and hardens (p. 455)

cell [SEL] The basic unit of structure and function in all living things (p. 104)

cell membrane [SEL MEM•brayn] The thin covering that surrounds every cell (p. 106)

chemical changes [KEM•ih•kuhl CHAYNJ•ez] Changes in one or more substances, caused by a reaction, that form new and different substances (p. 599)

chlorophyll [KLAWR•uh•fil] A green pigment in plants that allows a plant cell to use light to make food (p. 293)

classification [klas•uh•fih•KAY•shuhn] The sorting of things into groups of similar items (p. 176)

comet [KAHM•it] A chunk of frozen gases, rock, ice, and dust orbiting the sun (p. 549)

community [kuh•MYOO•nih•tee] A group of organisms that live in the same area and interact with each other (p. 250)

© Houghton Mifflin Harcourt Publishing Company HMH Credits

complete metamorphosis [kuhm•PLEET met•uh•MAWR•fuh•sis] A complex change that most insects undergo that includes larva and pupa stages (p. 217)

consumer [kuhn•SOOM•er] A living thing that cannot make its own food and must eat other living things (p. 295)

compound [KAHM•pownd] A substance made of two or more types of atoms that are chemically combined (p. 634)

continental shelf [kahnt•uhn•ENT•uhl SHELF] A gradually sloping portion of the ocean floor that is made of continental crust (p. 496)

conservation [kahn•ser•VAY•shuhn] The process of preserving and protecting an ecosystem or a resource (p. 344)

continental slope [kahnt•uhn•ENT•uhl SLOHP] The part of the ocean floor that slopes steeply (p. 496)

conservation of mass [kahn•ser•VAY•shuhn uhv MAS] A law that states that matter cannot be made or destroyed; however, matter can be changed into a new form (p. 604)

control [kuhn•TROHL] The experimental setup to which you will compare all other setups (p. 29)

© Houghton Mifflin Harcourt Publishing Company   HMH credits

Interactive Glossary

coral reef [KAWR•uhl REEF] Branch-like structures formed by the skeletons of colonies of coral polyps (p. 523)

core [KAWR] The layer of Earth extending from Earth's center to the bottom of the mantle. It is mostly metallic iron and nickel (p. 389)

criteria [kry•TEER•ee•uh] The standards for measuring success (p. 70)

crust [KRUHST] The thin outer layer of Earth, including dry land and the ocean floor (p. 389)

current [KER•uhnt] A continuous flow of water in a regular pattern in the ocean. (p. 508)

D

decomposer [dee•kuhm•POHZ•er] A living thing that gets energy by breaking down dead organisms and animal wastes into simpler substances (p. 299)

deposition [dep•uh•ZISH•uhn] The dropping or settling of eroded materials (p. 368)

dichotomous key [dy•KAHT•uh•muhs KEE] A tool used to identify organisms based on contrasting pairs of characteristics (p. 177)

© Houghton Mifflin Harcourt Publishing Company   HMH Credits

domain [doh•MAYN] The broadest level of classification of organisms (p. 179)

ecosystem [EE•koh•sis•tuhm] A community of organisms and the environment in which they live (p. 249)

dominant trait [DAHM•ih•nuhnt TRAYT] A trait that appears if an organism has one factor for that trait (p. 115)

electromagnetic spectrum [ee•lek•troh•mag•NET•ik SPEK•truhm] All energy waves that travel at the speed of light in a vacuum; includes radio, infrared, visible, ultraviolet, x-rays, and gamma rays (p. 671)

dwarf planet [DWORF PLAN•it] A nearly round body, slightly smaller than a planet, whose orbit crosses the orbit of another body (p. 548)

element [EL•uh•muhnt] Matter that is made of only one kind of atom (p. 632)

E

earthquake [ERTH•kwayk] A shaking of Earth's surface that can cause land to rise and fall (p. 394)

energy pyramid [EN•er•jee PIR•uh•mid] A diagram that shows that energy is lost at each level in a food chain (p. 312)

© Houghton Mifflin Harcourt Publishing Company   HMH credits

Interactive Glossary

engineering [en•juh•NEER•ing] The use of science and math for practical uses such as the design of structures, machines, and systems (p. 65)

evidence [EV•uh•duhns] Information collected during a scientific investigation (p. 6)

environment [en•VEYE•ruhn•muhnt] All the living and nonliving things that surround and affect an organism (p. 248)

experiment [ik•SPAIR•uh•muhnt] An investigation in which all the conditions are controlled to test a hypothesis (p. 23)

epicenter [EP•ih•sent•er] The point on Earth's surface directly above the focus of an earthquake (p. 394)

extinction [ek•STINGKT•shuhn] A plant or an animal species that is no longer living or existing (p. 274)

erosion [uh•ROH•zhuhn] The process of moving sediment from one place to another (p. 368)

fault [FAWLT] A break in Earth's crust where rock on one side moves in relation to rock on the other side (p. 394)

© Houghton Mifflin Harcourt Publishing Company   HMH Credits

food chain [FOOD CHAYN] The transfer of food energy between organisms in an ecosystem (p. 309)

fossil fuel [FAHS•uhl FYOO•uhl] Fuel formed from the remains of once-living things. Coal, oil, and natural gas are fossil fuels. (p. 456)

food web [FOOD WEB] A group of food chains that overlap (p. 310)

frequency [FREE•kwuhn•see] A measure of the number of waves that pass a point in a second (p. 650)

force [FAWRS] A push or pull, which may cause a change in an object's motion (p. 700)

friction [FRIK•shuhn] A force that acts between two touching objects and that opposes motion (p. 703)

fossil [FAHS•uhl] The remains or traces of a plant or an animal that lived long ago (p. 454)

G

galaxy [GAL•uhk•see] A group containing billions of stars, objects that orbit those stars, gas, and dust (p. 565)

© Houghton Mifflin Harcourt Publishing Company HMH credits

Interactive Glossary

gas [GAS] The state of matter in which a substance does not have a definite shape or volume (p. 584)

gymnosperm [JIM•noh•sperm] A vascular plant that produces seeds that are not surrounded by a fruit (p. 196)

genus [JEE•nuhs] In the classification of organisms, a subdivision of a family (p. 179)

H

habitat [HAB•ih•tat] The place where an organism lives and can find everything it needs to survive (p. 252)

germinate [JER•muh•nayt] To begin to grow (a seed, spore, or bud) (p. 200)

heart [HART] The muscular organ that pumps blood through the rest of the circulatory system (p. 148)

gravity [GRAV•ih•tee] The force of attraction between objects, such as the attraction between Earth and objects on it (p. 702)

© Houghton Mifflin Harcourt Publishing Company HMH Credits

I

igneous rock [IG•nee•uhs RAHK] A type of rock that forms from melted rock that cools and hardens (p. 429)

inherited trait [in•HAIR•it•ed TRAYT] A characteristic passed from parents to their offspring (p. 112)

incomplete metamorphosis [in•kuhm•PLEET met•uh•MAWR•fuh•sis] Developmental change in some insects in which a nymph hatches from an egg and gradually develops into an adult (p. 218)

instinct [IN•stinkt] Behavior that an organism inherits and knows how to do without being taught (p. 232)

index fossil [IN•deks FAHS•uhl] A fossil of a type of organism that lived in many places during a relatively short time span (p. 469)

intertidal zone [in•ter•TYD•uhl ZOHN] The area between the land and the ocean that is covered by water at high tide and uncovered at low tide (p. 521)

inertia [ih•NUR•shuh] The tendency for an object to resist change in motion (p. 725)

invertebrate [in•VER•tuh•brit] An animal without a backbone (p. 212)

© Houghton Mifflin Harcourt Publishing Company   HMH credits

Interactive Glossary

investigation [in•ves•tuh•GAY•shuhn]
A procedure carried out to carefully observe, study, or test something in order to learn more about it (p. 4)

L

life cycle [LYF SEYE•kuhl] The stages that a living thing passes through as it grows and changes (p. 216)

J

jetty [JET•ee] A wall-like structure that sticks out into the ocean to prevent sand from being carried away (p. 513)

light [LYT] A form of energy that can travel through space and lies partly within the visible range (p. 668)

K

kidneys [KID•neez] Organs in the human excretory system that remove waste materials from the blood (p. 159)

liquid [LIK•wid] The state of matter in which a substance has a definite volume but no definite shape (p. 584)

liver [LIV•er] A large organ that makes a digestive juice called bile (p. 155)

© Houghton Mifflin Harcourt Publishing Company HMH Credits

lungs [LUNGZ] The large organs in the respiratory system that bring oxygen from the air into the body and release carbon dioxide (p. 144)

meiosis [my•OH•sis] The process that produces reproductive cells (p. 111)

M

mantle [MAN•tuhl] The thick layer of Earth beneath the crust (p. 389)

metamorphic rock [met•uh•MAWR•fik RAHK] A type of rock that forms when heat or pressure changes an existing rock (p. 432)

mass extinction [MAS ek•STINGK•shuhn] A period in which a large number of species become extinct (p. 475)

microscopic [my•kruh•SKAHP•ik] Too small to be seen without using a microscope (p. 43)

mineral [MIN•er•uhl] A nonliving solid that has a crystal form (p. 414)

matter [MAT•er] Anything that has mass and takes up space (p. 580)

© Houghton Mifflin Harcourt Publishing Company HMH credits

Interactive Glossary

mitosis [my•TOH•sis] The process by which most cells divide (p. 110)

muscles [MUHS•uhlz] Organs made of bundles of long fibers that can contract to produce movement in living things (p. 142)

mixture [MIKS•cher] A combination of two or more different substances in which the substances keep their identities (p. 615)

N

natural resource [NACH•er•uhl REE•sawrs] Anything from nature that people can use (p. 330)

mold [MOHLD] An impression of an organism, formed when sediment hardens around the organism (p. 455)

niche [NICH] The role a plant or an animal plays in its habitat (p. 252)

molecule [MAHL•ih•kyool] A single particle of matter made up of two or more atoms joined together chemically (p. 634)

nonrenewable resource [nahn•rih•NOO•uh•buhl REE•sawrs] A resource that, once used, cannot be replaced in a reasonable amount of time (p. 331)

© Houghton Mifflin Harcourt Publishing Company HMH Credits

nonvascular plant [nahn•VAS•kyuh•ler PLANT] A plant that lacks tissues for carrying water, food, and nutrients (p. 192)

organ [AWR•guhn] A group of tissues that work together to perform a certain function (p. 126)

nucleus [NOO•klee•uhs] The control center of a cell that directs the cell's activities (p. 106)

organ system [AWR•guhn SIS•tuhm] A group of organs that work together to do a job for the body (p. 126)

O

opaque [oh•PAYK] Not allowing light to pass through (p. 678)

organism [AWR•guh•niz•uhm] A living thing (p. 104)

P

opinion [uh•PIN•yuhn] A personal belief or judgment based on what a person thinks or feels but not necessarily based on evidence (p. 9)

pancreas [PAN•kree•uhs] An organ in the body that makes a digestive juice as well as insulin (p. 155)

© Houghton Mifflin Harcourt Publishing Company   HMH credits

Interactive Glossary

photosynthesis [foh•toh•SIN•thuh•sis] The process that plants use to make sugar (p. 293)

plate tectonics [PLAYT tek•TAHN•iks] The theory that Earth's crust is divided into plates that are always moving (p. 390)

physical changes [FIZ•i•kuhl CHAYNJ•ez] Changes in which the form or shape of a substance changes but the substance still has the same chemical makeup (p. 598)

plankton [PLANK•tuhn] Small organisms that float, or drift, in great numbers in bodies of salt water or fresh water (p. 526)

pitch [PICH] The highness or lowness of a sound (p. 650)

pollution [puh•LOO•shuhn] Any waste product or contamination that harms or dirties an ecosystem and harms organisms (p. 337)

planet [PLAN•it] A large, round body that revolves around a star (p. 540)

population [pahp•yuh•LAY•shuhn] All the organisms of the same kind that live together in an ecosystem (p. 250)

© Houghton Mifflin Harcourt Publishing Company   HMH Credits

prism [PRIZ•uhm] A transparent object that separates white light into the colors of the rainbow (p. 683)

recessive trait [ree•SES•iv TRAYT] A trait that appears only if an organism has two factors for that trait (p. 115)

producer [pruh•DOOS•er] A living thing, such as a plant, that can make its own food (p. 294)

reflection [rih•FLEHK•shuhn] The bouncing of light waves when they encounter an obstacle (p. 680)

prototype [PROH•tuh•typ] The original or test model on which a product is based (p. 68)

refraction [rih•FRAK•shuhn] The bending of light waves as they pass from one material to another (p. 682)

R

renewable resource [rih•NOO•uh•buhl REE•sawrs] A resource that can be replaced within a reasonable amount of time (p. 330)

reaction [ree•AK•shuhn] The process through which new substances are formed during a chemical change (p. 599)

© Houghton Mifflin Harcourt Publishing Company   HMH credits

Interactive Glossary

rock [RAHK] A naturally formed solid made of one or more minerals (p. 428)

sediment [SED•uh•ment] Sand, bits of rock, fossils, and other matter carried and deposited by water, wind, or ice (p. 369)

S

salinity [suh•LIN•uh•tee] The saltiness of water (p. 495)

sedimentary rock [sed•uh•MEN•tuh•ree RAHK] A type of rock that forms when layers of sediment are pressed together (p. 430)

science [SY•uhns] The study of the natural world through observation and investigation (p. 5)

shore [SHAWR] The area where the ocean and the land meet and interact (p. 513)

skin [SKIN] The human body's largest organ, covering the outside of the body (p. 134)

scientific methods [SY•uhn•TIF•ik METH•uhds] The different ways that scientists perform investigations and collect reliable data (p. 22)

© Houghton Mifflin Harcourt Publishing Company HMH Credits

solar system [SOH•ler SIS•tuhm] A star and all the planets and other bodies that revolve around it (p. 540)

spore [SPAWR] A reproductive structure made by some plants, including mosses and ferns, that can grow into a new plant (p. 194)

solid [SAHL•id] The state of matter in which a substance has a definite shape and a definite volume (p. 585)

spring scale [SPRING SKAYL] A tool used to measure force (p. 47)

solution [suh•LOO•shuhn] A mixture that has the same composition throughout because all its parts are mixed evenly (p. 616)

stars [STARZ] Huge balls of very hot, glowing gases in space that produce their own light and heat (p. 562)

species [SPEE•sheez] In the classification of organisms, the smallest group of closely related individuals (p. 179)

stomach [STUHM•uhk] A baglike organ in which food is mixed with digestive juices and squeezed by muscles (p. 154)

© Houghton Mifflin Harcourt Publishing Company   HMH credits

Interactive Glossary

succession [suhk•SESH•uhn] A gradual change in the kinds of organisms in an ecosystem (p. 266)

tissue [TISH•OO] A group of similar cells that work together, such as muscle tissue and stomach tissue (p. 126)

T

technology [tek•NAHL•uh•jee] The use of scientific knowledge to solve practical problems (p. 66)

translucent [trahns•LOO•suhnt] Allows only some light to pass through (p. 679)

temperature [TEM•per•uh•cher] The measure of the energy of motion of particles of matter, which we feel as how hot or cold something is (p. 582)

transparent [trahns•PAIR•uhnt] Allows light to pass through (p. 679)

U

tide [TYD] The regular rise and fall of the ocean's surface, caused mostly by the moon's gravitational pull on Earth's oceans (p. 511)

unbalanced forces [uhn•BAL•uhnst FAWRS•iz] Forces that cause a change in an object's motion because they don't cancel each other out (p. 704)

© Houghton Mifflin Harcourt Publishing Company HMH Credits

universe [YOO•nuh•vers] Everything that exists, including galaxies and everything in them (p. 564)

volcano [vahl•KAY•noh] A place where hot gases, smoke, and melted rock come out of the ground onto Earth's surface (p. 398)

V

variable [VAIR•ee•uh•buhl] Any condition that can be changed in an experiment (p. 29)

volume [VAHL•yoom] The amount of space something takes up (p. 580)

volume [VAHL•yoom] The loudness of a sound (p. 651)

vascular plant [VAS•kyuh•ler PLANT] A plant that has transport tissues for carrying water, food, and nutrients to its cells (p. 193)

W

vertebrate [VER•tuh•brit] An animal with a backbone (p. 210)

water pressure [WAW•ter PRESH•er] The downward push of water (p. 495)

© Houghton Mifflin Harcourt Publishing Company   HMH credits

Interactive Glossary

wave [WAYV] The up-and-down movement of surface water (p. 506)

wavelength [WAYV•length] The distance between a point on one wave and the identical point on the next wave (p. 652)

wave [WAYV] A disturbance that carries energy, such as sound or light, through matter or space (p. 648)

weathering [WETH•er•ing] The breaking down of rocks on Earth's surface into smaller pieces (p. 367)

© Houghton Mifflin Harcourt Publishing Company   HMH Credits

Index

© Houghton Mifflin Harcourt Publishing Company

© Houghton Mifflin Harcourt Publishing Company

© Houghton Mifflin Harcourt Publishing Company

© Houghton Mifflin Harcourt Publishing Company

© Houghton Mifflin Harcourt Publishing Company

speed of, 669
transmission of, 678–679
visible, 671
waves, 668, 670–671
light bulbs, 72–73, 350, 602
light emitting diodes (LEDs),
350
light microscopes, 45
limestones, 431, 437
limiting factors, 251
Lincoln Memorial, 436
line graphs, 34
liquids, 584–589, 600
liter (L), 50
liver, 155, 158
low tides, 511
lungs, 144–145
luster, 416–417

magma, 398, 428–429
magnetic force, 619
magnitude of earthquake,
396–397
Main Idea and Details, 103, 175,
209, 343, 465, 491, 667
Main Ideas, 139, 247, 453
make a prediction, 595
mammals, 181, 211
mantle, 389
marble, 432, 436
marrow, 140
Mars, 543
Mars Rover, 710–711
mass, 48, 726–727, 730
conservation of, 604–605
forces and, 708–709
matter and, 580, 583
mass extinctions, 474–475
matter, 580–589

changes of state, 586–587
chemical changes in, 599,
605–606
gases, 584–589, 601
liquids, 584–589, 600
mass and, 580, 583
mixtures, 614–621
physical changes in, 598, 604
properties of, 581–583,
588–589
solids, 584–589
states of, 584–585
temperature and, 582,
586–587, 600–603, 606
volume and, 580, 582
measurement
of earthquakes, 396–397
of force, 49
of length, 46
of mass, 48
of temperature, 47
of time, 47
tools, 46–51
of volume, 50–51
meiosis, 111
melting, 586–587, 602
Mendel, Gregor, 114–115
Mendeleev, Dmitri, 632
meniscus, 51
Mercury, 542
mercury (element), 632
mesh screens, 619
Mesosaurus, 470–471
Mesozoic Era, 468–469
metamorphic rocks, 432–433
metamorphosis, 218–219
meteor impacts, 475
meteorites, 549
meteoroids, 549
meteorologists, 17–18
meteors, 549

meter (m), 46
metric system, 46
mica, 419
microscopes, 45, 105, 684
migration, 233
Milky Way, 564–565
mimicry, 231
minerals, 414–419
Mohs scale, 416–417
properties of, 416–419
mining, 272
mitochondria, 106–107
mitosis, 110–111
mixtures, 614–621
alloys, 620–621
separating, 618–619
solutions, 616–617
models, 25, 28–29
Mohs, Friedrich, 416
Mohs scale, 416–417
mold, 182
molecules, 634–635
mollusks, 212
molting, 219
moon (of Earth)
impacts upon, 550
tides and, 511
moons, 540–541, 548
moraines, 373
mosses, 180, 194
motion
animal, 463–464
forces and, 700–701
Newton's Laws of, 724–731
in space, 730–731
Mount St. Helens, 399
MP3 players, 87
muscles, 142–143
muscle tissue, 126–127
mushrooms, 182

© Houghton Mifflin Harcourt Publishing Company

© Houghton Mifflin Harcourt Publishing Company

© Houghton Mifflin Harcourt Publishing Company

© Houghton Mifflin Harcourt Publishing Company